I0799910

IMAGES
of America

LEE COUNTY
TEXAS

IMAGES
of America

LEE COUNTY
TEXAS

Nancy Hamilton
Lee County Historical Commission

ARCADIA
PUBLISHING

ISBN 978-0-7385-0296-0

Published by Arcadia Publishing
Charleston, South Carolina

Printed in the United States of America

Library of Congress Catalog Card Number: 99-066583

For all general information contact Arcadia Publishing at:
Telephone 843-853-2070
Fax 843-853-0044
E-Mail sales@arcadiapublishing.com
For customer service and orders:
Toll-Free 1-888-313-2665

Visit us on the Internet at www.arcadiapublishing.com

CONTENTS

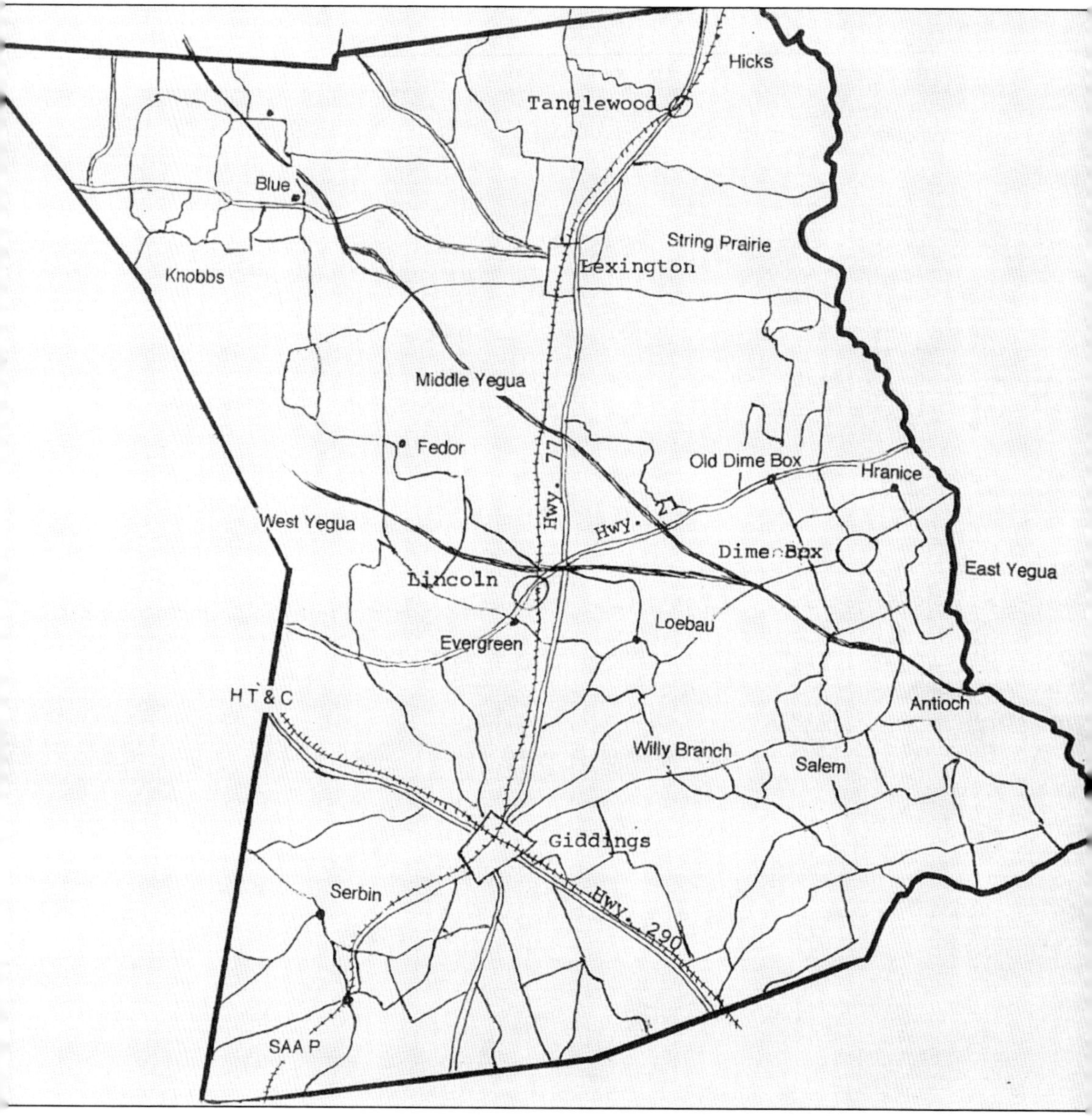
Hicks
Tanglewood
Blue
String Prairie
Lexington
Knobbs
Middle Yegua
Fedor
Old Dime Box
Hranice
Hwy. 77
Hwy. 21
West Yegua
Dime Box
East Yegua
Lincoln
Loebau
Evergreen
H T & C
Antioch
Willy Branch
Salem
Giddings
Serbin
Hwy. 290
SAA P

INTRODUCTION

Lee County, Texas, is located in the center of the triangle whose vertices are Houston, Dallas, and San Antonio. The county does not contain any very early settlements. Before the days of the Republic, it was largely unknown to any men but Native Americans. Then the dense Post Oak woodlands dominated, with short and narrow open prairies interspersed. The waters of the many-branched Yegua ("wild mare" in Spanish) fanned out and tangled to the northwest toward geologically ancient shoreline benches. Trade and travel routes of early explorers avoided the area.

Now the grassland prairies cover the rolling hills and the erect, round-topped Post Oaks appear here and there in isolated groves. Graceful junipers and outliers of the "lost" pines of Bastrop dot the area. Open spaces dominate, providing good grazing for animals and a pleasing prospect to the eye.

In the early days of the Texas Republic, there was a proposal for the creation of a county in this area to be called, appropriately, Centre County. But that proposal failed, and it was not until after the Civil War, in 1874, that parts of Burleson and Washington Counties, a corner of Bastrop County, and a small strip of Fayette County were composed into a new county named for Robert E. Lee. Giddings was selected as the county seat, probably because it was benefiting from energetic new growth stimulated by the advent of the railroads. Giddings grew and many of the older towns declined. They finally lost their post offices and disappeared from maps, but not from the memories of the Texans of Lee County.

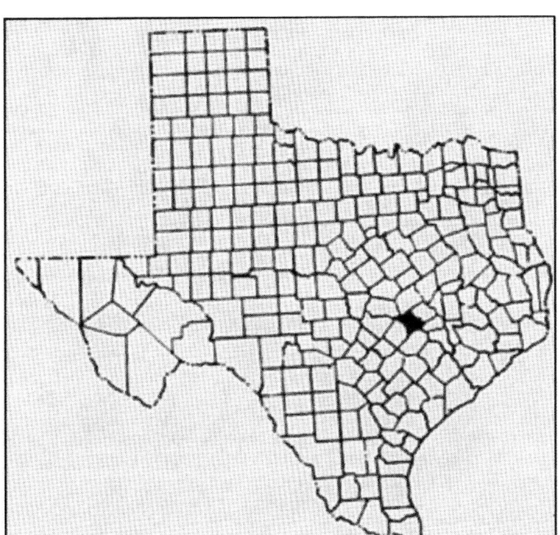

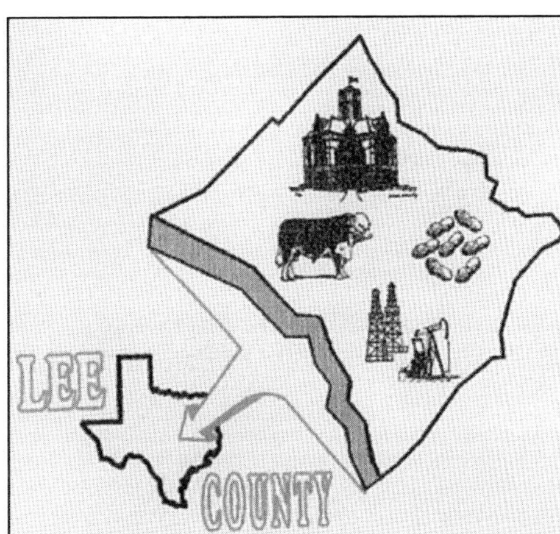

ACKNOWLEDGMENTS AND CREDITS

FOR PHOTOGRAPHS OF SERBIN AND DIME BOX:

The Texas Wendish Heritage Museum Archive
The Albert Blaha Collection, courtesy of Jean Davis

FOR TEXT EXCERPTS IN THE CAPTIONS:

The diaries of Annie Baumgaertner Rousseau for the years from 1882 to 1928, courtesy of the Lee County Historical Commission.

A memoir of DeWitt Clinton Thomas, written in 1878, transcribed in 1964 by his grandnephew James B. Thomas, courtesy of J.D. Turner

Letters of the Adam Turner family spanning 1865–95, courtesy of Jerry Pierce

A *History of Lee County, Texas* by the Lee County Historical Survey Committee, 1974

SPECIAL THANKS TO THE MANY INDIVIDUALS WHO LOANED PICTURES AND PROVIDED AID AND INFORMATION:

Jessie Opal Beard, Sandra Botard, Eloise Brademan, Joyce Carleston, Marcella and Morris Chapple, David Collins, Jean Davis, Dan Durow, Dorothy Edwards, Vivian Francis, J.B. Gersch, Lummus Hannes, Blanche Franklin Horton, Bonnie Langham, Carolyn Marble, James Marburger, Waldeen Hillsberg Moerbe, Dan Morse, Joyce Schroeder Nelson, Carol Nolen, Erwin Pavlik, Sue Placke, Charles Ramsel, Lydia Siegmund, Johnny Simpson, Arnold Smith, Jerry C. Spain, J.D. Turner, Ruby Vance, Emma Jackson Wisdom, and Alonzo and Beverly Wood.

One

String Prairie, Lexington, and the Knobbs

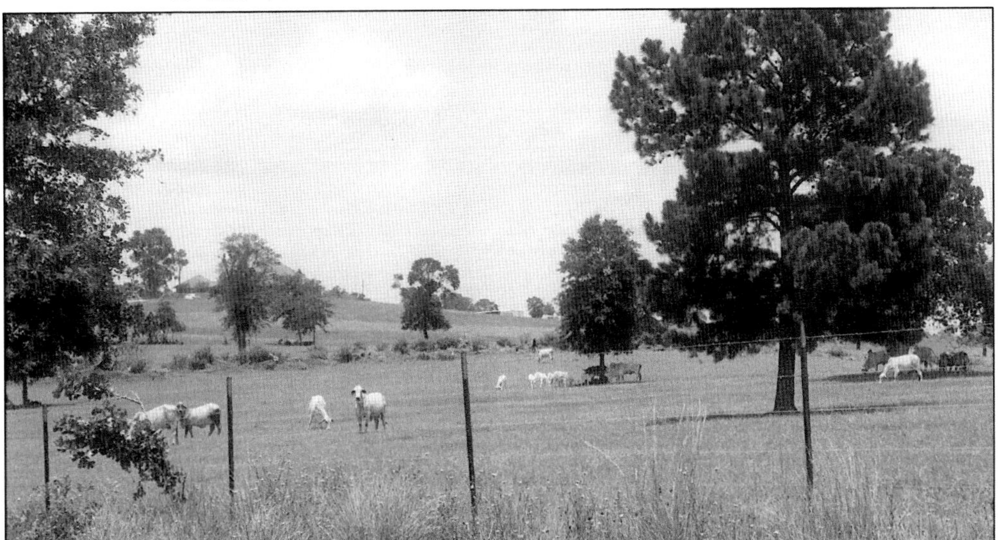

About 1847, the Thomas family moved westward from the Brazos bottoms, because many were "afflicted with chills and fever, so that another horse had to be sold to pay the doctor's bills . . . String Prairie [near what is now Lexington, Texas] was then a wilderness country, there being but five settlers between East and Middle Yegua creeks, a distance of some ten miles." The Thomases built a log cabin with a dirt floor and "lived together, all of us, black and white in this cabin, ground corn on a steel mill for our bread, worked all day, and took turns at grinding after supper each night, Sundays always excepted . . . The country was beautiful beyond description, wild and picturesque . . . Horses, cattle, and hogs kept in fine condition on the range without feed. Deer, turkeys, and all kinds of small game abounded everywhere. The streams were full of fish and all my spare moments were spent in the woods. I loved my gun and dog . . . It was a glorious country, and we were happy, almost contented." —Thomas memoirs.

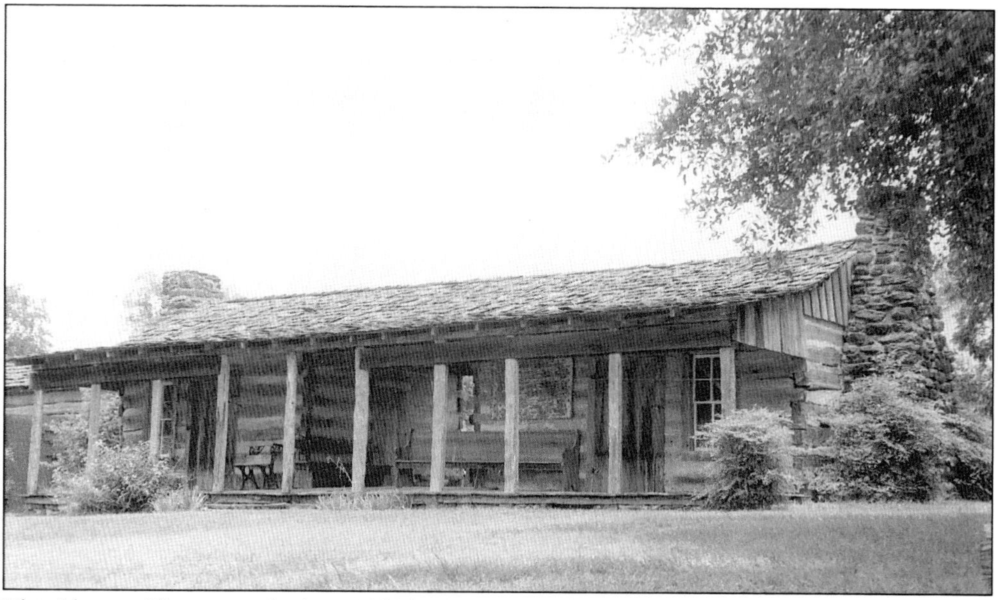

This "dog trot" house was built in 1850 by George Washington Guthrie (1824–1902), a veteran of the Texas Revolution. The Guthrie house was moved to Heritage Square in Lexington during the bicentennial in 1976.

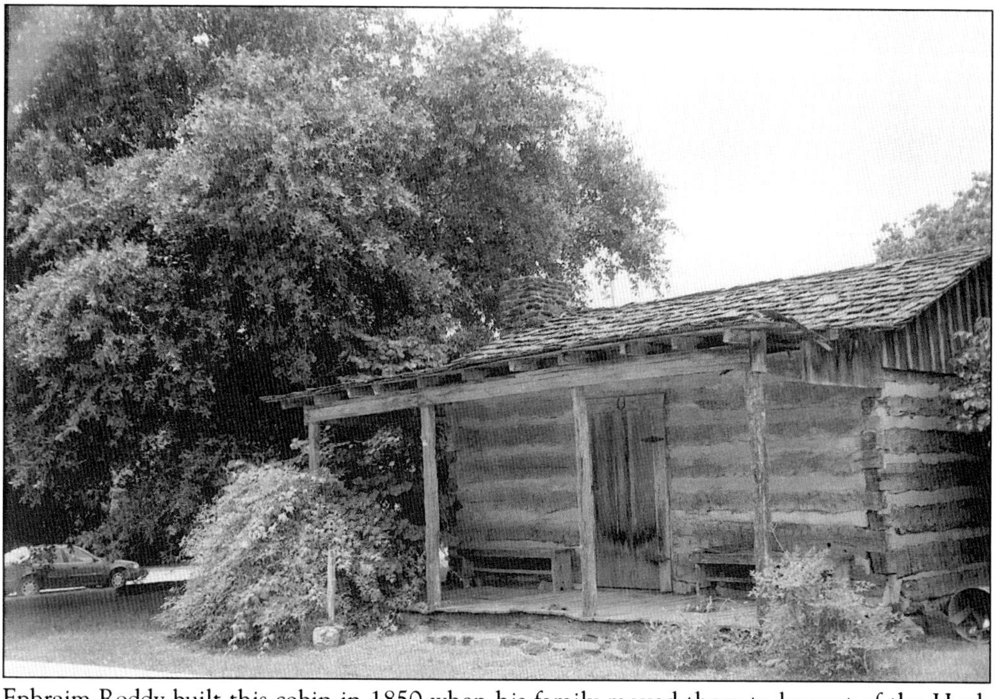

Ephraim Roddy built this cabin in 1850 when his family moved there to be part of the Hugh Wilson Presbyterian Church, which was built about 1860 near Tanglewood north of Lexington in the String Prairie area. Wilson, who was a missionary to the Chickasaw Indians, is known as the "father of Texas Presbyterians." Roddy had practiced law in San Felipe when it was capital of the Austin Colony, and was well acquainted with Stephen F. Austin, James Bowie, and David Crockett. This cabin is also in Heritage Square, Lexington.

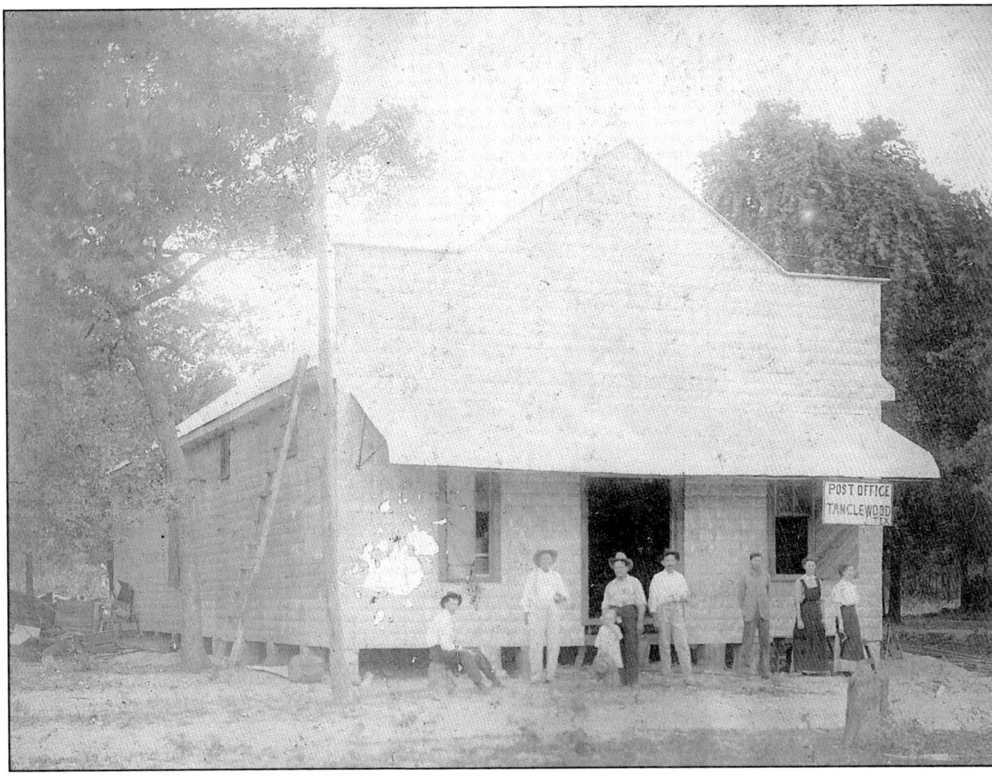

Sheriff J.H. Kelly is pictured second from the left in this photograph of the Tanglewood Post Office. Tanglewood was a thriving community around 1900, with three general stores, a cotton gin and oil mill, four churches, and three doctors.

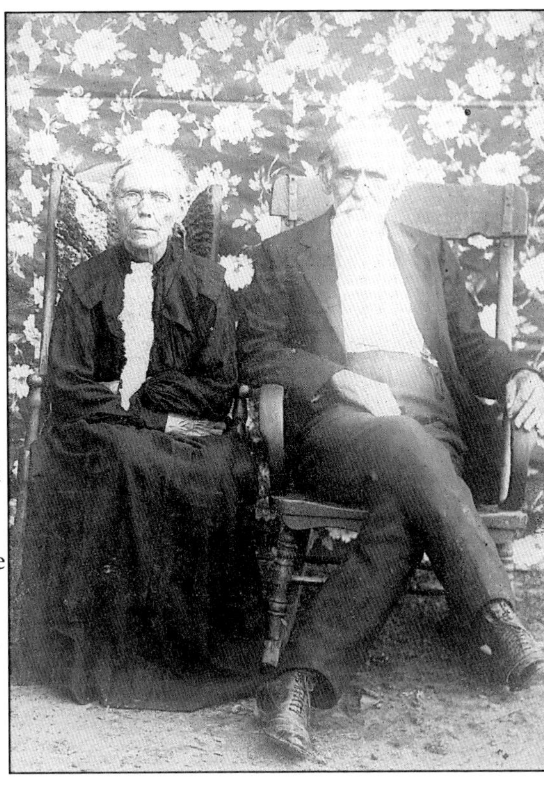

John Byrom Vance operated the store and post office and was postmaster at Adina and Blue, located near the Knobbs, an area named for three prominent hills since decapitated to surface a road through the area. His wife, Martha Heffington Vance (1843–1907), was a granddaughter of Isaac and Zillah Jackson, participants in the 1836 flight of settlers (after the fall of the Alamo) that is known as the "Runaway Scrape."

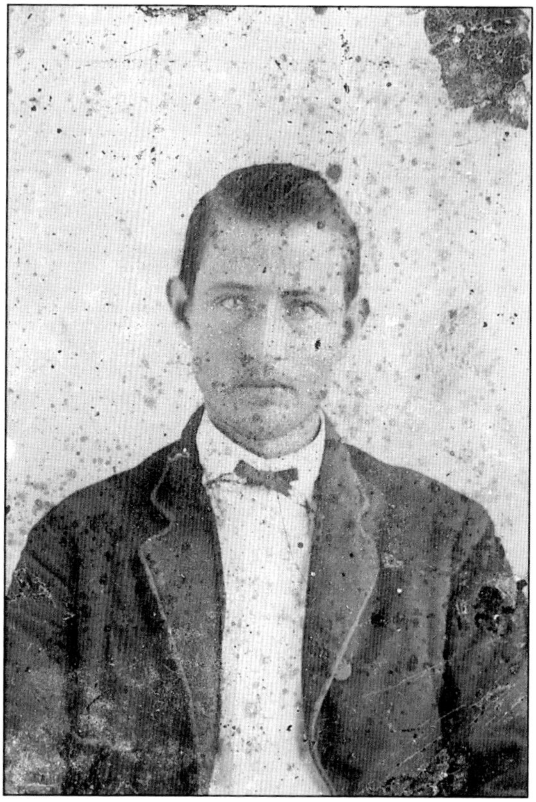

This tintype pictures an early settler in the Knobbs, either Adam Turner (1807–1896) or his son-in-law, Jerome Smith. According to a June 1876 letter from the Thornhills of Bosque County, Texas, to Turners of the Knobbs, this wild and remote area had a reputation for sheltering outlaws. "You said there had bin a great deal of hanging and killing going on in your country. It must be horrible country you live in. You wanted to know if there was fussing up here. They are all peasble in our own country. Men seem to be glad to see one another." A July 1884 letter between members of the Turner family reads, "Well Marg times is pretty squaley here yet. They have comensed taken men from behind the brush. Pete Allen was waylayed and shot killed dead. They got the horse the man was a riding that done the work. The poney was turned over to the constable for safe keeping and the man com that night and got the poney. [Pete] had been to Simins Store after medicen for his sick child and on his way home was killed." —Turner letters.

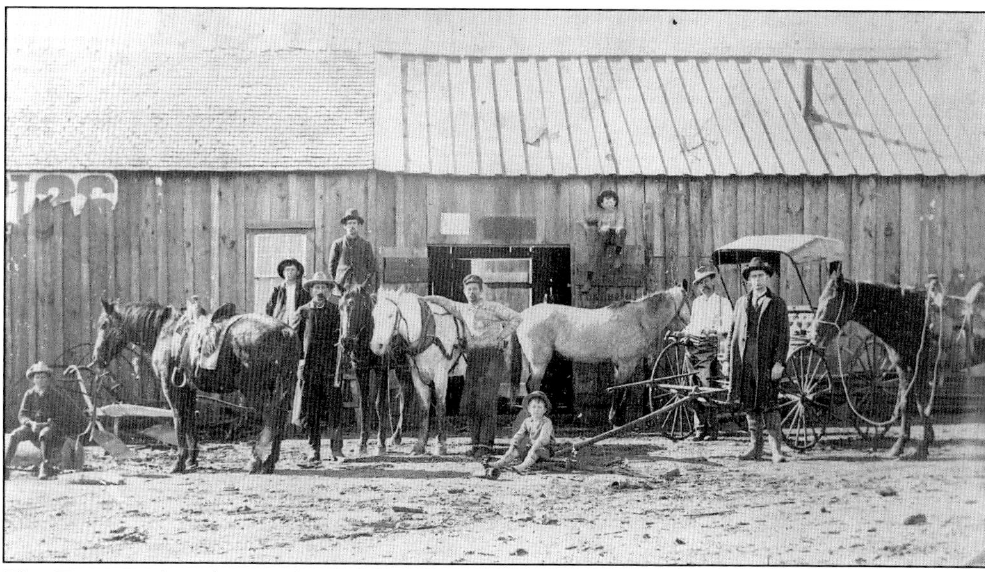

The Turners often discussed economic conditions in their letters. In 1876 they wrote, "Land is cheap you can by good prairie for three dollars a acre." In 1886, "I have bought me a place 7 miles north of Lexington. There is 80 acres in the tract and 40 in cultivation. It is all the country i no of that aint finced up." A letter dated November 14, 1896, read, "Fanny [Turner] had out nearly 13 bales of cotton. She wont quite pay for her place this year I think. She can pay for it next year if she has no bad luck." —Turner letters.

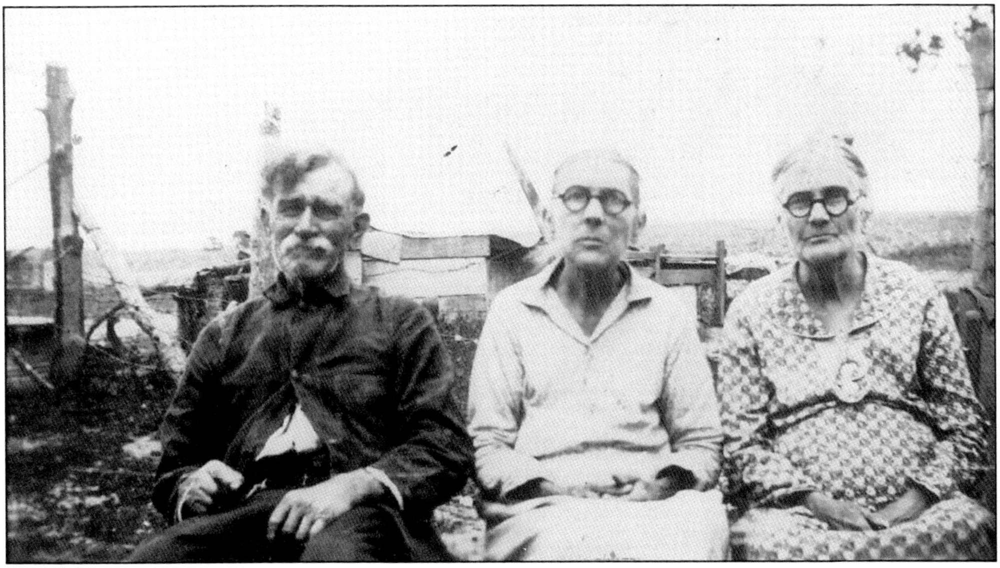

The respectable George Bowers Turner (no relation to Adam) of Blue Branch was a brother of Turk Turner, who was suspected of stealing cattle from a man named Craddock. The case was so clear cut that his lawyer advised him the only way out without conviction was to kill the witness, Craddock. After Craddock was found dead, direct action seemed indicated. Turk Turner and a pal were found shot to death and wrapped up in the hide of a beef they were thought to have stolen and butchered.

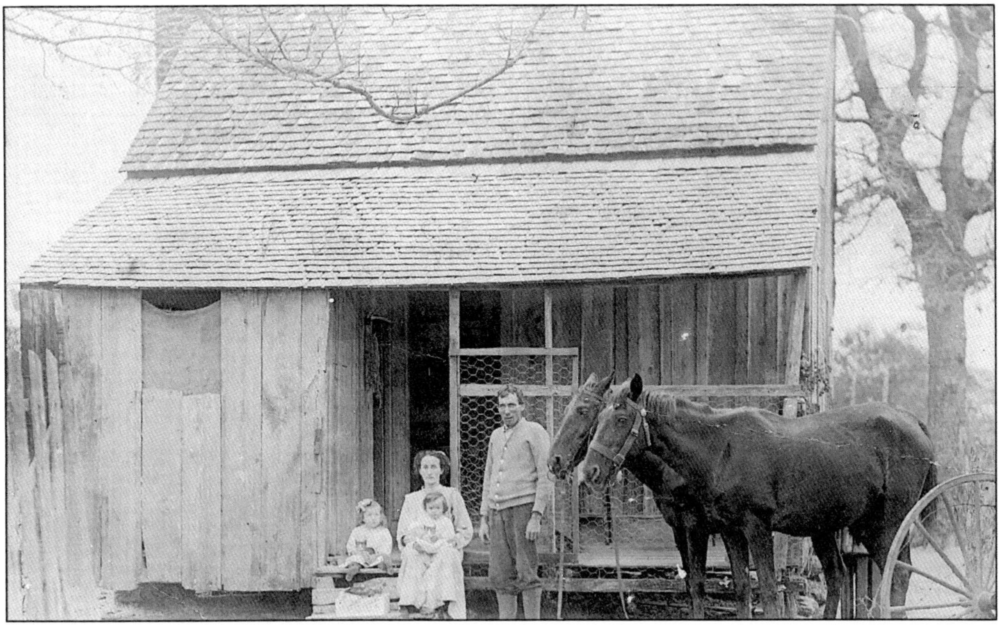

Life was hard. The mesh on the porch was to keep animals out and the boarded porch was a bedroom for a hired man. Farming was prey to bad weather and plagues. One of the Thornhill daughters wrote, "You said you had plenty to eat. We all have plenty of fried grasshoppers here whenever we want them." And again in 1893, "The grasshoppers like to have overtaken the country. They eat up fields of corn and cotton. They would eat up from one to five acres in a night time just as clean as if you had plowed it up." —Turner letters.

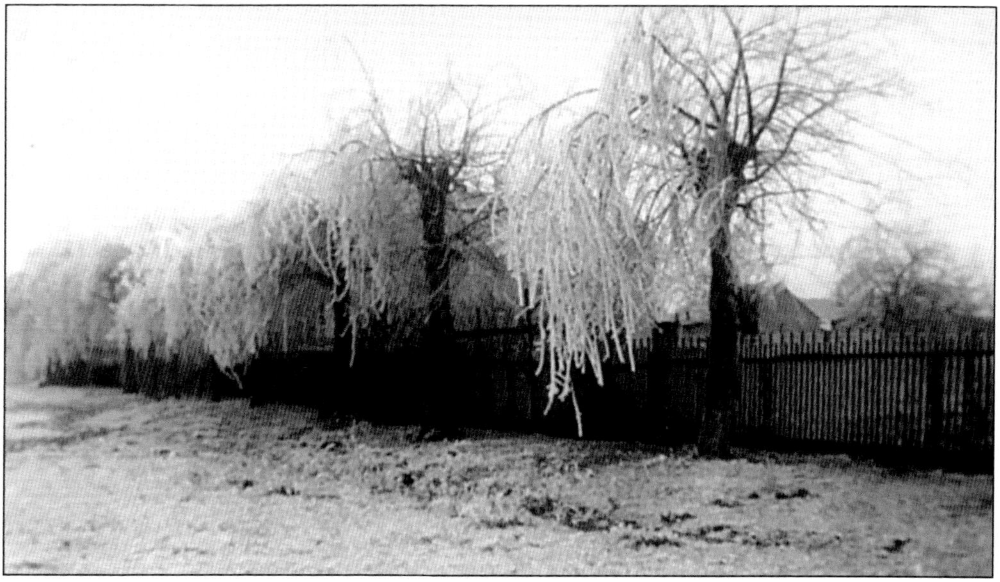

Texas is famed for heat, but cold could be equally extreme. An entry from February 11, 1899, read, "Freezing cold. After supper, 13 degrees below freezing, bitter cold." The next day, the entry read, "Extremely cold. One degree below zero. Every thing froze. No Sunday school and church, but Joe went up and made a fire and rang the bell." —Rousseau diaries.

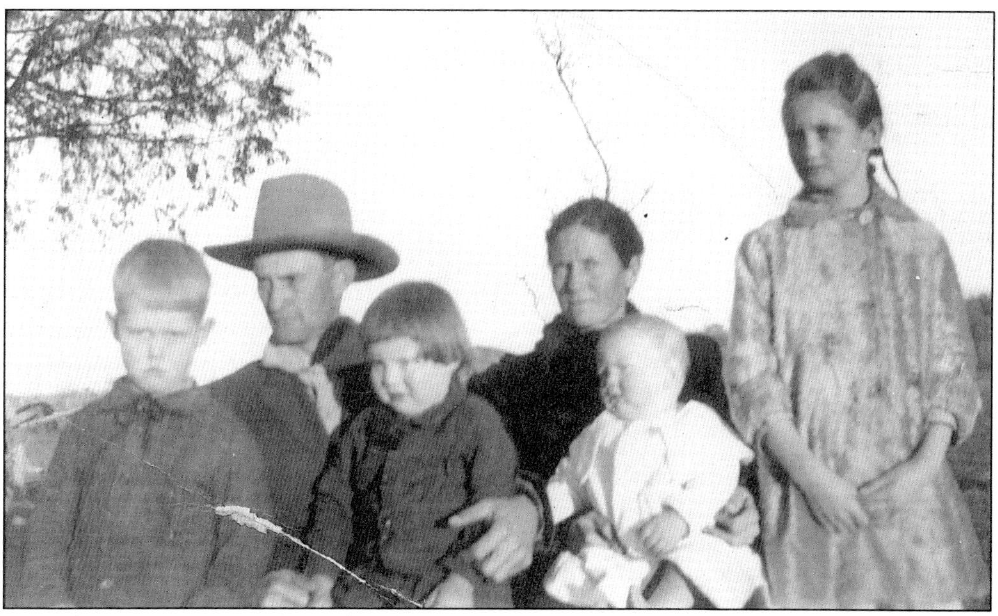

Joe and Carrie Yeager Nettles and children—Frank, McLarty, Wallace, and Ruby—are pictured here during the winter of either 1918 or 1919. Ruby Nettles Vance, on the right wearing a beloved coat long after she had outgrown it, is an outstanding Lee County historian who documented county cemeteries and was a major contributor to *A History of lee County, Texas.*

Even into the 1900s, washing and ironing for a family was a full two days work for one or two women.

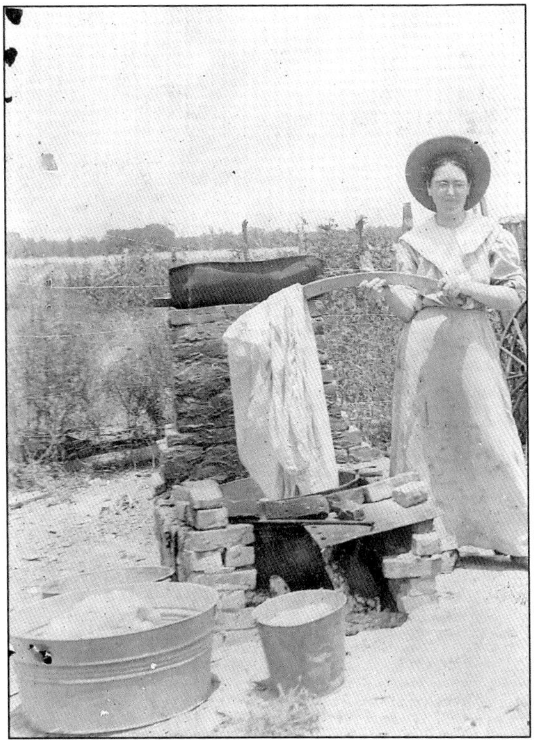

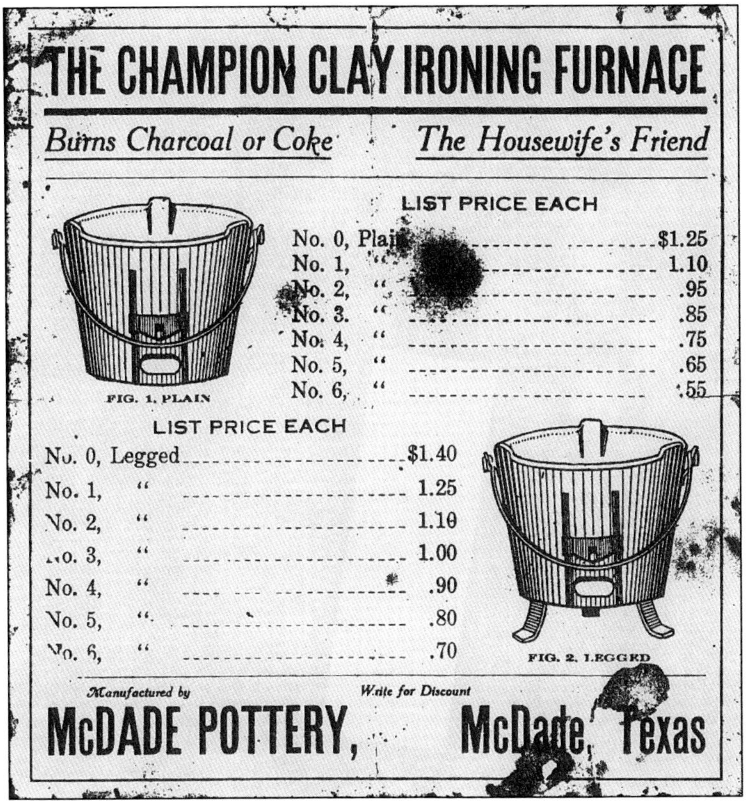

This clay ironing furnace was a product of the local pottery works, produced in McDade just over the county line in Bastrop County. It was used to heat sad irons and also as a foot warmer in buggies. Area clay was also used to make bricks, and the abundant wood was used to make furniture. One of the area potters was the father of Pete Allen, whose murder was reported in the Turner letter of July 1884.

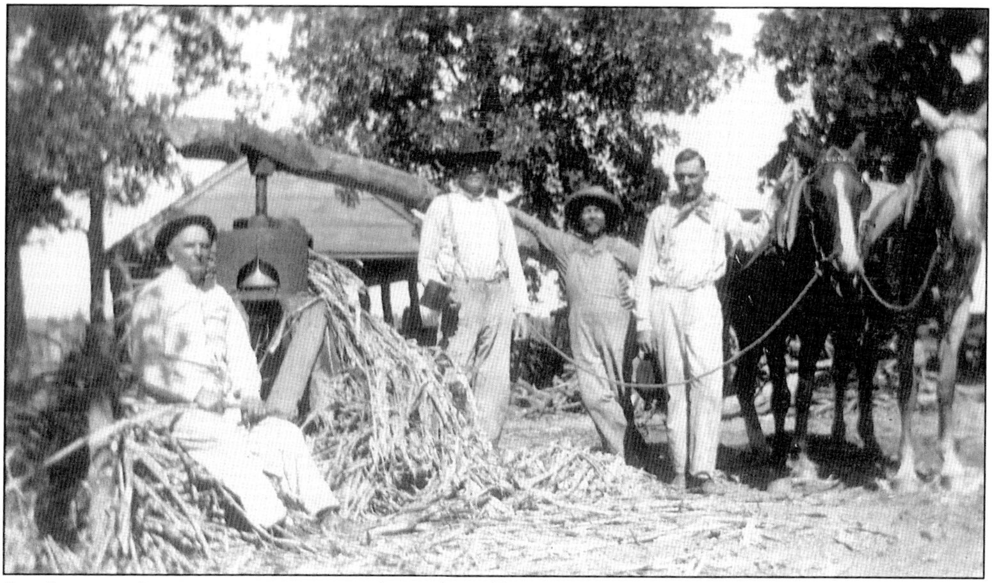

Sorghum and strip cane were put through mills to extract the sweet juice, which was then boiled down in wide flat pans to make syrup or molasses. Shown here are, from left to right, Fritz Retzlaff, Gus Retzlaff, Bob Vance, and Frank Retzlaff.

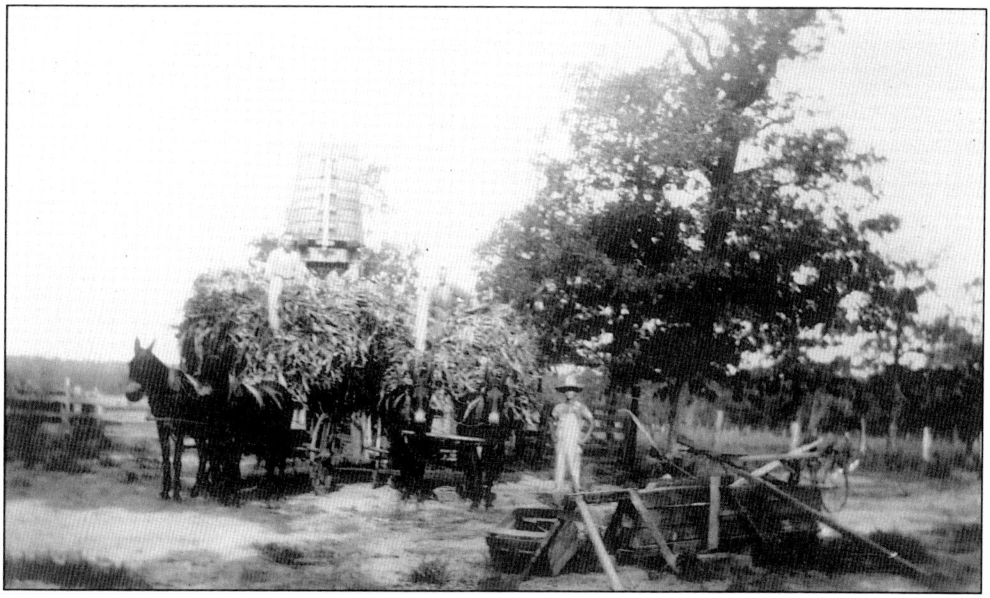

Corn was a major crop and every bit of it was used. The tops of the corn, above the ripened ears, were gathered in bundles in the early morning while they were still damp, then stacked to make fodder to feed the cattle. And corn seed could be expensive. A letter from November 14, 1896, read, "Fanny had to buy corn. She bought seventy bu. and Luke bought 26 bu. They sent to Kansas for it so that made 96 bu. in all! The corn was 8 cts a bu. back there but by the time it got to McDade it was 41 cts. a bushel. You see they had to pay freight." —Turner letters.

Luther Byrum was a circuit Missionary Baptist. Rev. Byrum conducted informal religious services called "Brush Arbor meetings" under shelters of vines and branches constructed to shade the gatherings. About 1880, Byrum arrived at the Pate home one morning and by the end of the day had persuaded 13-year-old Laura Ann to run away and marry him. Her father never forgave Luther.

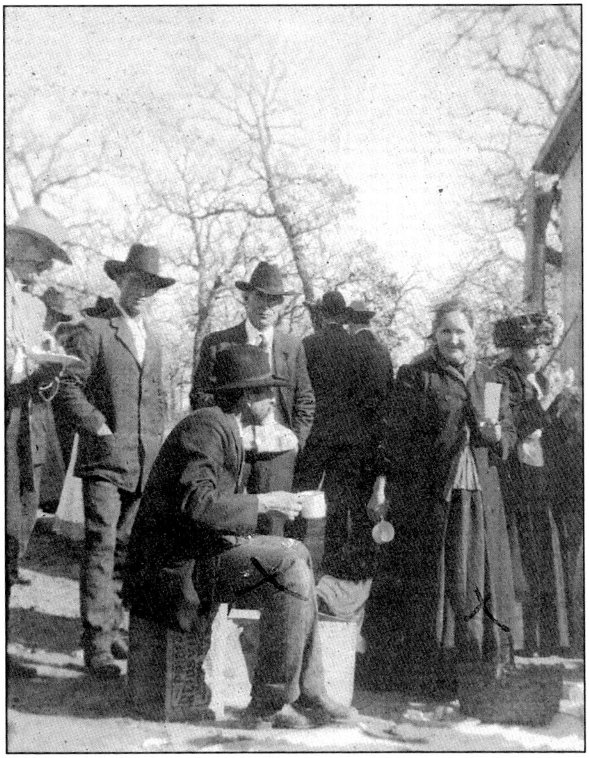

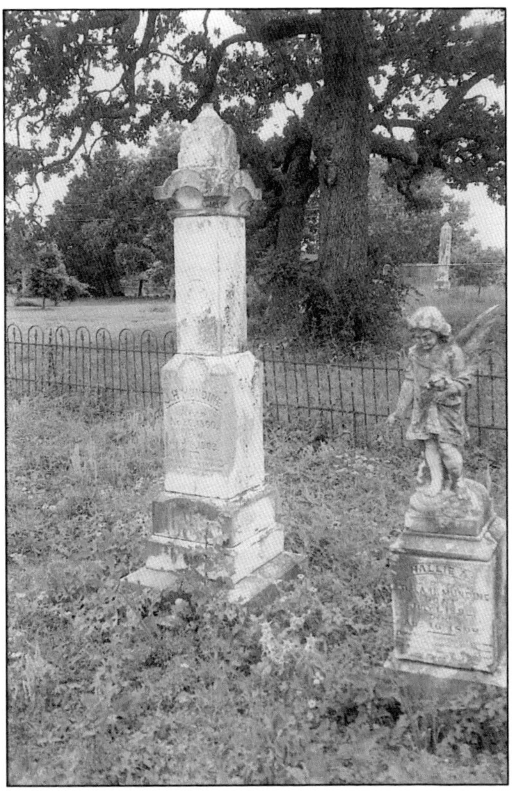

Children often died young. These Lexington monuments commemorate J.H. Mundine (1860–1903) and his young daughter, Hallie A. Mundine (1892–1896). The inscription on his tombstone reads, "Another link is broken, In our household band, But a chain is forming, In a better land," while her stone reads, "Dear lovely baby, to part with you, Hath racked our hearts with pain, But though our loss is great, we trust, Tis your eternal gain." Mr. Mundine's stone was erected by the Woodmen of the World; its seal contains a stump surrounded by a laurel wreath.

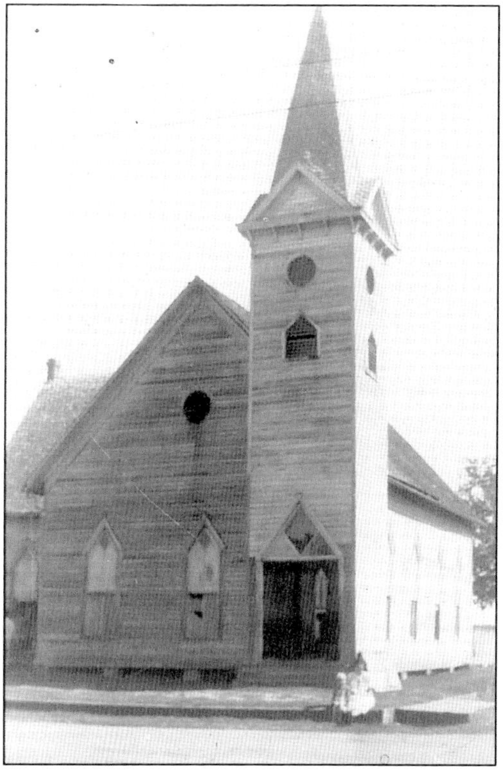

This is the Lexington Methodist Episcopal Church, South, which was built in 1892 and replaced by a new structure, which still stands, in 1928. In 1939 this congregation combined with that of the German Methodist Church near Lexington.

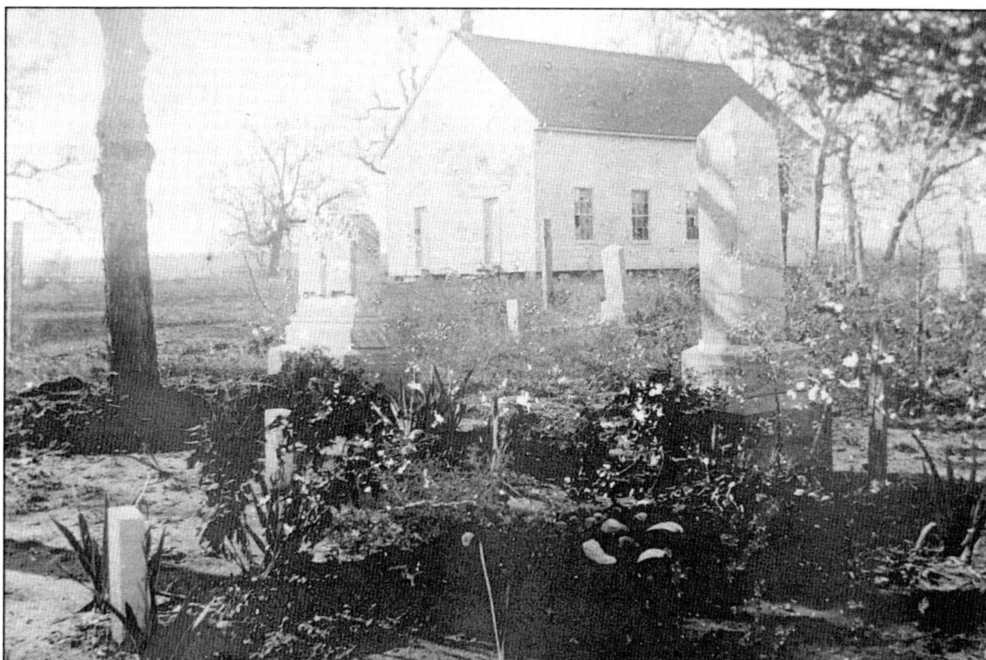

Early Chapel, Methodist Episcopal Church, South, is the oldest church land in Lee County, deeded in 1850. The graveyard contains the graves of W.W. Hawkins and James W. Shaw, veterans of the Battle of San Jacinto. The chapel was torn down in 1928.

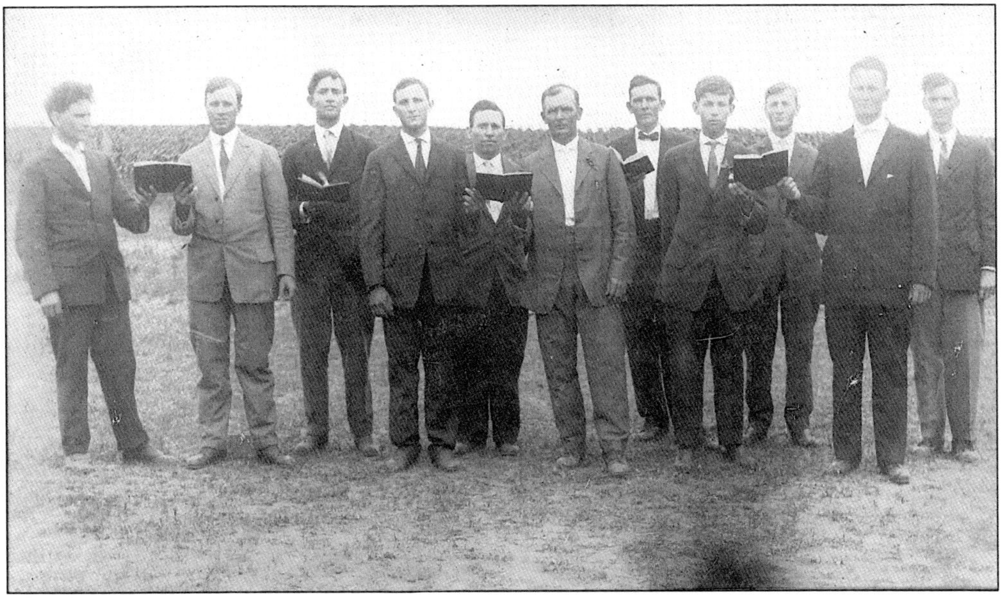

From about 1882, there was a community of German farmers around Lexington. Many of the original 12 families—the Seiferts, Petersons, Retzlaffs, Hornungs, Urbantkes, Ottos, Bauers, Hillegeists, Raeseners, Raschkes, Grusendorfs, and Lettermans—had come to the area from the town of Industry in Austin County to the south. The German men's choir in 1915 was comprised of, from left to right, Hugo Urbantke, Julius Bauer, Arthur Peterson, Gus Bauer, Adolph Peterson, Fritz Retzlaff, Gus Retzlaff, Ed Peterson, Ernest Bauer, Rev. A.A. Liefeste, and Frank Retzlaff.

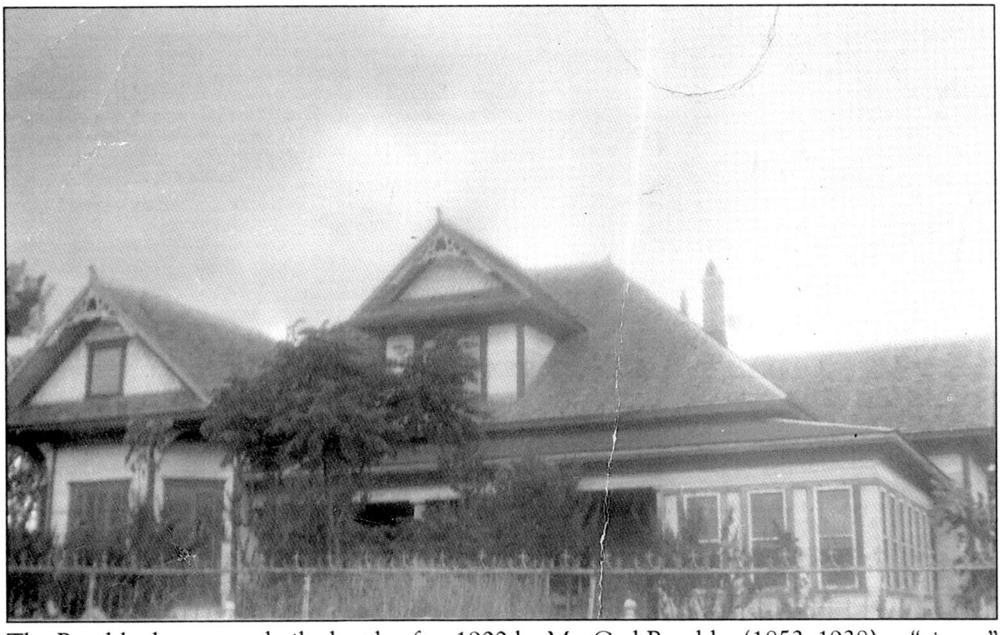

The Raschke house was built shortly after 1900 by Mr. Carl Raschke (1853–1938), a "ginner" (owner of cotton gins) who married Louise Grusendorf. It was one of the most beautiful houses in Lexington and it still stands, though it is in considerable disrepair. This picture was taken in 1952. Raschke's son and partner, Charles, lost his arm in a gin accident.

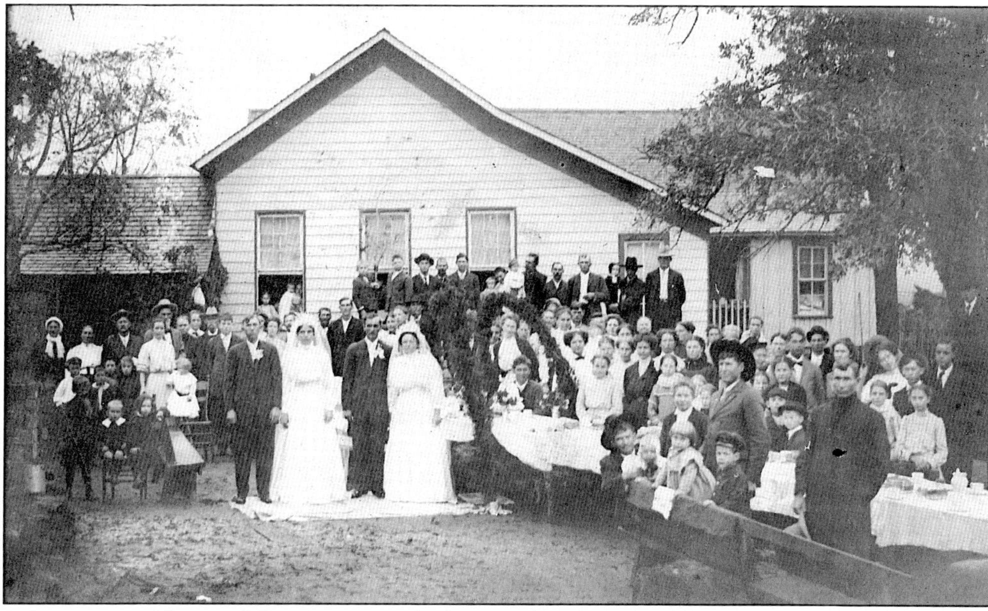

When sisters Alice and Emma Grusendorf married into the Hillegeist and Retzlaff families in 1910, the three families attended en masse. Note the white cloth on the ground under the brides' feet to keep the hems of their white dresses clean and off the dirt ground.

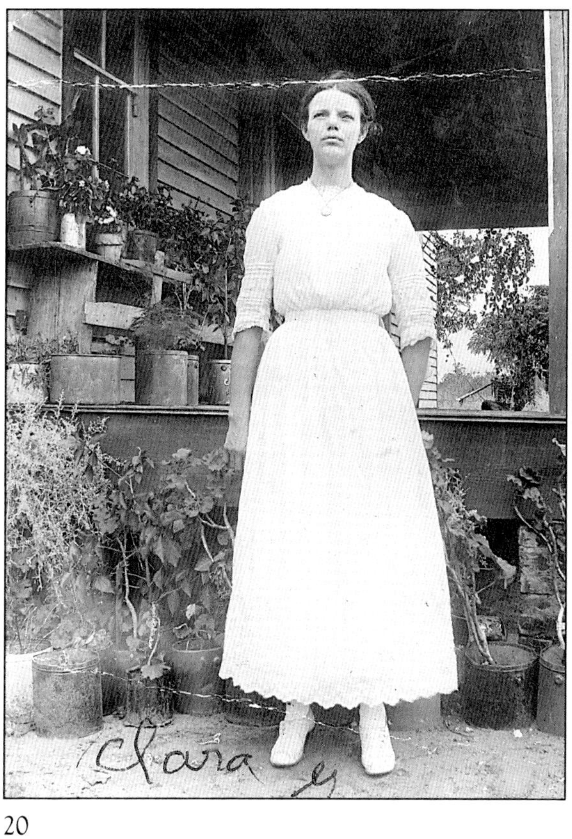

Clara Grusendorf (1889–1963) is pictured here about 1910. Even in large extended German families in Lexington, some independent daughters, such as Clara, never married.

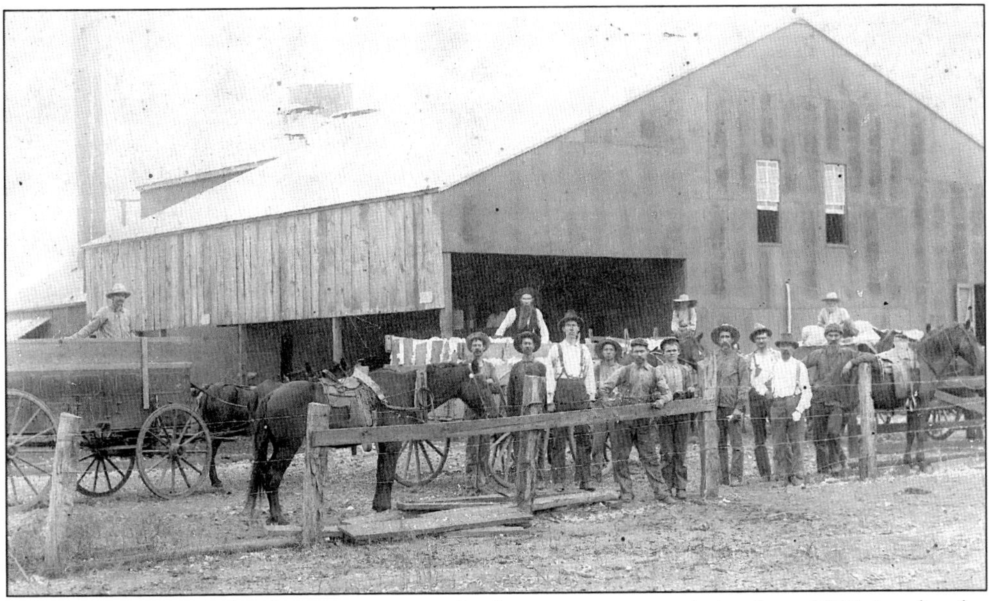

Blacksmith Jacob Seifert drives a wagon to the Lexington cotton gin in about 1900. Jacob, who was born in Wurtenberg, Germany, in 1841, was the first member of the 12 German families to arrive in Lexington.

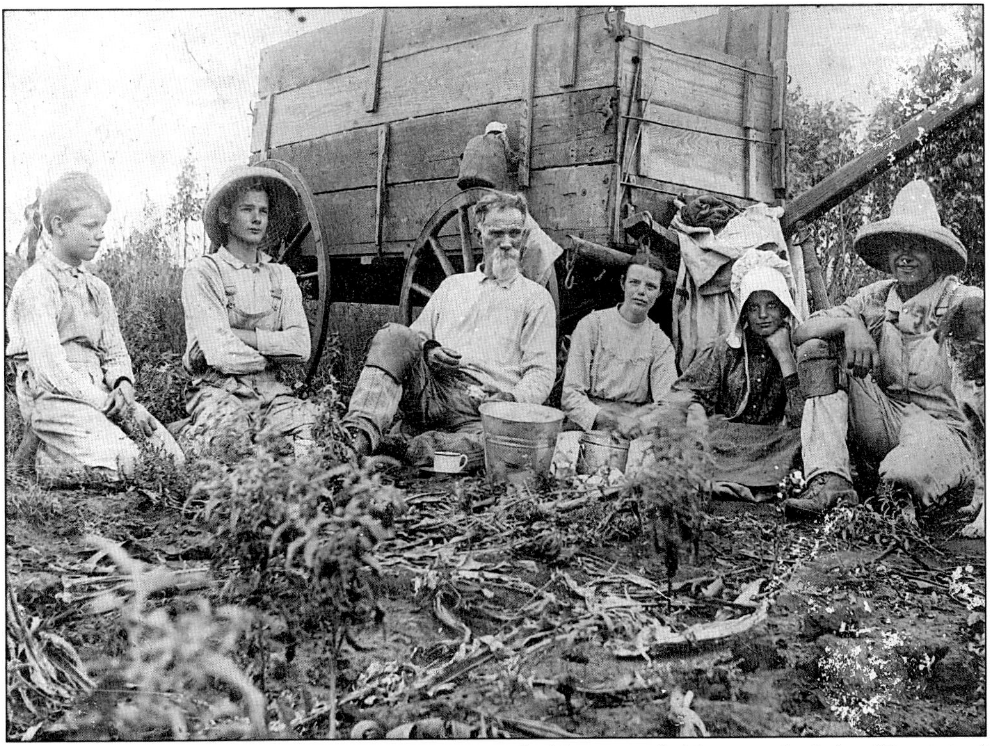

Henry Grusendorf was connected by marriage of siblings or children to 6 of the 12 original families. He and his family rest after a good day's work in the fields in about 1910. Probable identifications, from left to right, are as follows: daughters Linda and Bertha, Henry, Bertha (Henry's wife), an older woman (perhaps sister Mary), and son Will or Arthur.

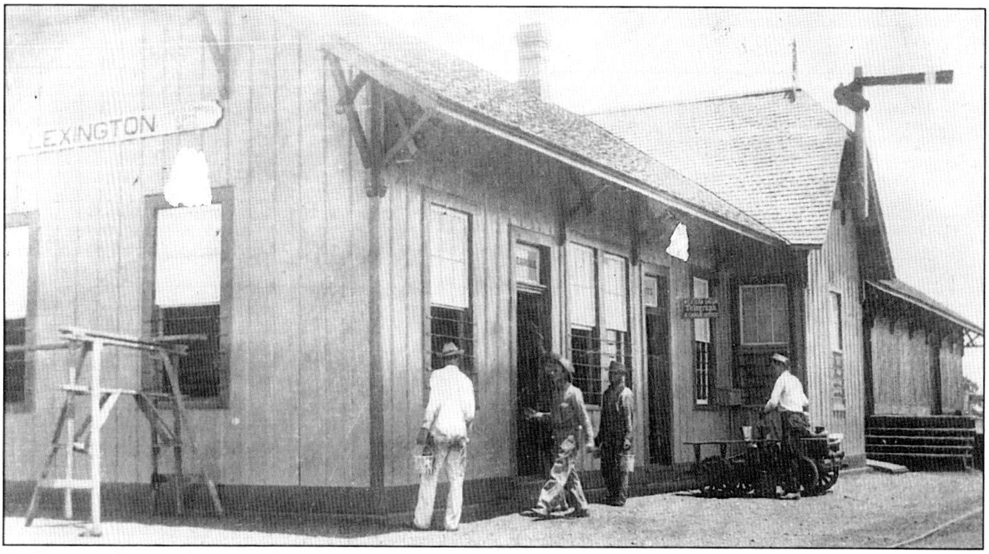

Galen Brademan (pictured center with his back facing the photographer) painted the Lexington depot in the early 1900s. An entry from Minnie Hester's diary on June 28, 1900, read, "Here Tena and I are bounding our way across Texas on our way to Colorado. We left Lexington at 1:17 a.m. and arrived in Fort Worth, after a change at Waco, at 5:00 p.m. We are now crossing the Panhandle. When we arrived at Quannah we were dirty! We had never been so filthy in our lives with the soot that came in on us through the car windows from the coal-burning engine. We got us some berths in a sleeper, which is screened and much cleaner. It is surely a lot more comfortable and we will sleep well tonight."

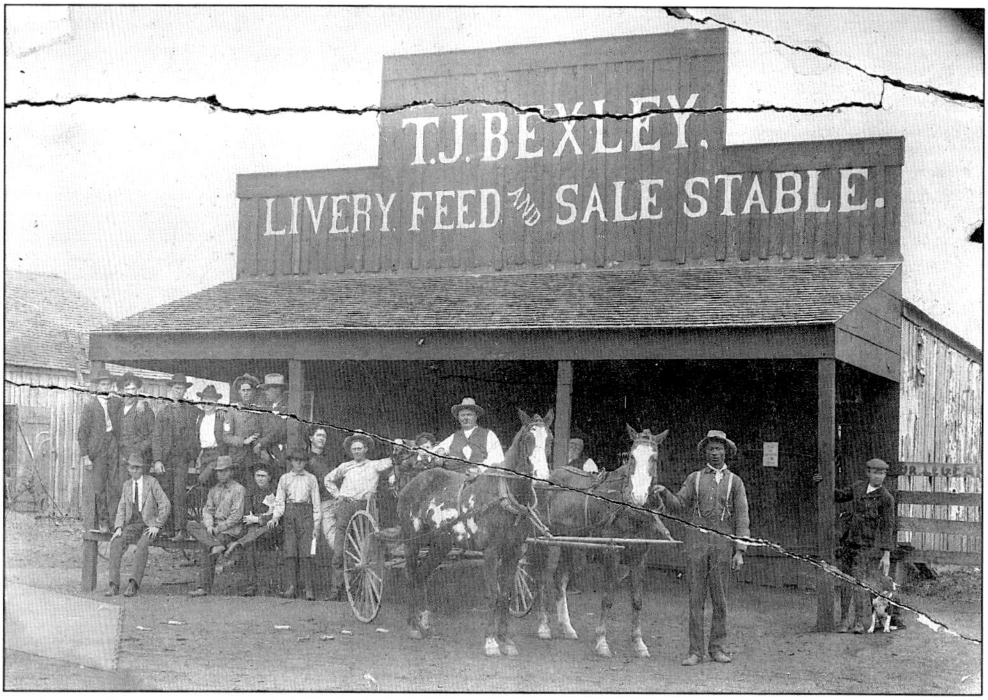

In this early 1900s view of the Bexley Livery and Stable, Mr. Thomas J. Bexley is in the center of the wagon. To Bexley's right is Galen F. Brademan.

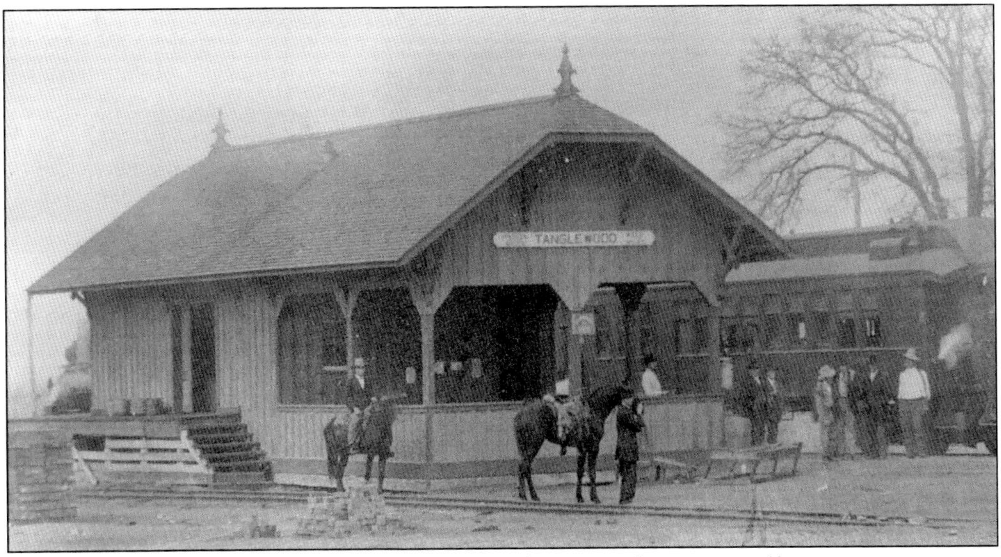

The "Dinky" was a one or two car train in which engine, baggage, and/or passenger sections were combined. It ran daily between Yoakum and Waco with a crew of three—an engineer, brakeman, and fireman. The Dinky familiar to Lee County is pictured here at the Tanglewood Depot. Eloise Brademan relates, "In 1945 Sikes and I had been married about a year—he was fresh out of the Army Signal Corps then—and we didn't have a car. My parents lived close to Hicks near Tanglewood. To go to see my parents we would board the Dinky on the SAAP line. The conductor was so nice he would let us off at the RR crossing in front of my parents home. When we were ready to come back home, all we had to do was to stand on the RR track and flag the Dinky and it would stop so we could board the train."

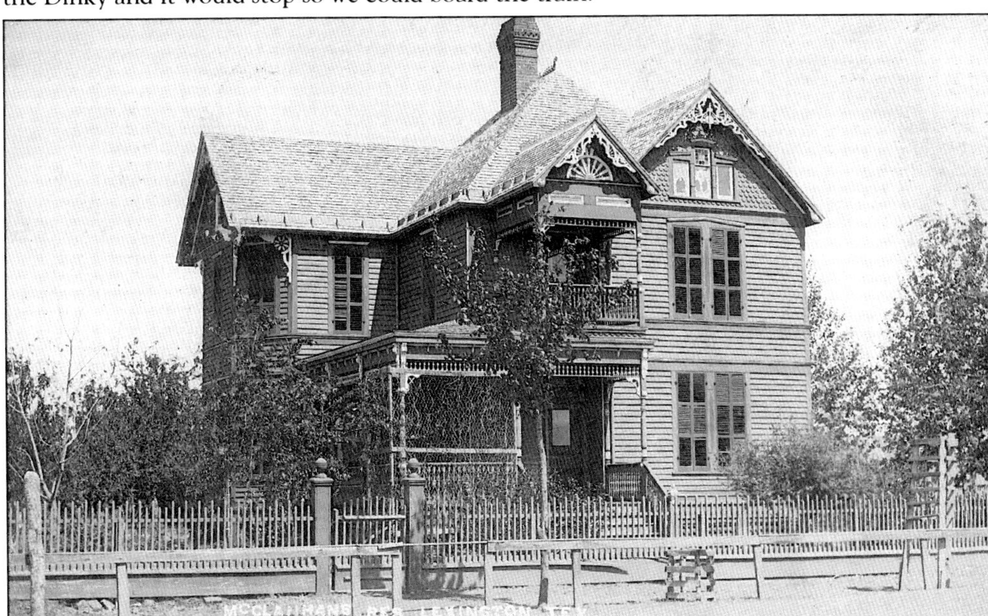

The McClanahan home, built in the late 1800s, still stands and is in excellent condition. It is now occupied by one of the Lexington teachers. Mr. and Mrs. James Heffington lived in the home, which Nell Heffington inherited from her parents, the McClanahans.

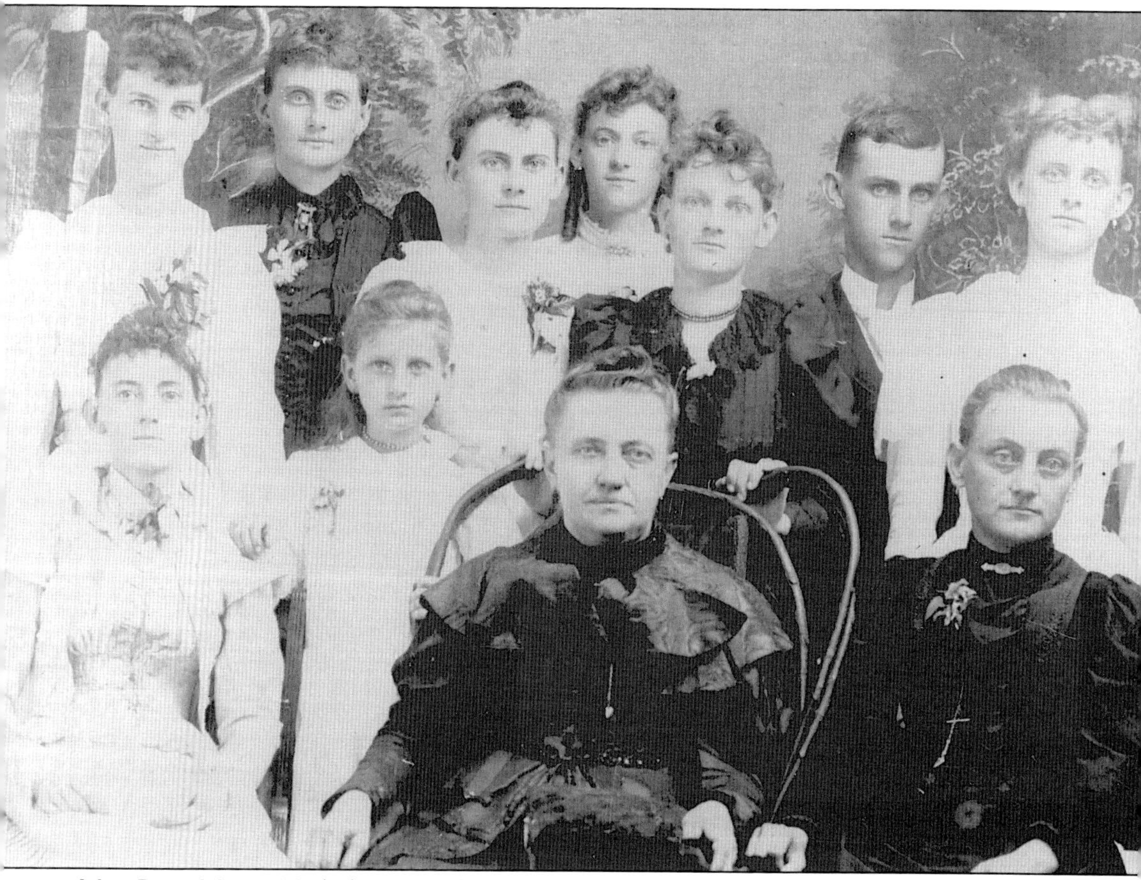

Mrs. Peter Martin Nicholas Bismark Hester, nee Louisa Wolf (1840–1923), appears in the center foreground surrounded by her nine daughters and one son. From left to right are as follows: (front row) Marie, Flora, and Dora; (middle row) Clara, Bella, Germania, and Minnie; (back row) Elvira, Tena, and Bismark. The family story is that Nicholas Hester fell in love with Louisa in Germany but could not marry her because of a social class difference. Nicholas came to Texas and, being a versatile and accomplished man, soon established himself as a merchant. He then sent for Louisa. They made quite a couple. The girls called their mother "the Queen" and always said "Mother was the strong one," but Nicholas was also remarkable and the girls all grew up to be strong women.

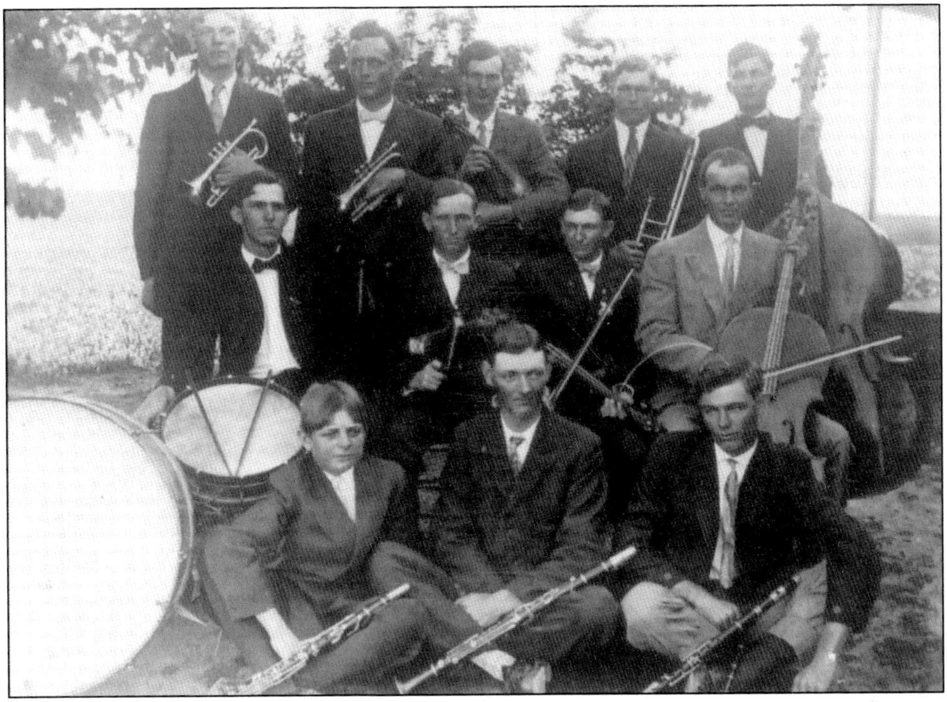

Louisa Wolf Hester's brothers were all musical. The Wolf boys used to arrive at the Hester Camp near Fedor with a variety of instruments, ready to perform. In the center rear is Willie Wolf, the "left-handed violinist." A number of Hester daughters inherited the musical trait and filled the Hester house with music.

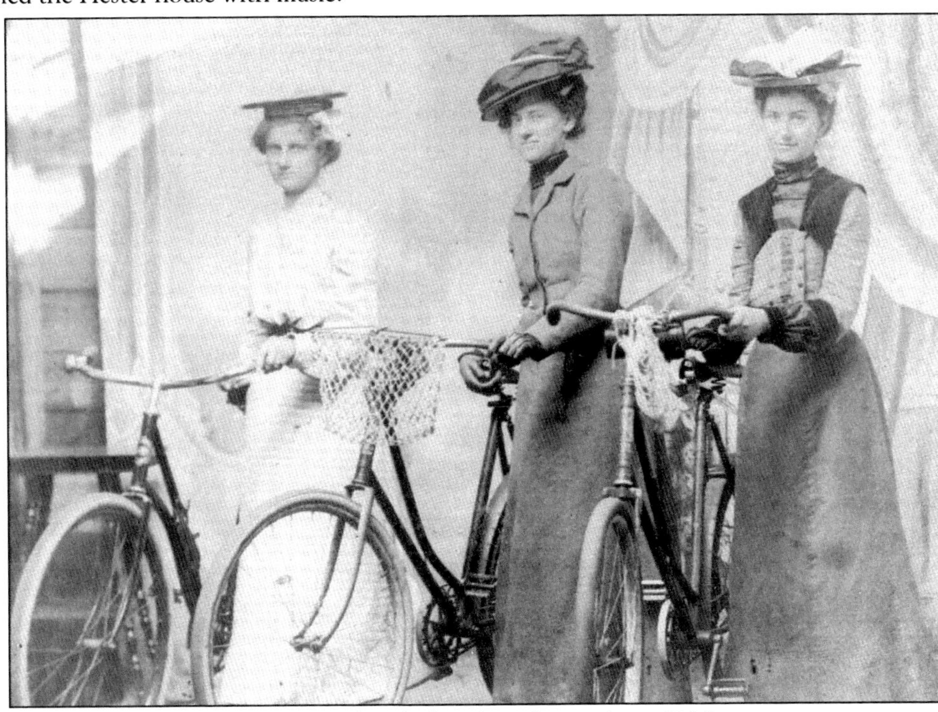

Clara, Tena, and Flora Hester posed with their bicycles in about 1900.

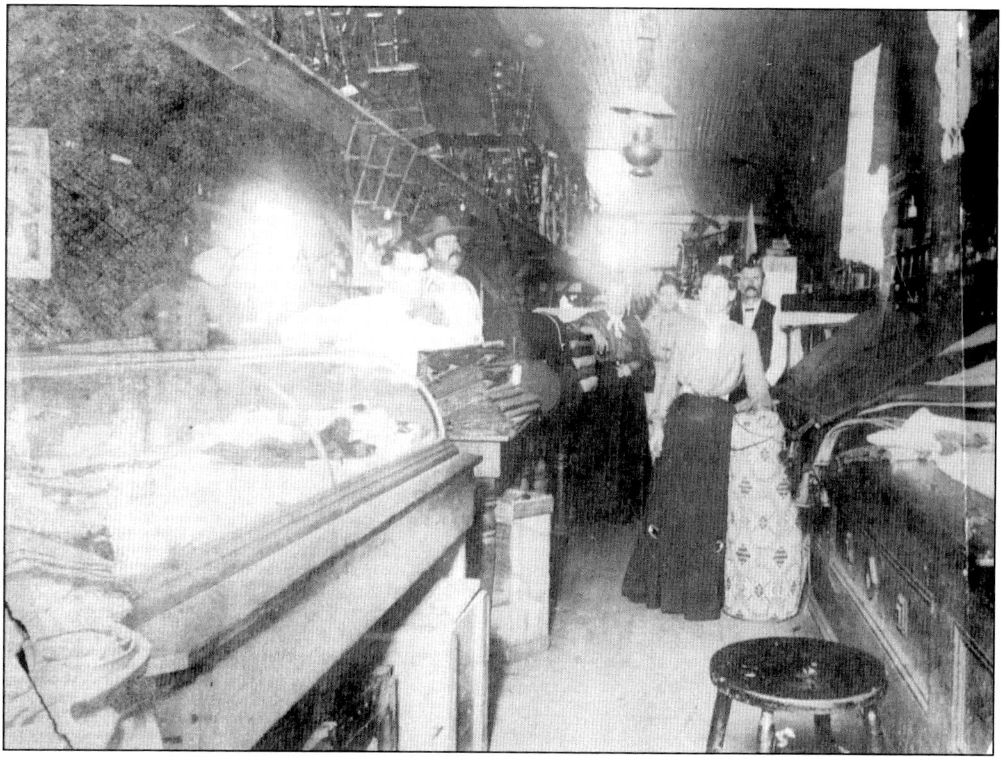

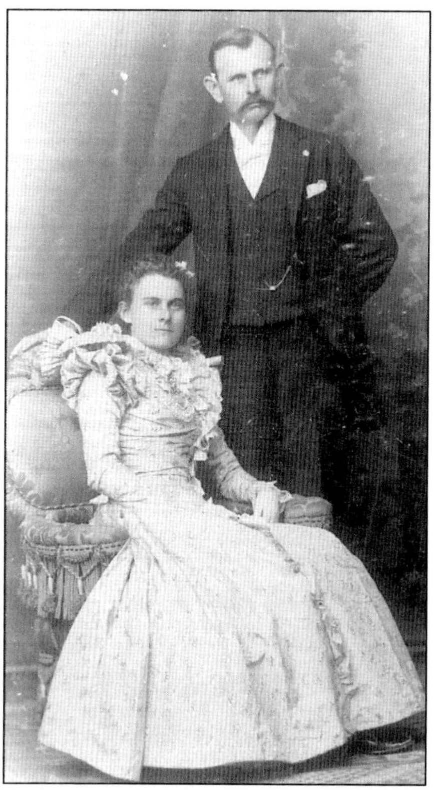

The interior of the Hester-Konzelman store was described as follows: "the building . . . a large shell of a structure about 25 x 100 feet. It would have made a wonderful fire, and in those days there would have been no way to stop it if it had a good start. In that event you could just say goodbye to half a dozen similarly combustible buildings along the block. We opened as soon after breakfast as possible and remained until sundown. We never opened at night but we did light 2 or 3 suspended lamps on dark days." They sold molasses, kerosene, vinegar, ribbons, laces, goods, and shoes—nothing that required refrigeration, such as eggs, milk, or butter. "Business was done chiefly on credit with full payment made during cotton harvesting time. We lost little to bad debts since most of our customers really wanted to pay if at all possible. Mortgages were taken, but I never heard of a foreclosure in our store." —Hester memoir.

Isabella Hester married Henry Engelhardt in 1897. They ran the Hester store until his death in 1917, then she ran it alone until she died in 1945. Among other duties, she graded cotton samples and sold them to Giddings buyers who represented Houston cotton factories. The Hester store was razed in 1967.

Roy Fletcher painted portraits of all nine of the Hester girls. Each painting is different, portraying something about the character of the subject. This one is remarkably romantic.

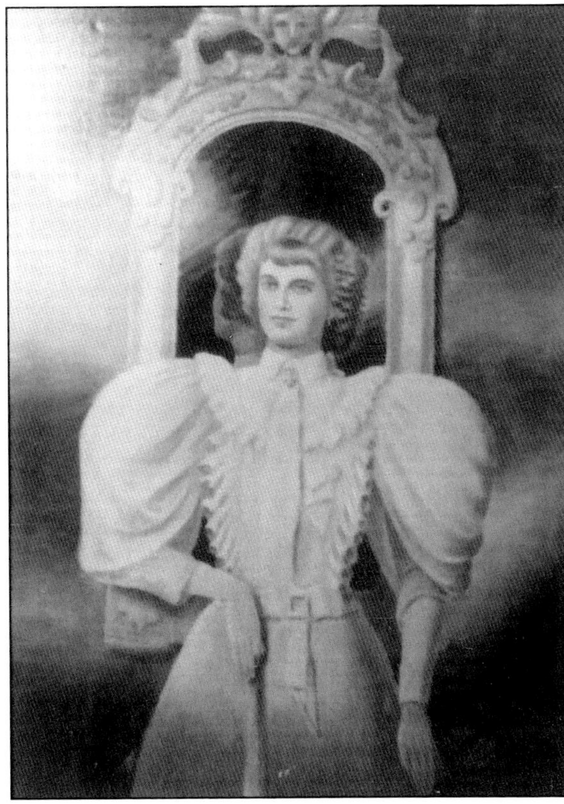

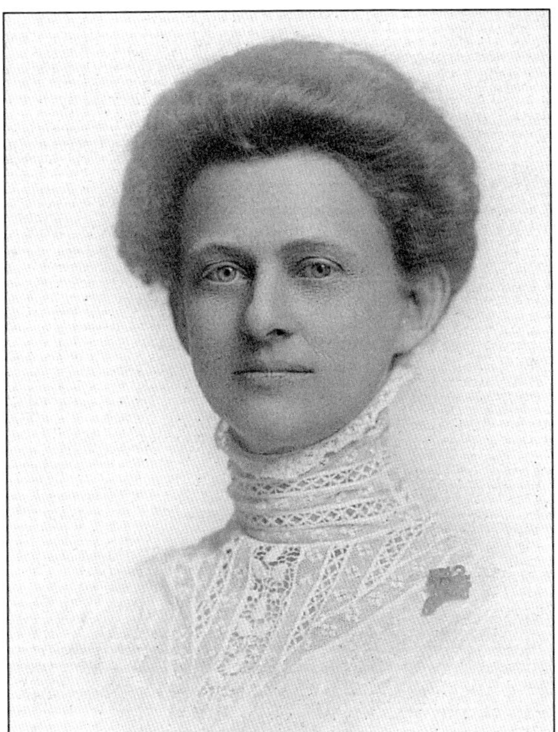

This is a photo depicting the fragile beauty of Minnie Hester. In reality she was a strong woman, an early feminist, and the first president of Texas Women Bankers.

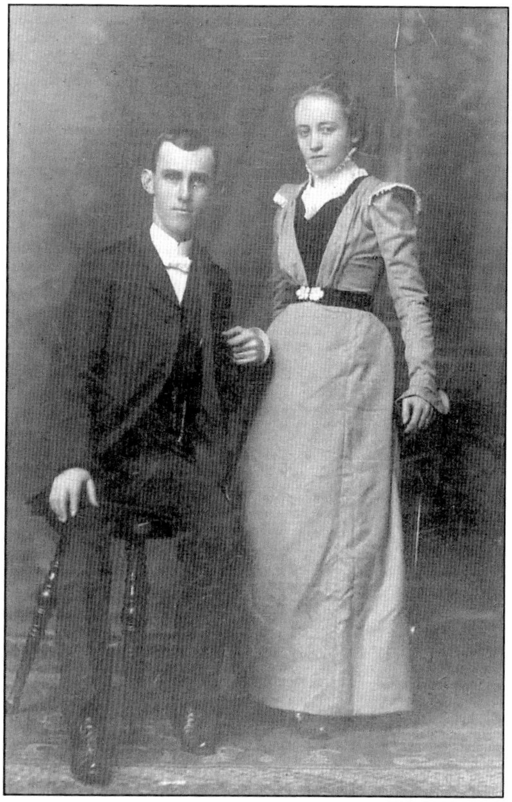

The only Hester son, Bismark, married flirtatious belle Lillie Perry in 1900.

This is one of a number of beaux whose photos Lillie Perry Hester kept. She noted in her scrapbook, "I went with him for a very long time."

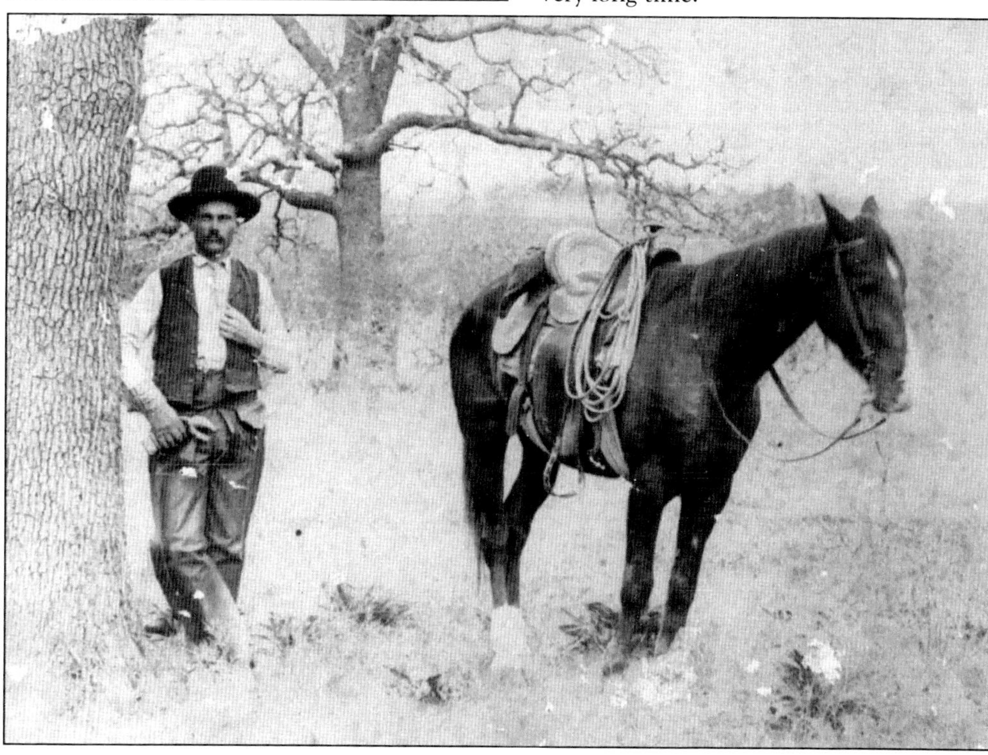

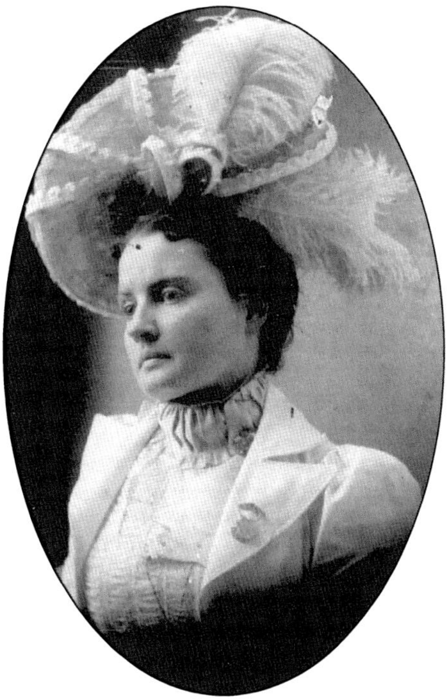

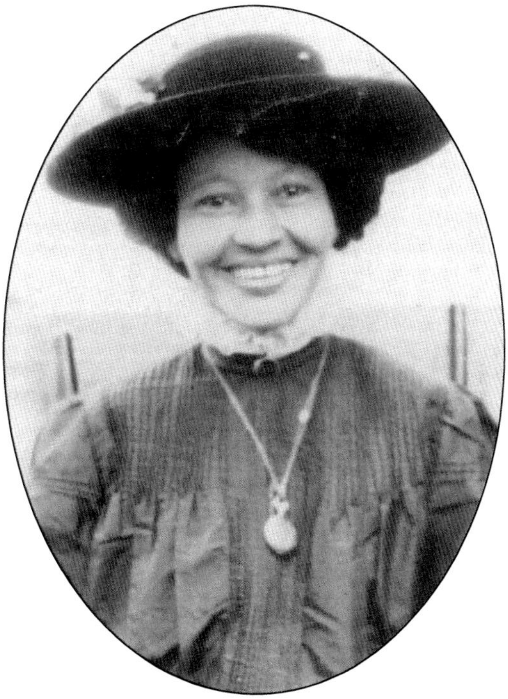

The years from 1900 to 1920 were a great time for hats. These three pretty young ladies, clockwise from upper left, are Maggie Dowdy, Eva Wormley, and Leila Roddy.

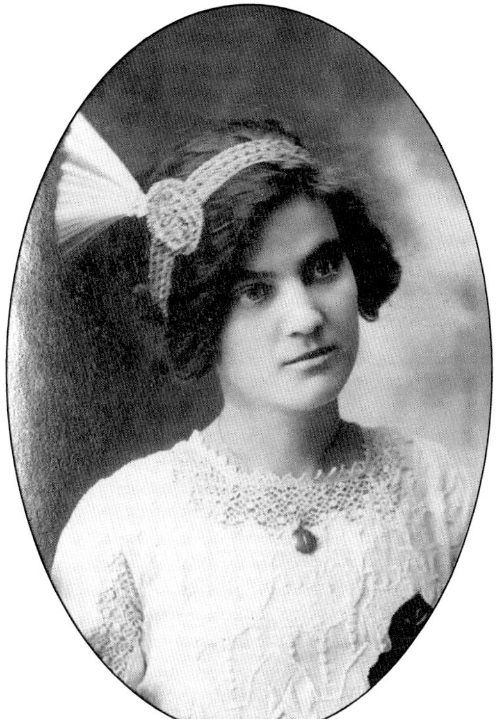

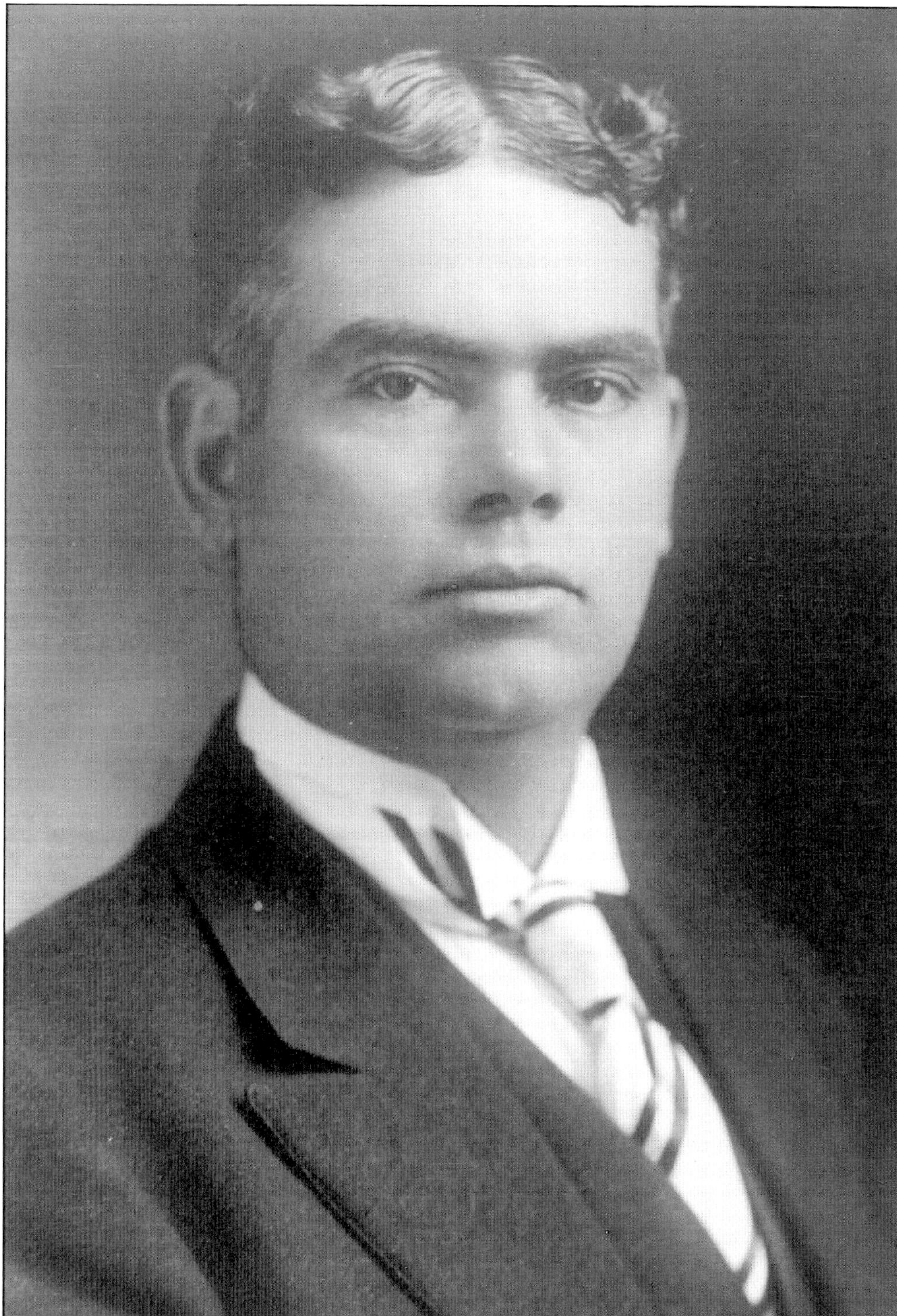

In 1896, the formidable Dora Hester married the also formidable Henry F. Schlosshan, a teacher, lawyer, newspaper founder, and Texas State Representative.

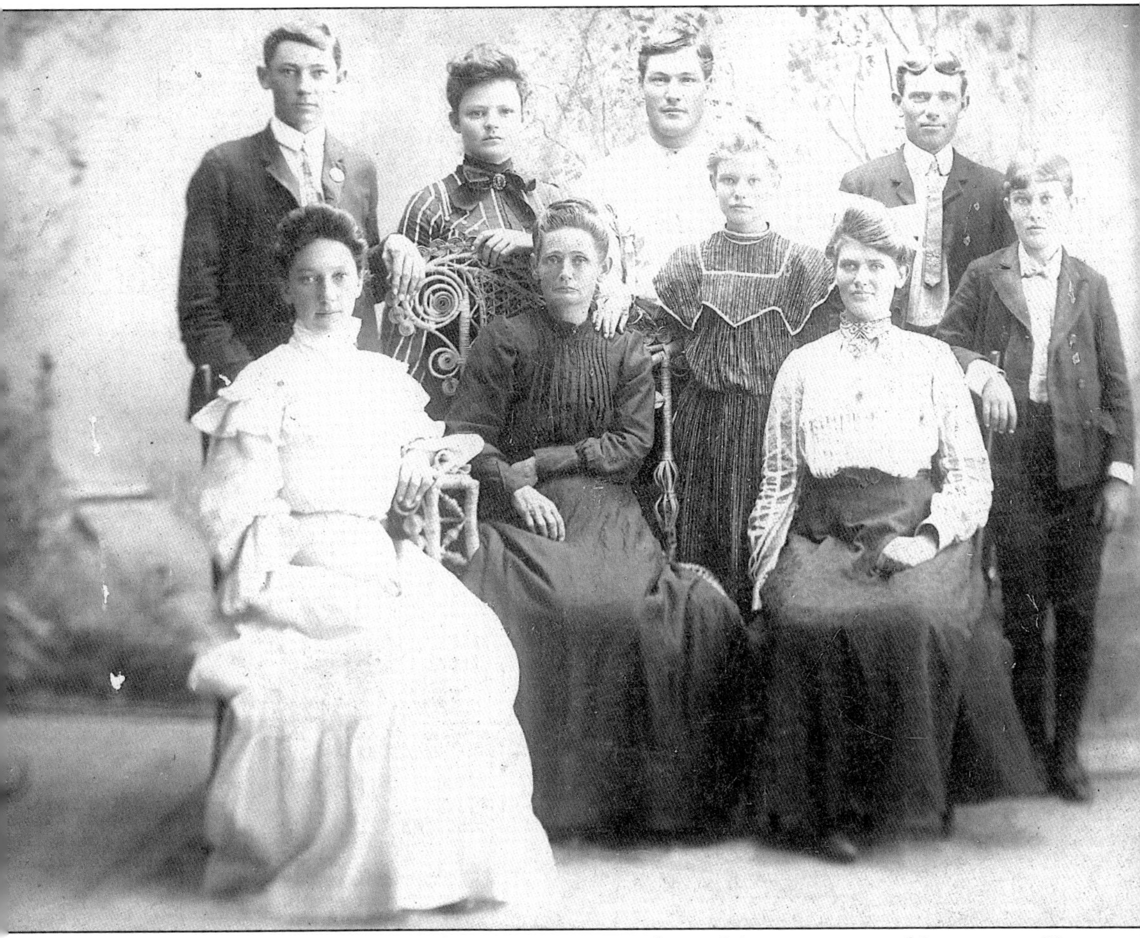

William H. Coffman (1831–1903) was a pioneer settler in Mesquite, west of Lexington. He and his young wife came to the area from Kentucky by covered wagon in 1855. He taught school, served as a county commissioner, and represented what became Lee County in the state legislature in 1883–84 (18th legislature). Coffman was married twice and had children in both marriages. This complex portrait taken after Coffman's death contains children of his second marriage—the rightmost foursome of Cleve, John, Nell, and Allie Coffman—and Coffman's second wife Mary Standlee (in the center of the front row). Coffman's daughter by his first marriage, Nolie Coffman Thomas Thompson, was married twice, the second time to Danish immigrant and widower Jens Thompson. The leftmost threesome in the picture is composed of Nolie's daughter, Neva Thomas (behind Mary), and her stepchildren, Lauris and Mary Thompson (on the left). The identity of the man in the center of the back row is unknown.

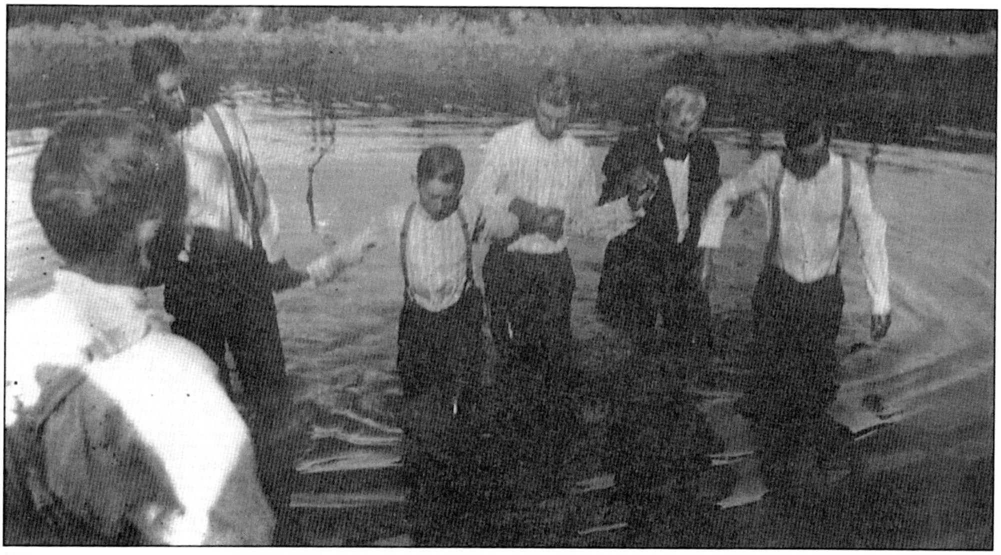

"Camp meetings were July and August experiences in the Baptist church, and Gum Springs on the Lexington-Giddings road was a favorite spot for building the brush arbor necessary for the protracted revival. The springs were dammed up to form a pool sufficiently deep for baptismal purposes." —*A History of Lee County, Texas.*

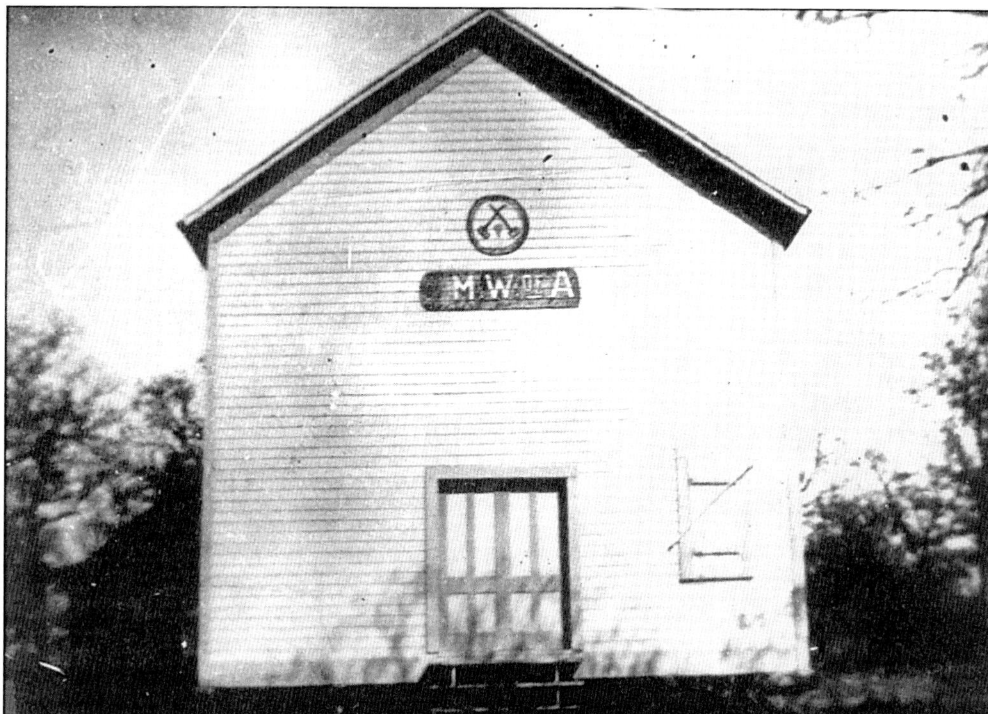

Fraternal societies were varied and prevalent in the 19th century. They often offered services such as insurance policies as well as social events. The crossed axes symbol over the door marks this austere building as the house of the Knobbs chapter of the Woodmen of the World, a fraternal benefit life insurance society. Many local cemeteries contain gravestones topped with stone logs or other insignia signifying the deceased's membership in this order.

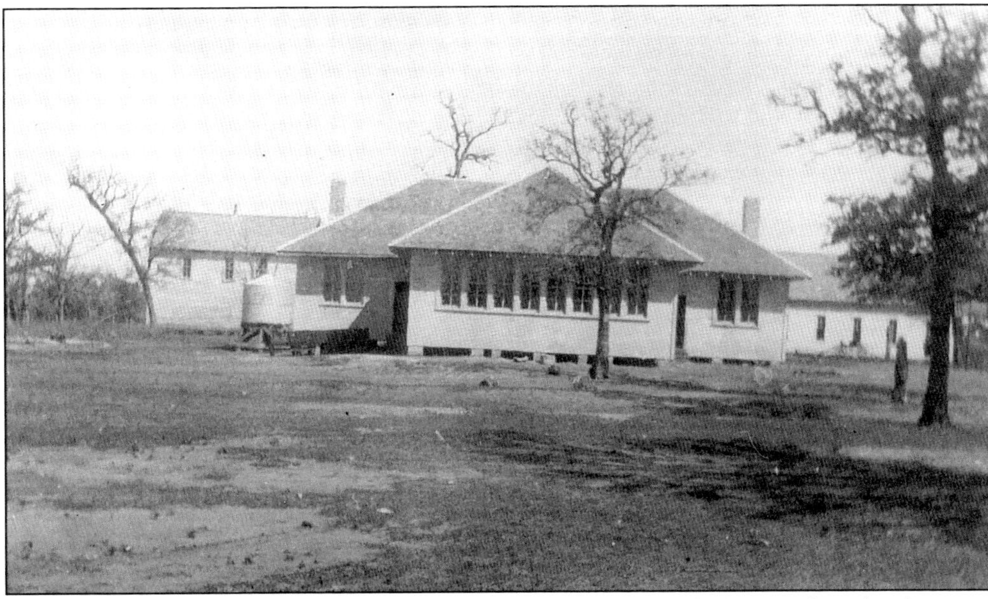

The Knobbs school is pictured with trees bare from a disastrous hailstorm that also destroyed the year's crops. "Our school building, made of pine, was little more than a windbreak. The wood heaters were good, but the fuel was too often green . . . good for nothing but generating smoke . . . we had little heat and a good deal of soot. On cold days we had to huddle as near the stove as possible to keep half comfortable . . . The tragedy of the early day schools was the lack of a library . . . children sat through the entire school term with one little reader." —*A History of Lee County, Texas.*

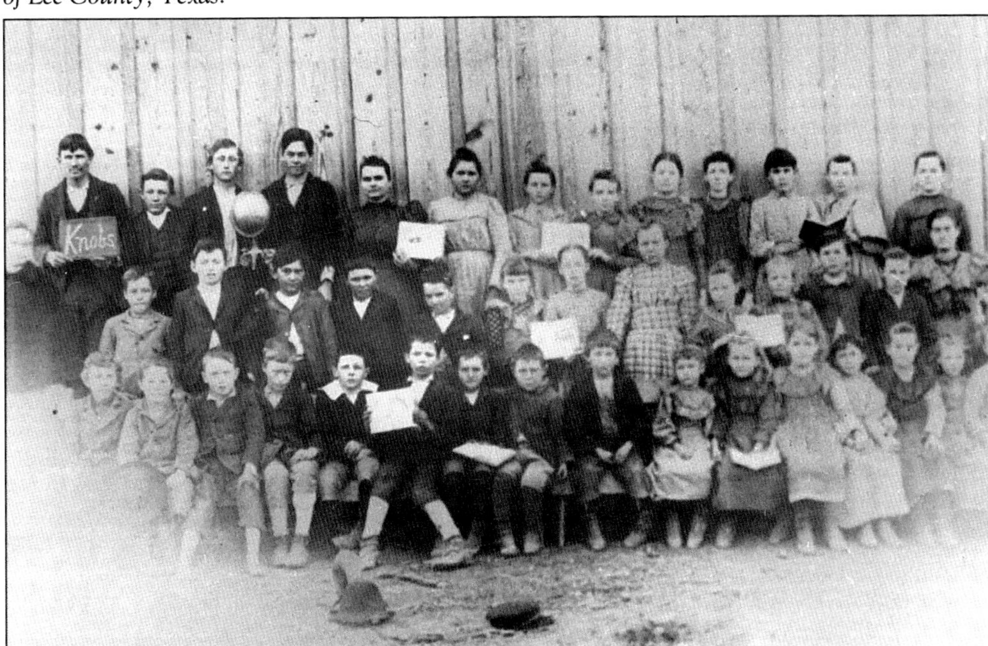

In this shot of the Knobbs school class, one member on the far left displays a sign reading "Knobs." This school, which was established in 1890, later became a one-room, two-teacher school. Two classes, each with its own teacher and stove, met at opposite ends of the classroom.

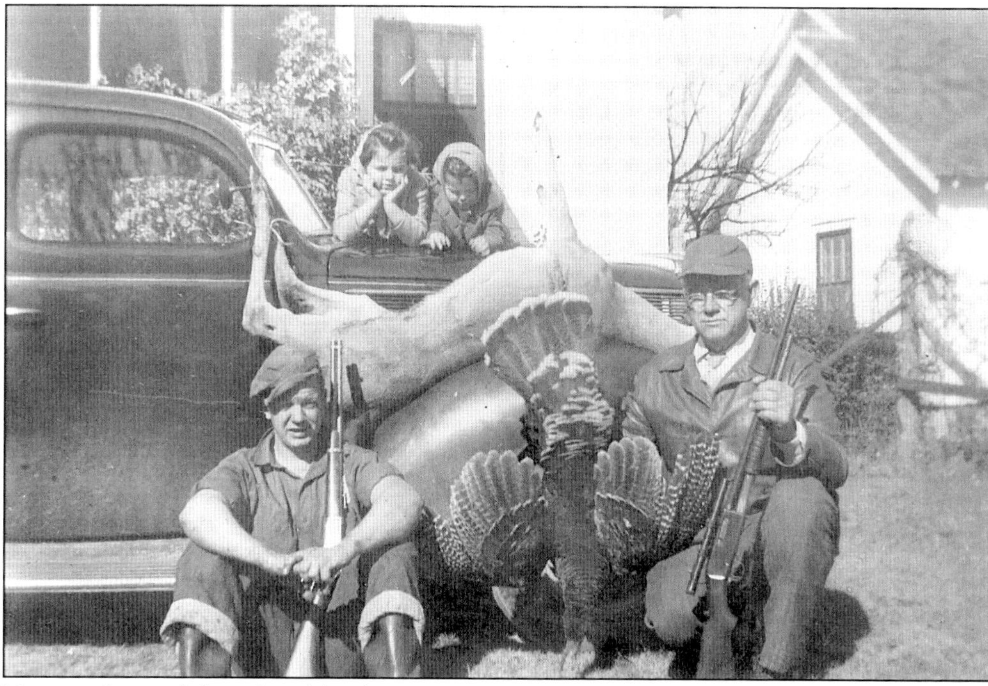

Hunting deer and the wily wild turkey continues to be a popular sport to this day.

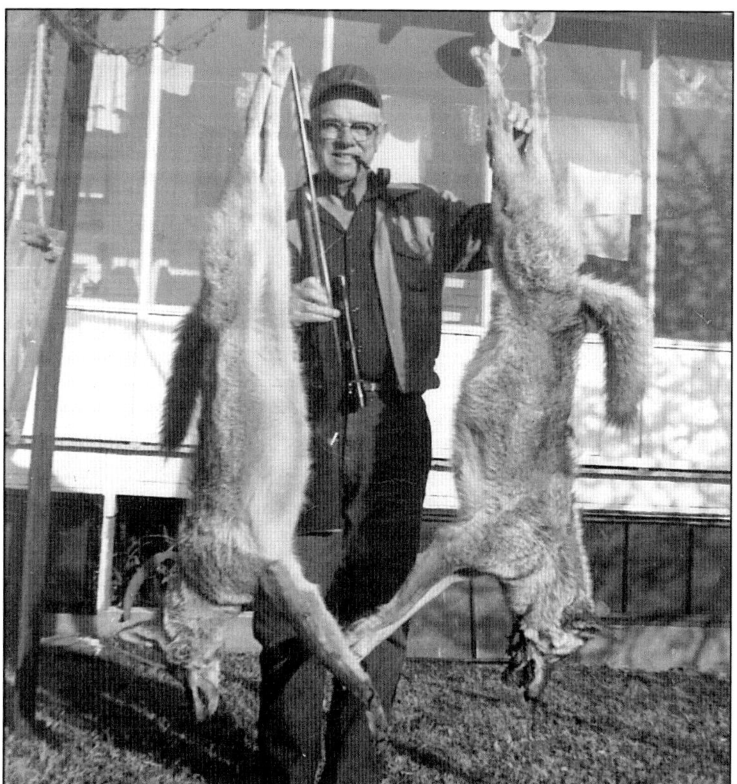

Will Grusendorf displays trophies from hunting coyote. They also hunted coons with dogs. The hunters could tell where each dog was by his "singing," the tone of his voice "just as plain as if you were looking at him," and they viewed with some alarm the hopeless ignorance of those who could not appreciate this music.

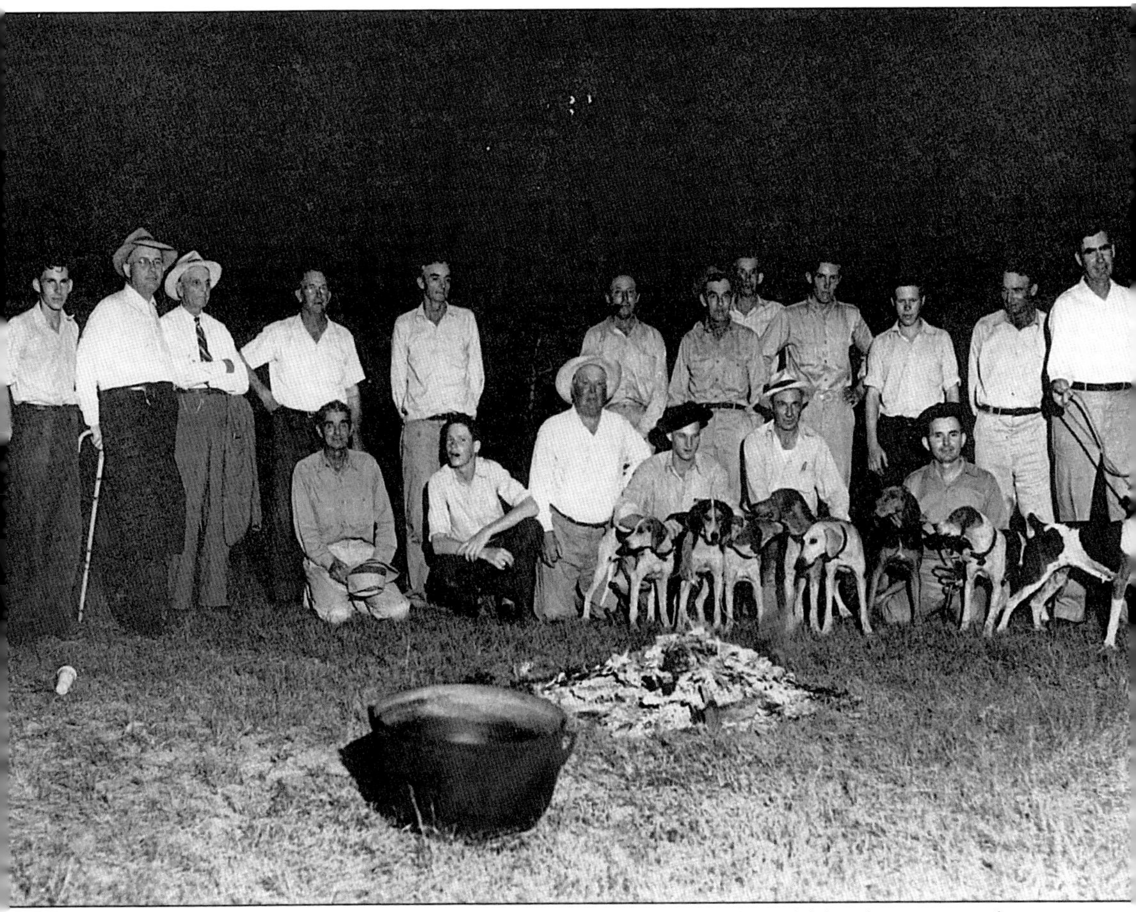

This Knobbs fox hunt took place about 1945. Customarily, a flavorful but bony squirrel stew, with onions, potatoes, carrots, corn, and tomatoes, would be prepared in the pot. Pictured left to right are as follows: (standing) P.A. Helms Jr., Dr. W.R. White, Rev. Ed Mobley, Albert Carnell, Charlie Eddleman, W.D. Stewart, Irvin Nance, "Doc" Euin Walker, Grady Edwards, J.V. Helms, Dee McDavid, P.A. Helms Sr., and Alfred Browning; (sitting) Clem Edwards, Waverly Helms, Dee Hughes, Bennie McDavid, Nelson Harrison, and Rev. Olen Miles.

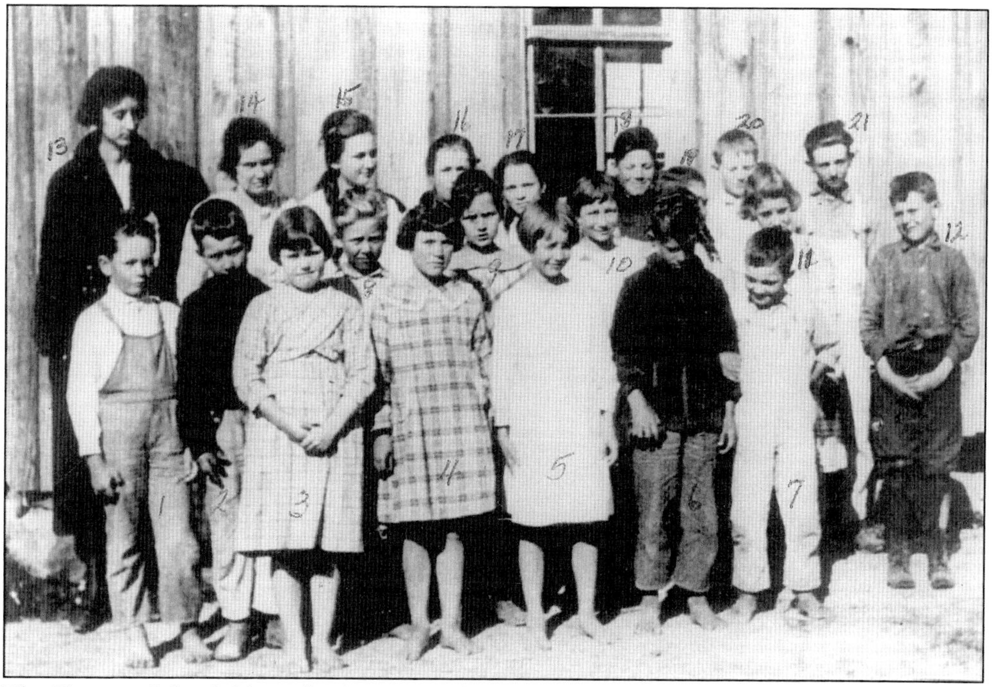

The Florence School Class of 1930 consisted of the following students, from left to right: (front row) Jim Bob Allen, Waymon Clare, Addie Byrum, Audrey Clare, Audrey Jensen, unidentified, and Wayne Yeager; (second row) Ardis Clare, unidentified, Mildred Jensen, unidentified, and unidentified; (back row) teacher Beulah Hadaway, Ola Byrum, Alpha Clare, Melissa Clare, Etha Yeager, unidentified, Lucile Yeager, Burt Poe, and Arnold Jensen.

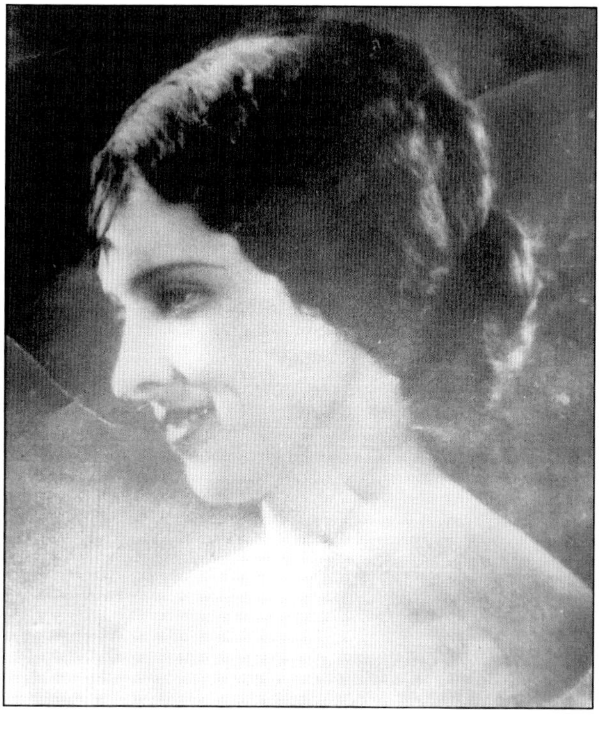

This photo of Blanche Franklin Horton was taken in 1922–23, when she taught at the Florence School. She signed a contract saying that she would leave if she could not control her pupils. Later she also taught at Leo School.

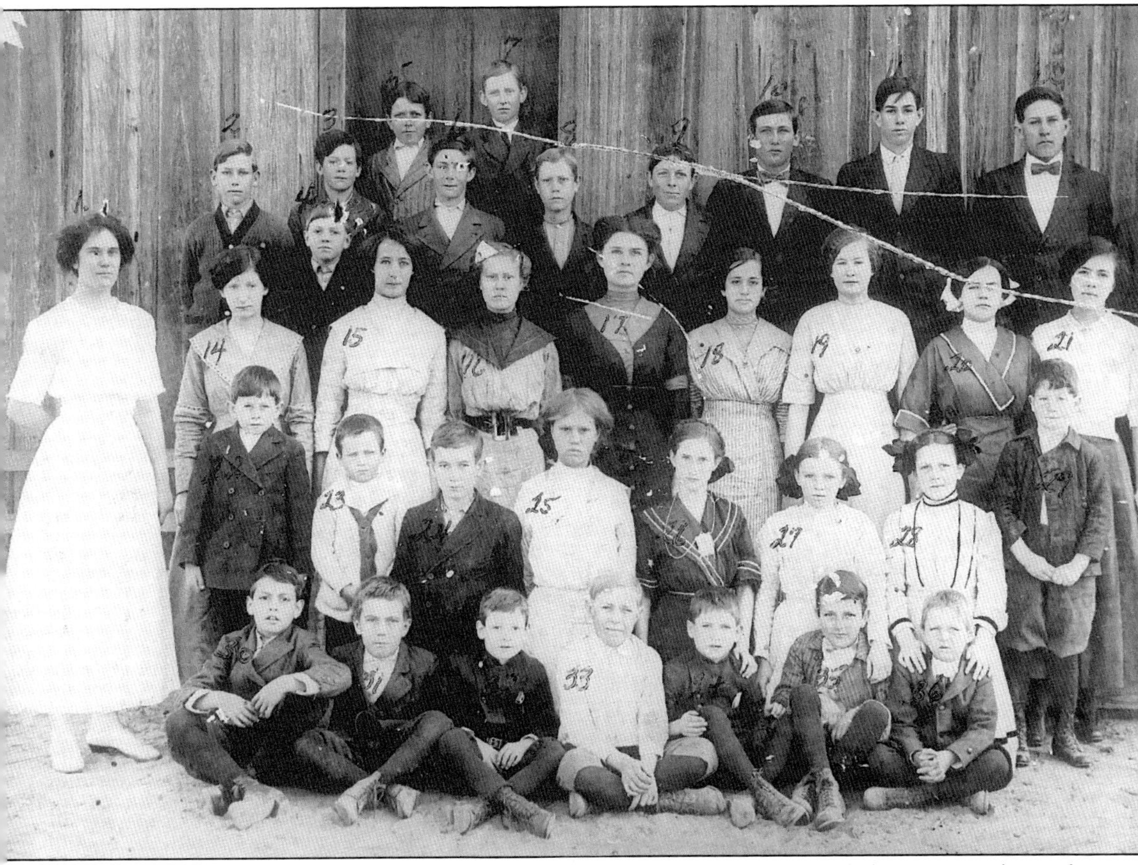

The Cole Springs School was located in northwest Lee County. The following members of the class of 1912 are shown here, from left to right, back to front: Hattie Davis McVoy, Virgil Swain, Andy Horton, Dick Gay, Roy Crouch, Charlie Horton, Guy Burroughs, Tommy Bryant, Willie Crouch, Marvin Bexley, Gilbert Cook, Gene Carder, Raphe Boswell, Ruth Moore, Nettie Horton, Ola Bryant, Lula Bell Corder, Agnes Cook, Blanche Moore, Eva Boswell, Elsie Gay, Hoodie Snodgrass, Guy Tabor, Earl Moore, Bettie Bryant, Grace Nettles, Hazel Gay, Mattie Crouch, Alfred Tabor, Adrian Boswell, Clyde Albritton, Luther Boswell, Irvin Williamson, Carl Moore, Robert Crouch, and Fayette Crouch.

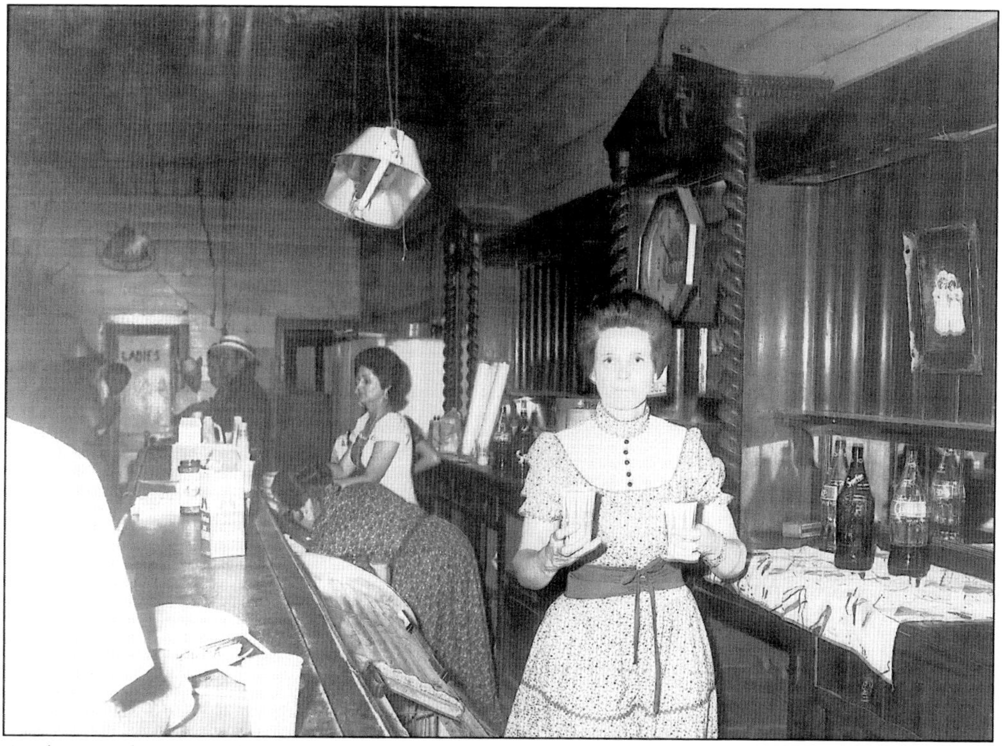

At the May homecoming in Lexington in 1974, they served "Sassparilla" in the "Longbranch."

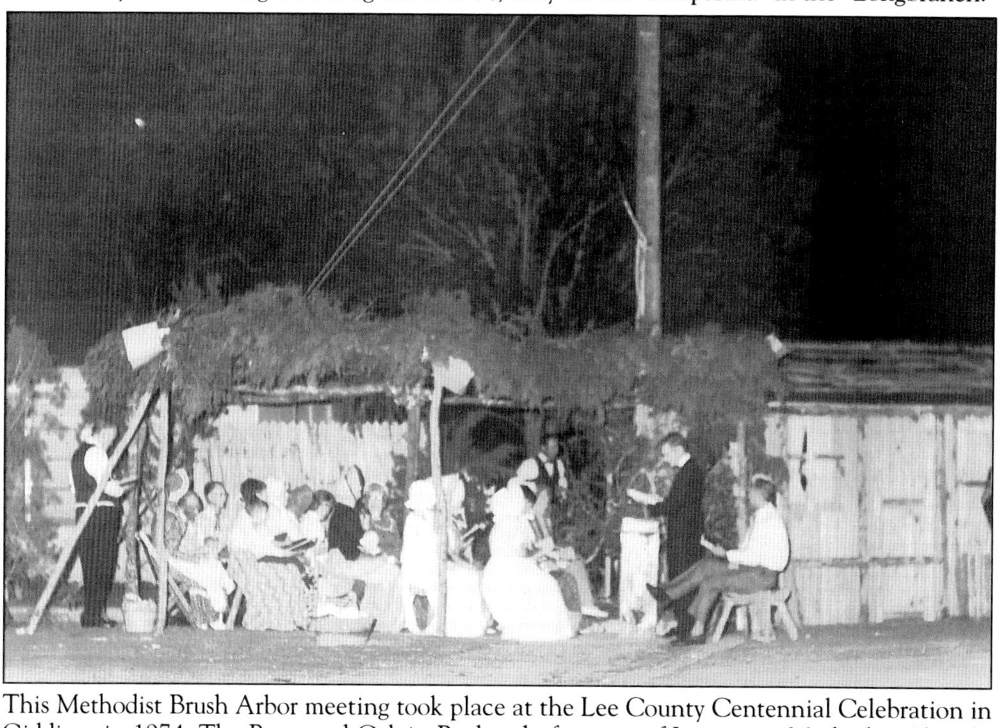

This Methodist Brush Arbor meeting took place at the Lee County Centennial Celebration in Giddings in 1974. The Reverend Calvin Beckendorf, pastor of Lexington Methodist Church, is at the altar.

Two

Communities along the Old San Antonio Road

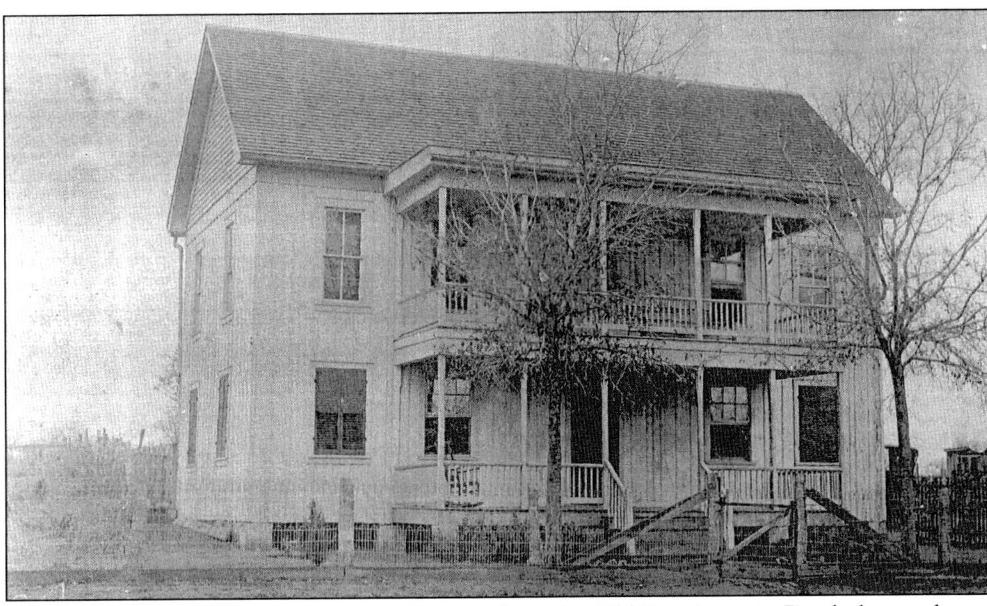

In the 1850s, Evergreen was a stagecoach stop along the Old San Antonio Road, the northeast-southwest trail between Nacogdoches and San Antonio, which is now approximated by Highway 21. In the mid-1880s, Sam Houston, among others, stayed at the Stockton Hotel at this intersection. Also located on Stockton's land was the famous Hanging Tree under which the justice of the peace held court—and upon which more than one horse thief was hung. In 1896, by which time Evergreen had become Lincoln, Johann Marburger built this house, which also served as a hotel. Marburger plied several other trades in which the Lincoln intersection was an advantage, including mail carrier and justice of the peace. The town Lincoln was named for a local Campbellite circuit rider, not for the President.

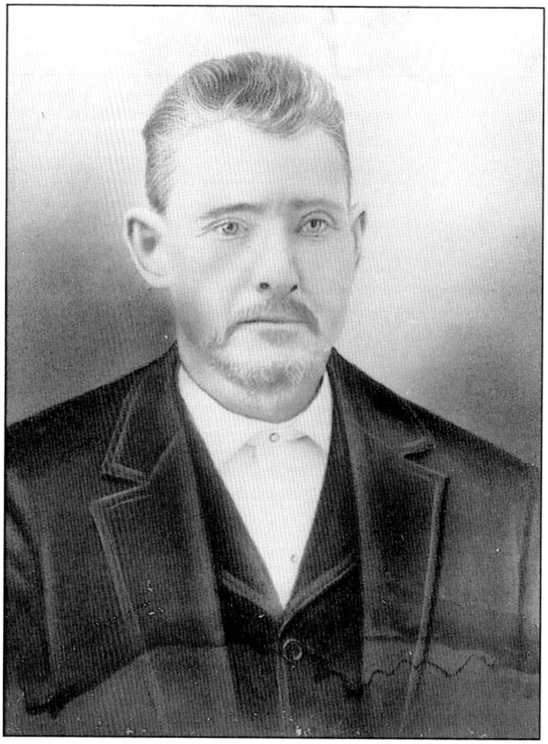

Born in 1834 in Alabama (he died in 1894 in Texas), William Holmes Fariss moved to Evergreen in 1853, just a couple of years before the historically severe droughts of 1856. In1860, his father, Thomas, who was still in Alabama, wrote, "I have 40 acres and I think [to] make 5 or 6 hundred bushels, half a crop. I have old corn and bacon to do until March cotton. Sorry half a crop. A word to Amelia [William's wife] to take care of my 3 grandsons. I am trying to make money to scholar them."

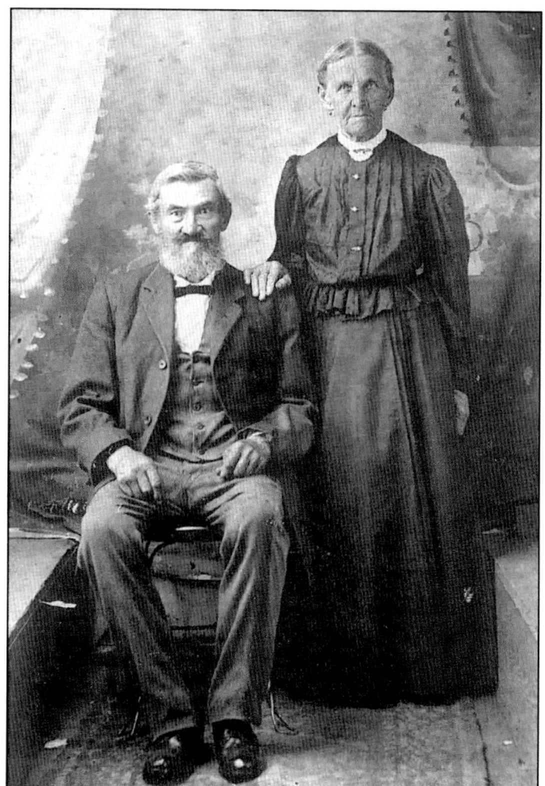

This is Carl F. Hannes and Emile Theresia Hunger Hannes, both born in 1836 in Germany. The Hannes family emigrated from Sachsen to Galveston in 1881 and went directly to Fedor in Lee County. Their son, Carl Hannes, who married Louisa Marburger (the daughter of Johann Marburger), was a successful farmer who could afford to buy the Brown's Mill (Dime Box) gin from John Krenek in 1896.

Reverend Daniel Morse was an itinerant Methodist preacher who came to Texas in 1850 from Mississippi and settled on land on the Middle Yegua. The old Morse homeplace was located about 10 miles north of Giddings on the Old San Antonio Road. Ever on circuit for the Methodist Episcopal Church, South, as he traveled districts up to his 70th year, he still maintained his home in the area until 1867. A memorialist writes, "He was endowed with elements of character combining the attributes of the isothermal line of latitude of his Northern and Southern homes. He brought with him extraordinary energy, strict economy, and an enterprise that never flagged. This indomitable spirit, emancipated from the domination of the isms of the region of his birth, was pervaded by the genial, sympathetic, ardent animus of the clime of his adoption."

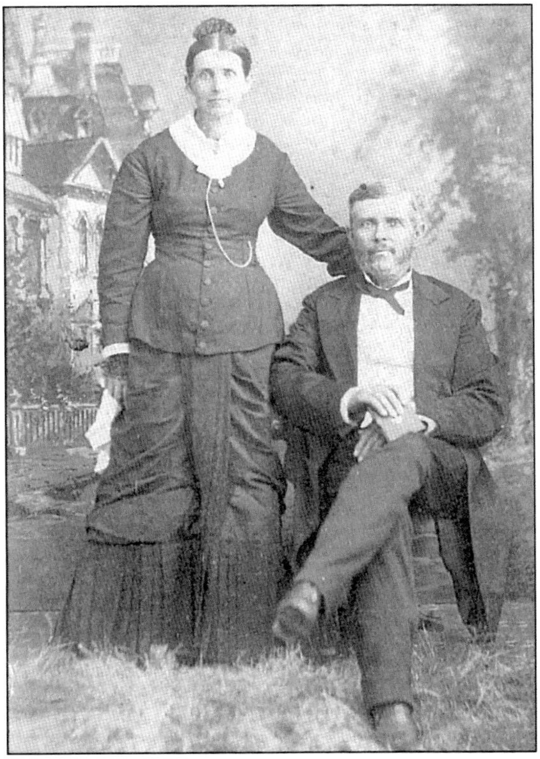

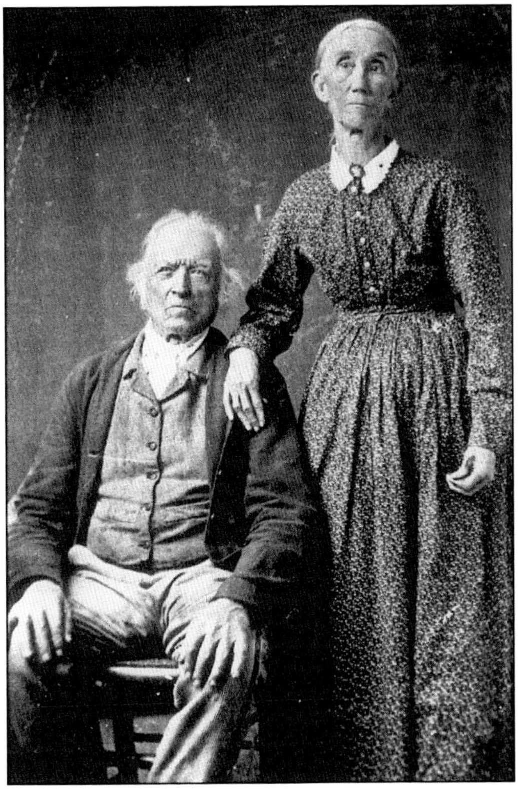

The first Eggers arrived in the Evergreen area before 1880. They were the sons of Moses Egger (1798–1883), shown here with his second wife, Liddie Vance Harris Egger. Their route from Chester County, S.C., went through Tennessee, down the Natchez trace, and took the sons nearly 15 years. Moses' journey took even longer, but he was in Evergreen by 1880. They were neighbors and friends of the Longley family. Egger later told his son Charles tales of the wild areas along the Yegua, where they often had to hunt for their wandering cattle.

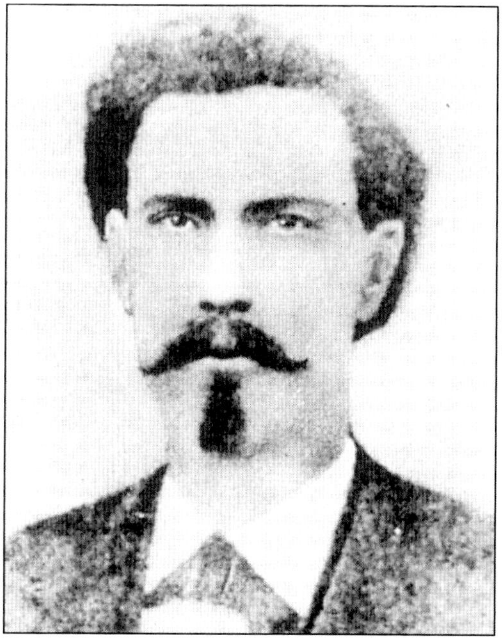

Bill Longley, who spent his youth in Evergreen, is the notorious outlaw of Lee County. His most famous distinction, aside from the number of men he is supposed to have killed, is being "hung twice." The first time, in 1867, the noose knot caught under his ear and he hung, strangulating slowly, until one of his captors shot a couple of times, accidentally severing the rope (and breaking one of Bill's teeth). The second time, in 1878 in Giddings, was fatal.

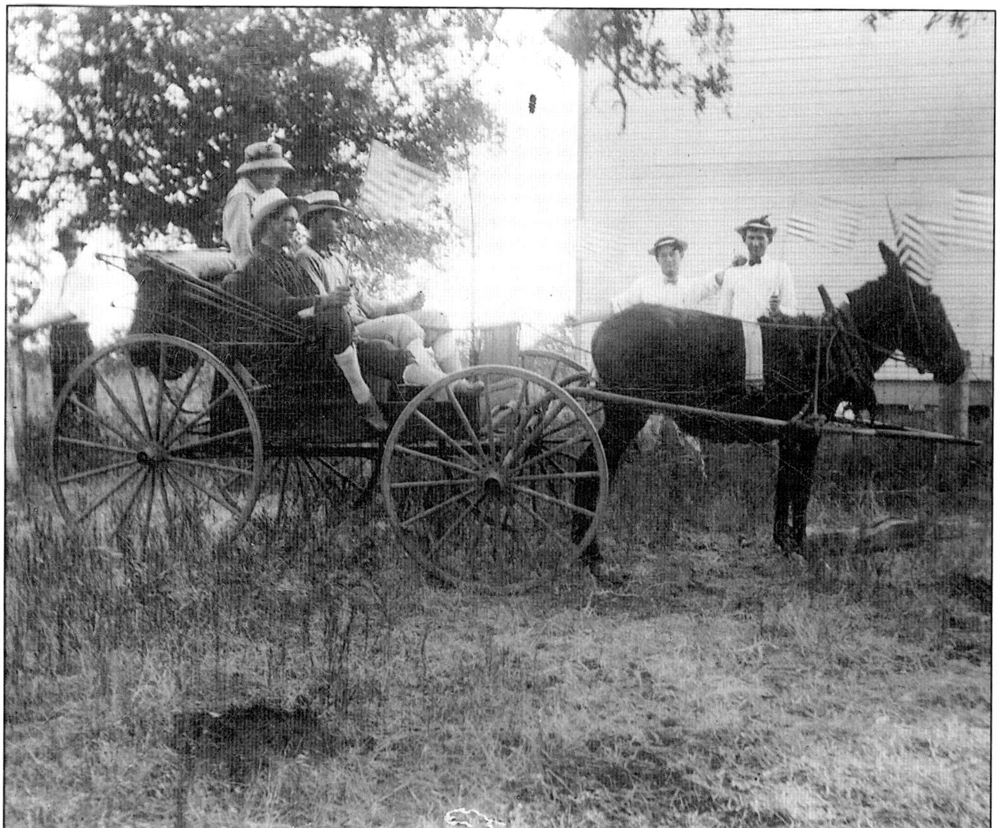

More God-fearing, law-abiding families (even Bill Longley's family fit that description) were the rule. A horse and buggy is shown here bringing a family to visit in Lincoln, Texas.

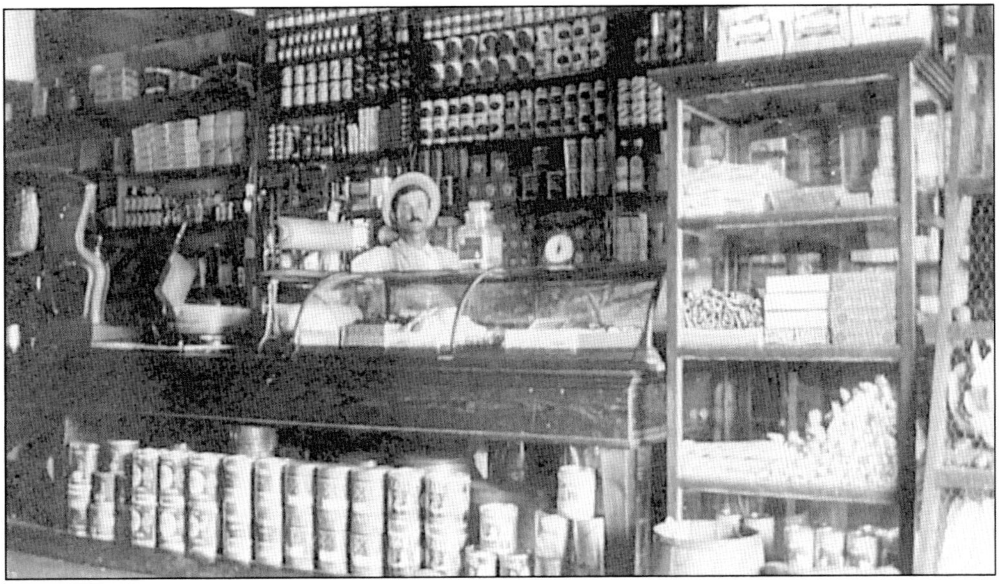

The Zwerneman & Schkade General Merchandise Store in Lincoln (known simply as Z&S), was established in 1905 by Frederick Ernst Schkade, shown here *c.* 1907 behind the counter, and Adolph Zwernemann. Johann Marburger's son Herman married Lena Schkade.

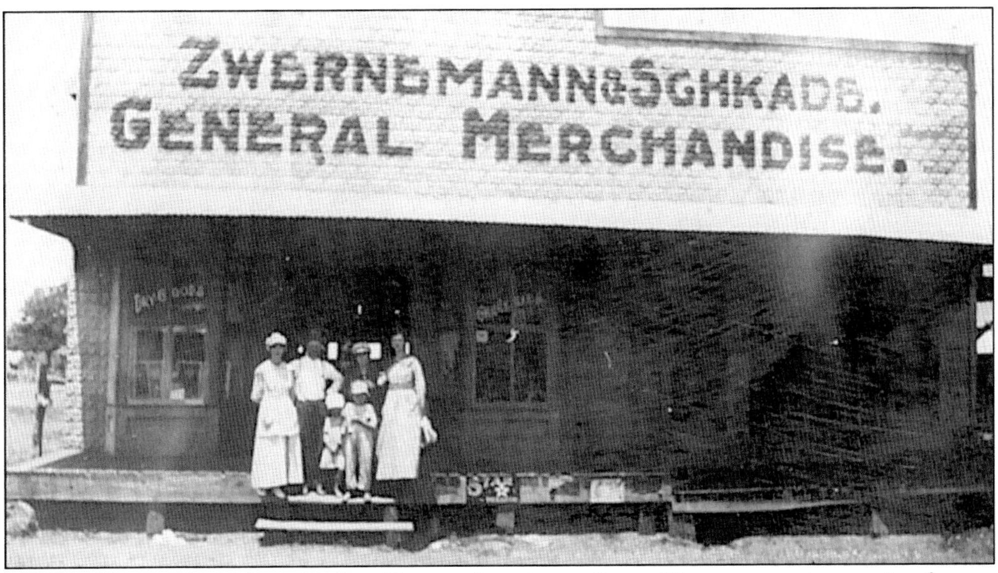

Z & S sold everything from food and beer to buggies and cars. There was an interesting feature of the store—buggies, wagons, and mowing machines were stored in the upper level. There was a 16-by-20-foot wooden door that faced outward and was hinged on the lower side so that it could fold out, controlled by ropes and pulleys, to be lowered at an angle, making a ramp on which equipment could be rolled down to the ground. F.E. Schkade later had the franchise for selling Oaklands in Giddings, and after the company began producing Chevrolets, he sold those.

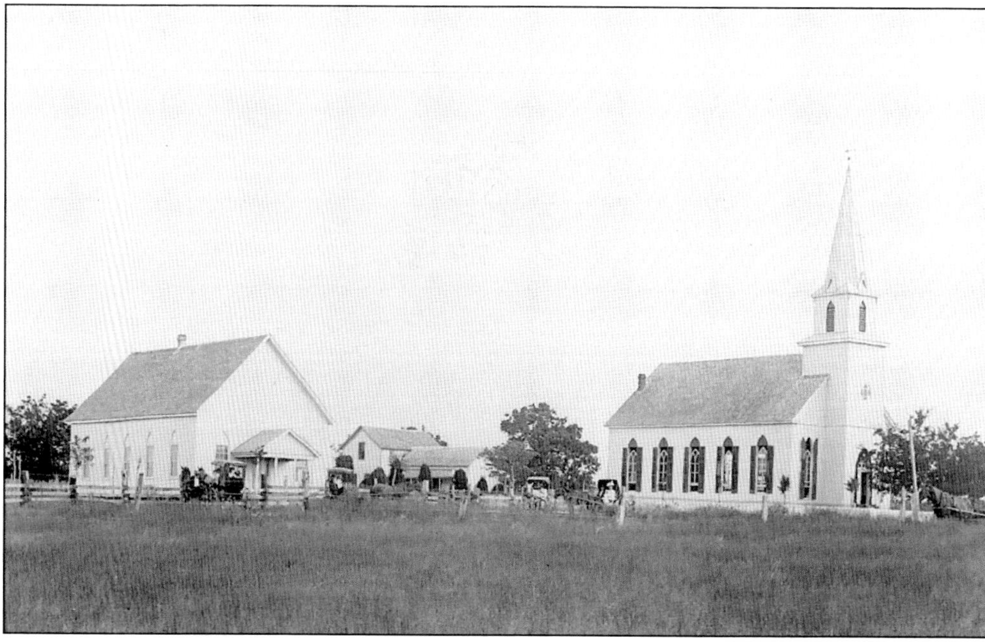

Before 1882, there were four Lutheran schools in the county, one each at Fedor and San Antonio Prairie and two at Serbin. The Lincoln School, on the left in this picture, was built in 1886 and used as a church until a new building was completed five years later to serve 138 baptized and 78 communing members. By 1903, the congregation had grown to 440 baptized members and 227 communicants. Services were in German only for many years. The church was so severely damaged by a windstorm in 1957 that a new church was built.

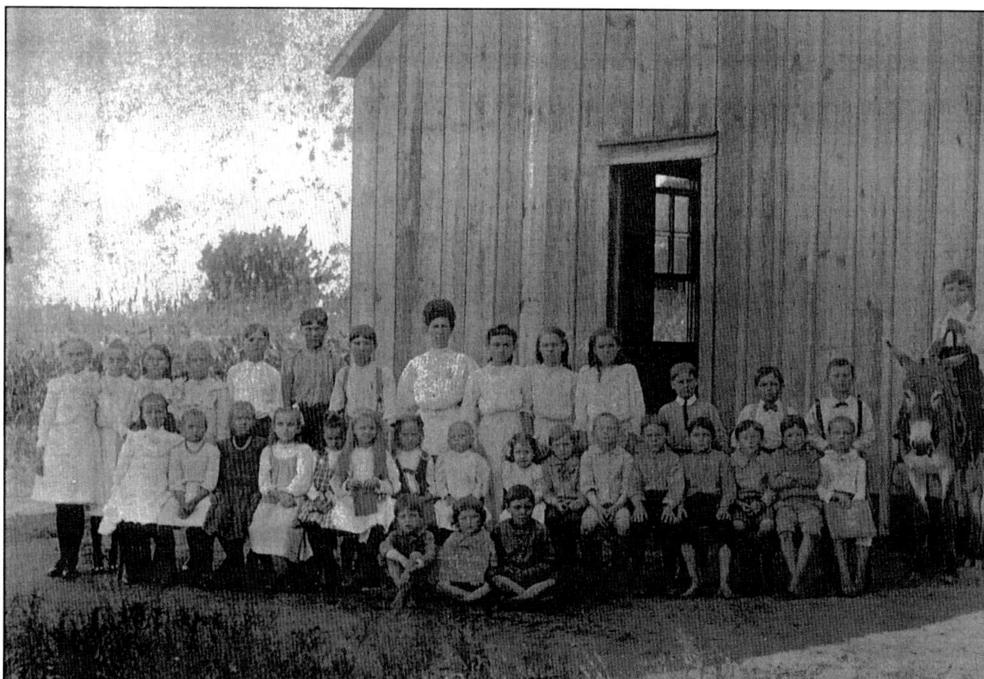

The Lincoln Public School Class of 1908 appears here.

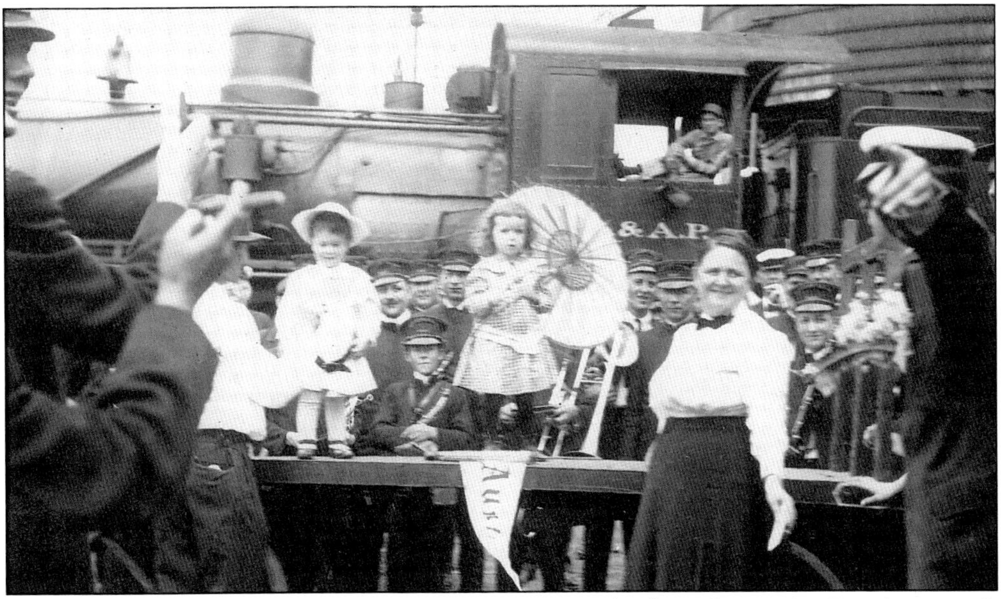

A band, a crowd, and a Sanders child with a pretty umbrella welcome the San Antonio & Aransas Pass train to the Lincoln Station. Was this a special run? Could it be the first run?

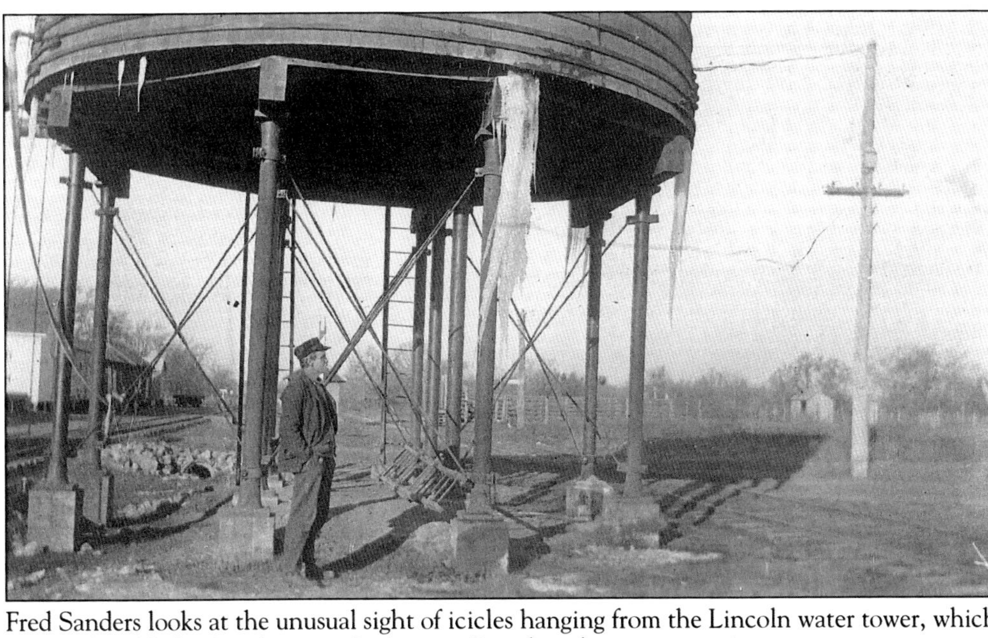

Fred Sanders looks at the unusual sight of icicles hanging from the Lincoln water tower, which was used to fill the San Antonio & Aransas Pass short line steam engines.

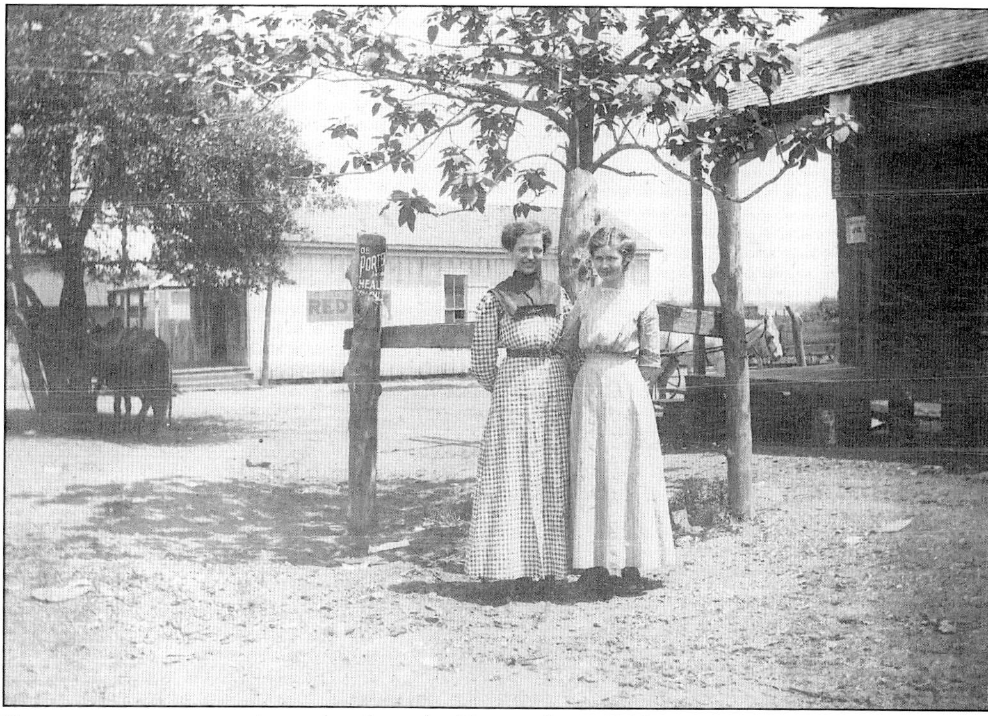

Two pretty women are pictured in Lincoln, Texas, about 1900.

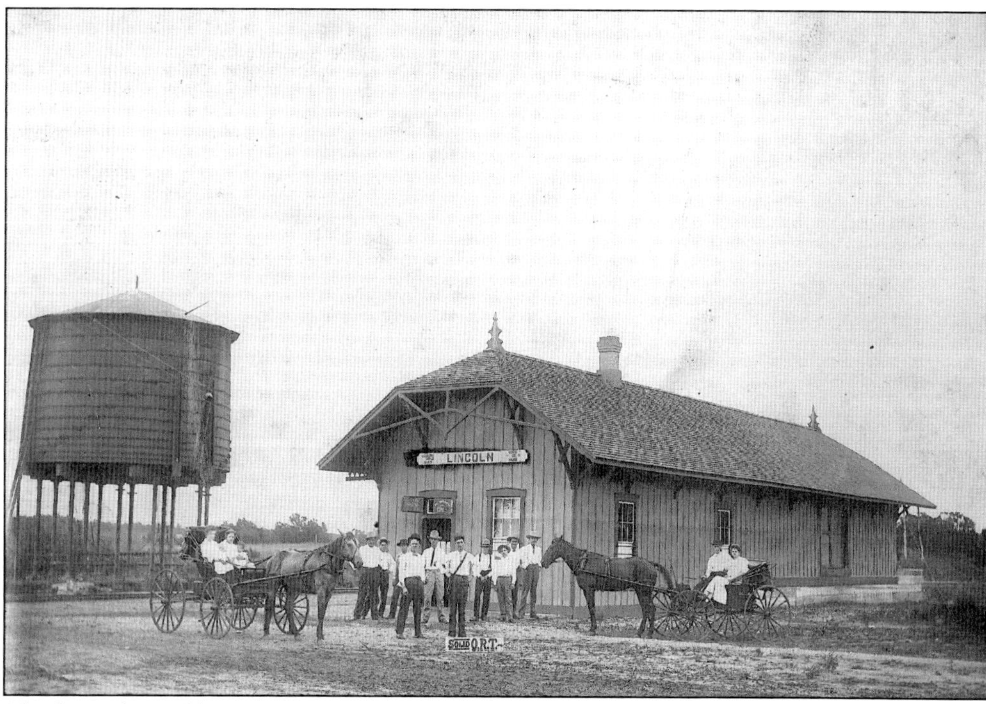

Charles and Matilda Tonn wait in their buggy for the train to arrive at the station in Lincoln. The legend Solid O.R.T. is a slogan of the Order of Railroad Telegraphers.

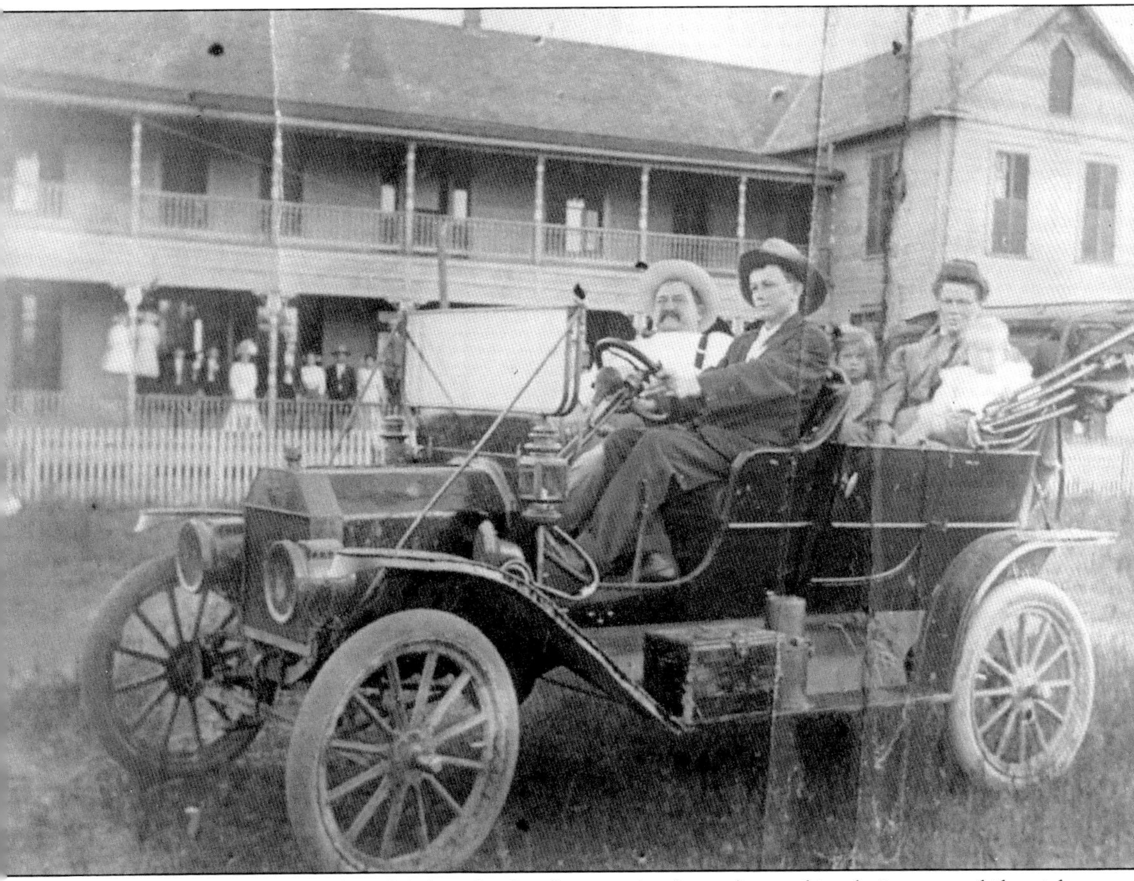

Charles (right, front seat) and Selma Jatzlau (center, back seat) posed in their automobile with some company, in front of their large new house in Fedor.

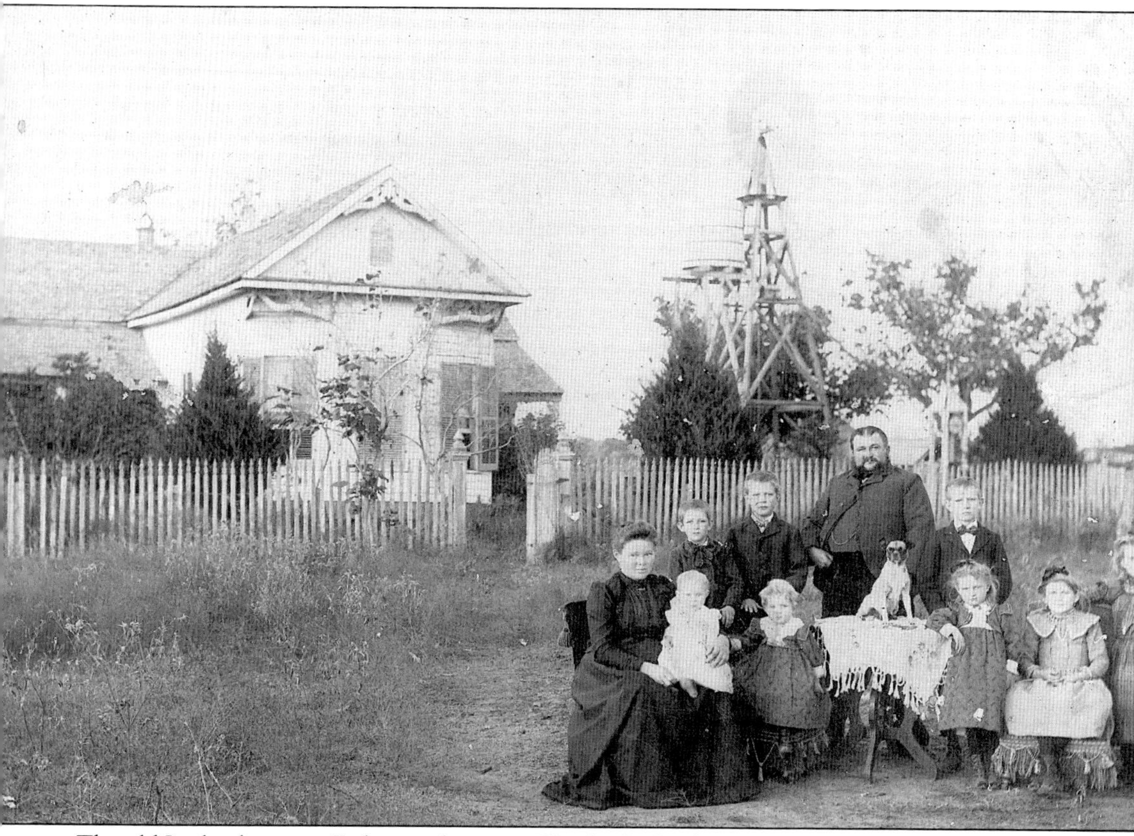

The old Jatzlau house in Fedor was home to Charles R. Jatzlau and family before 1905.

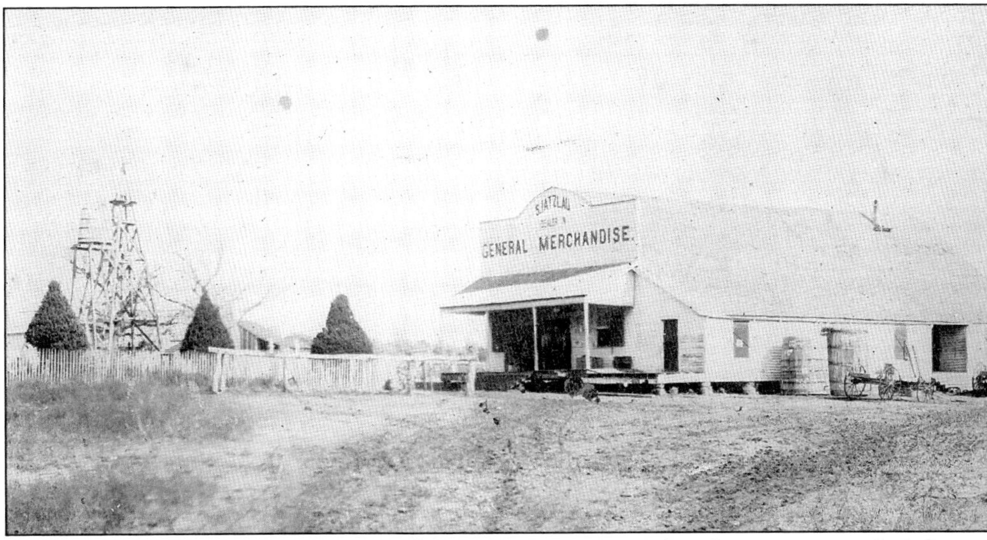

Charles Jatzlau bought this store in Fedor in 1886, two years after the manager and clerk were shot and killed by an armed robber. He ran it successfully until his death in 1919.

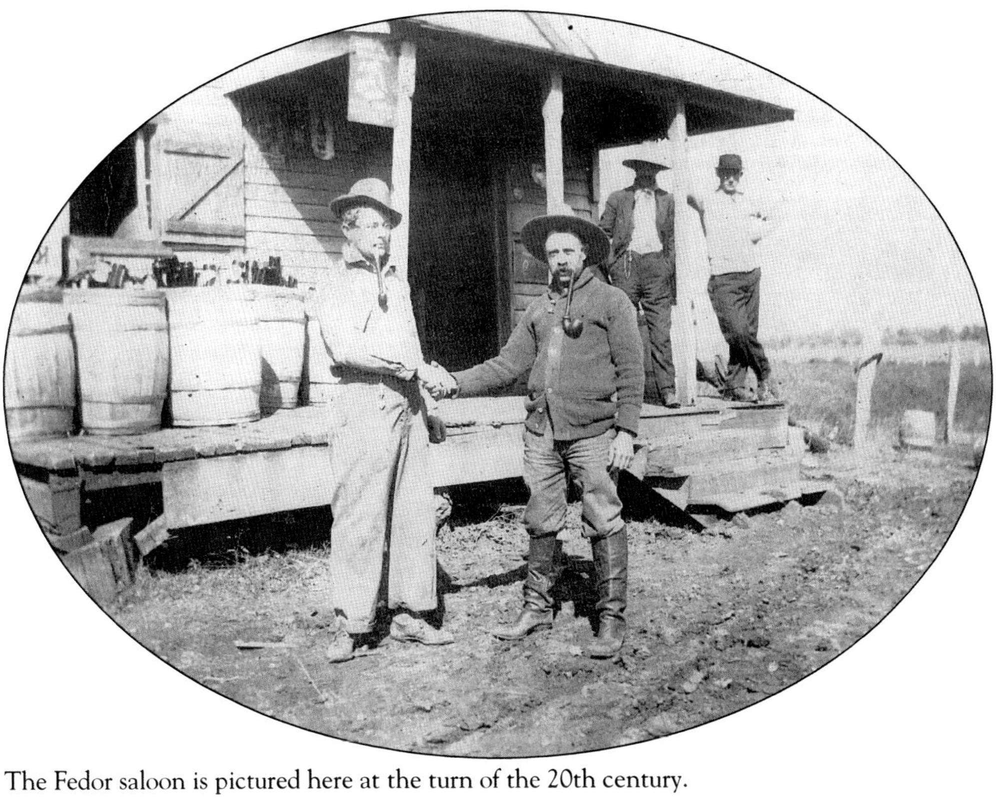

The Fedor saloon is pictured here at the turn of the 20th century.

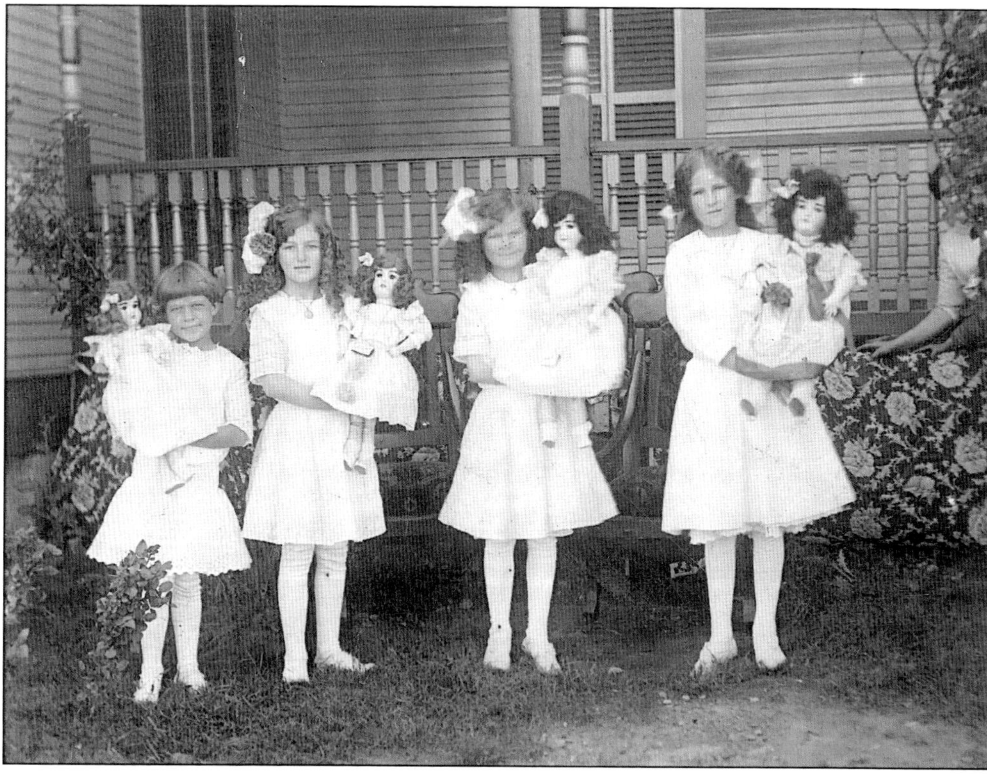

Four Jatzlau daughters—Meta, Sallie, Winnie [Alwine], and Minnie—pose with their new dolls.

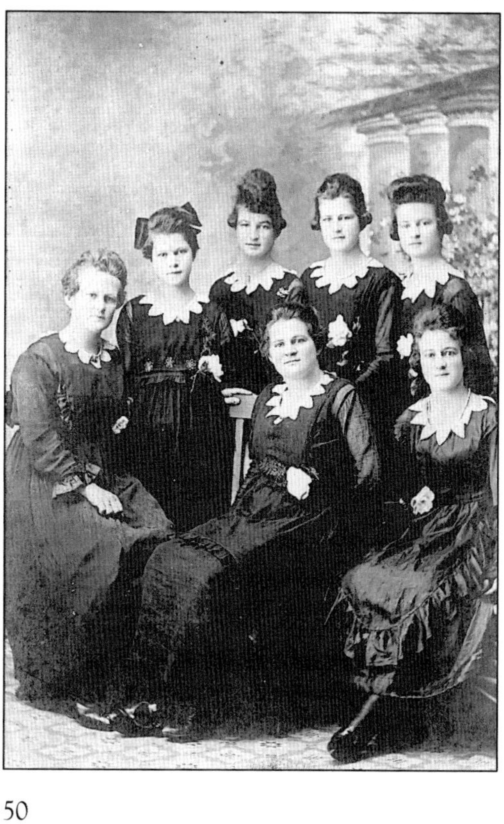

Seven Jatzlau daughters—clockwise from the left, Martha (Becker), Meta (Schkade), Sallie (Woelfel), Minnie (Wagner), Winnie [Alwine] (Zwerneman), Clara (Winkler), and Alma (Domann)—were in identical mourning for their father, Charles R. Jatzlau, in 1919.

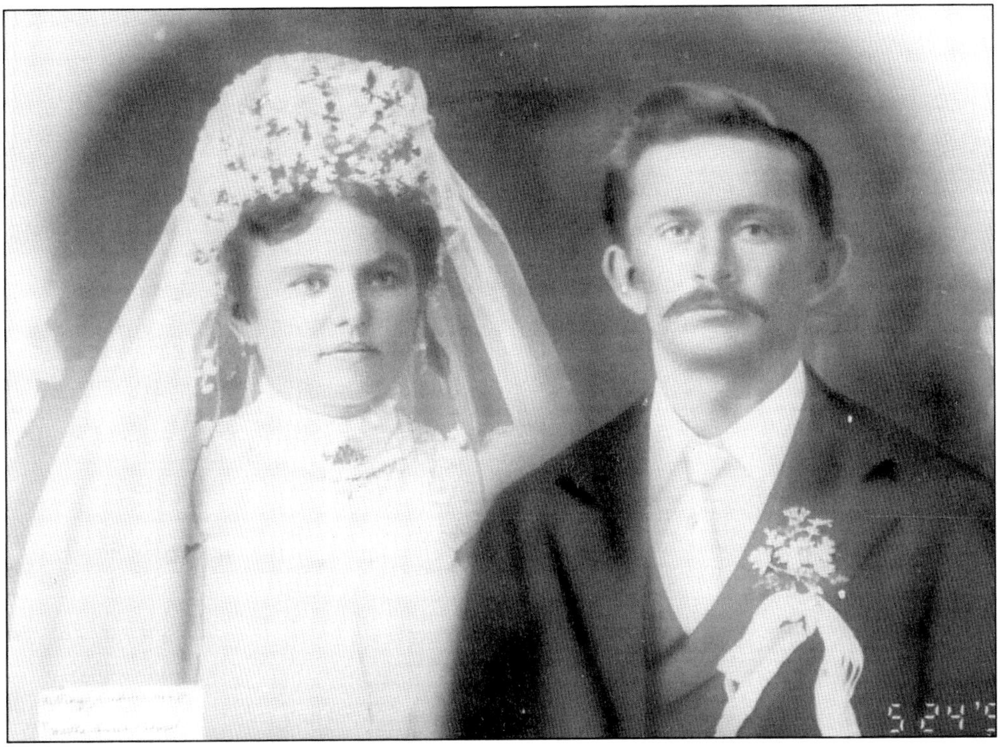

William Hamff (1876–1950) and Martha Frenzel Hamff (1880–1955) are pictured here. William Hamff had a gristmill near Serbin on the western side of Lee County. There were several large gristmills in the area and also a few portable gristmills, so that the miller could go out to the farms and grind small batches of corn on site.

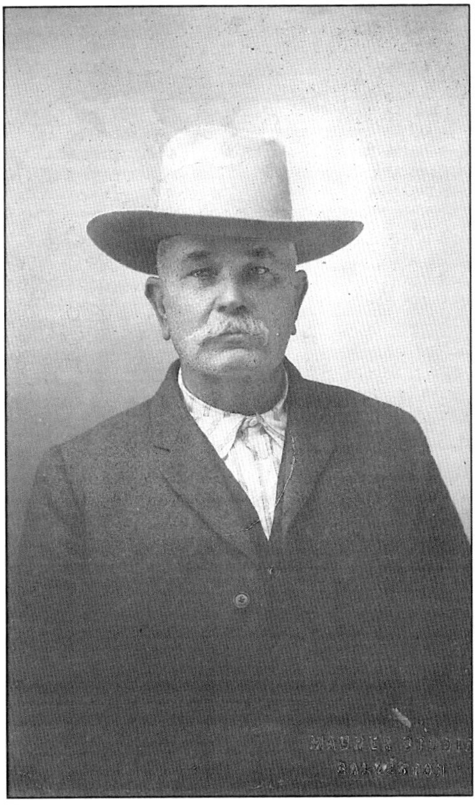

Gustavus Adolph Ramsel (1853–1936) was an enterprising cotton gin owner. Ramsel's father visited Texas in 1848, went back to Germany to marry, and returned to Texas to settle. Gus, who was born in Texas, had experience ginning cotton before he came to Lee County, and he carved a large wooden screw for pressing the bales early on when the mill still used animal power to turn the press. Gus's brother William also had a gin a few miles to the west, closer to Giddings.

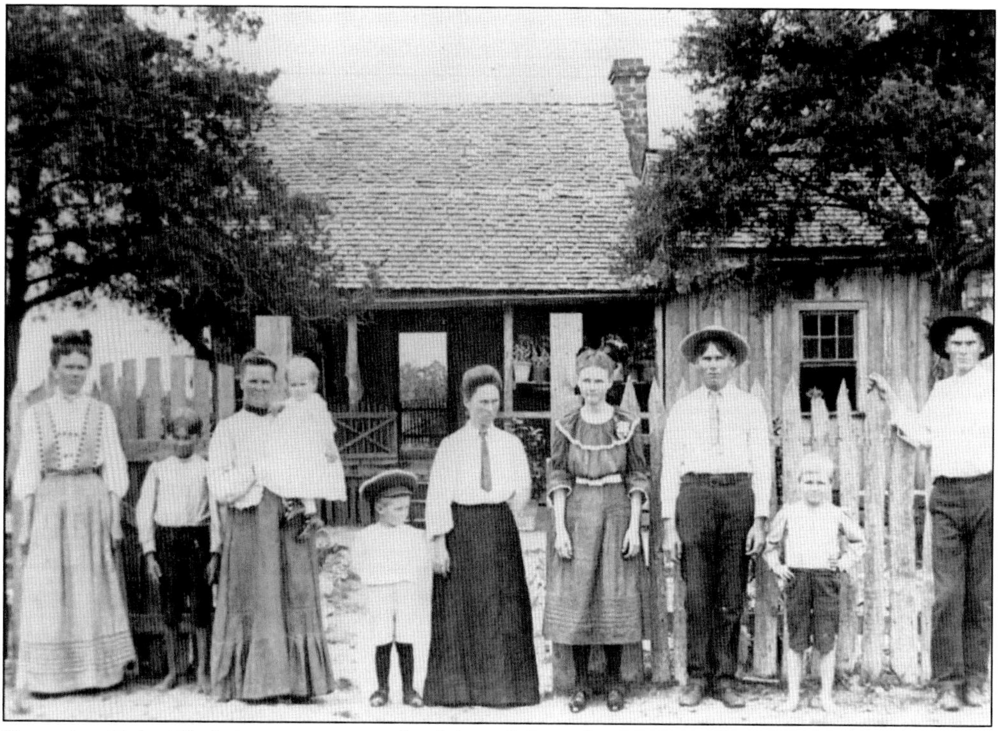

Ernestine Dube Christianson appears third from left in this *c.* 1906 photograph of the family of August Christianson (not shown).

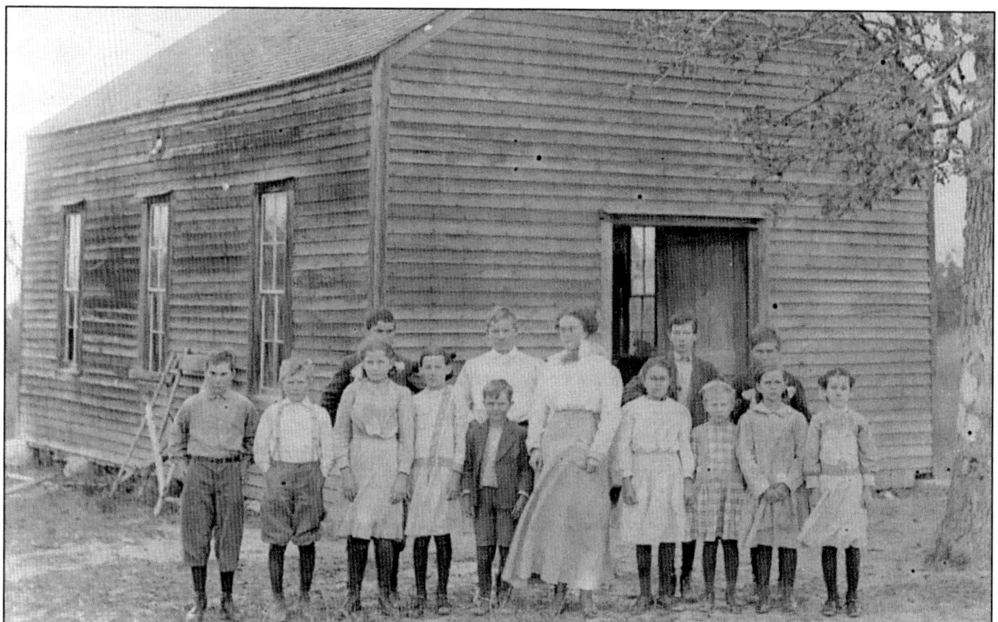

Lee County was divided into five beats or precincts. Beat Five was the mainly rural southeastern section centered on Dime Box. This area had an identity of its own and its residents referred to their locality as simply "Beat Five." This class at Salem School in the Beat Five area had first-year teacher Bess Black, who later became a historian of Lee County.

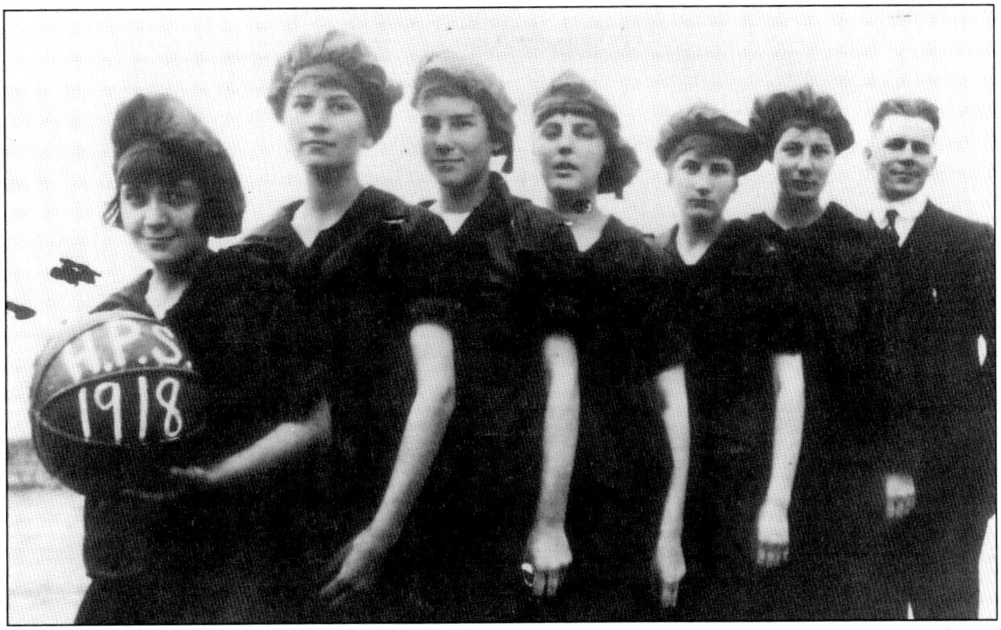

The 1918 High Prairie School basketball team from Beat Five (near Dime Box) is pictured here. They are, from left to right, Norine McLarty Reat, Annie Ross Teague Thompson, Ellen Green Bolander. Sue Wood Dodd, Mae Teague Stanley, Flora Green Thompson, and Grover Reat.

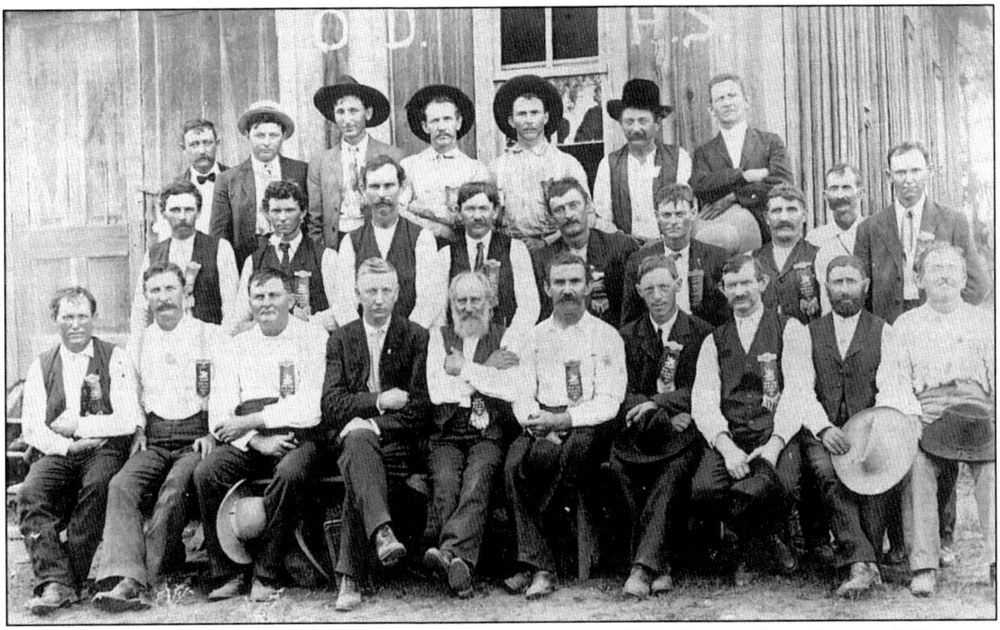

One of the German fraternal organizations was the Old Dime Box Sons of Herman "Morganroth" Lodge. Shown here are, from left to right, as follows: (front row) Herman Etzel, Christian Gloyna, August Karcher, unidentified, ? Boehme, Herman Hannes, Henry Fenzlein, ? Spitzenberger, and two unidentified men; (middle row) Paul Wolf, Arnold Hannes, Henry Marburger, John Nimtz, Gustalph Maluchka, Butch Grundman, Willie Bage, Will Phears, and unidentified; (back row) Willie Reuther, Paul Wendler, unidentified, Charlie Hannes, Oswald Hannes, Engelbert Reuther, and unidentified.

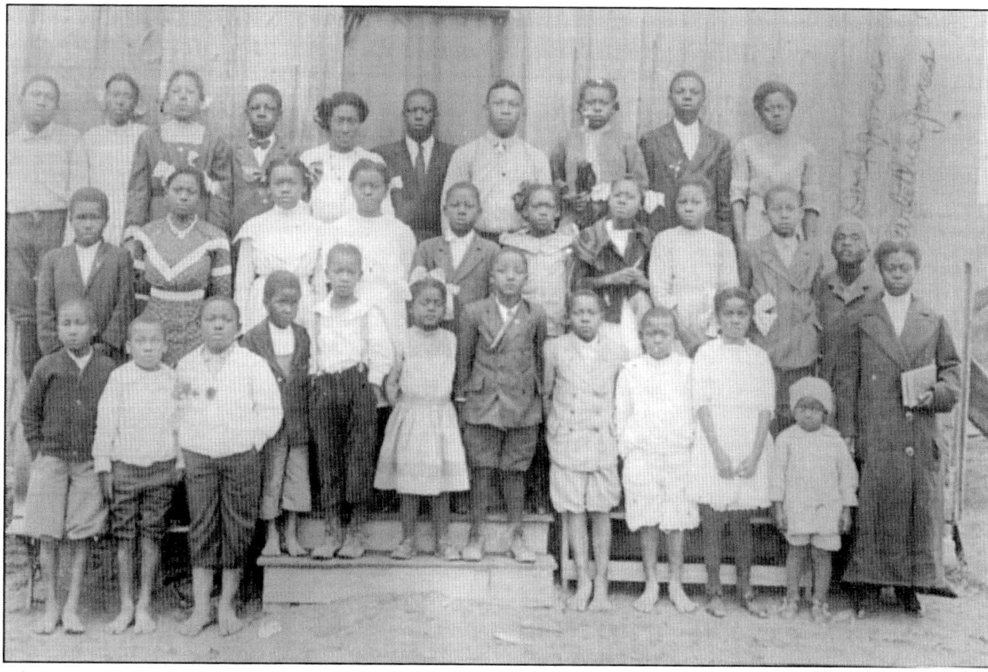

This picture of the Sweet Home School class includes teacher Arlethia Jones, on the extreme right, and Father "Doc" Jones (one of the founders in 1880 of Sweet Home Church), just behind to her right.

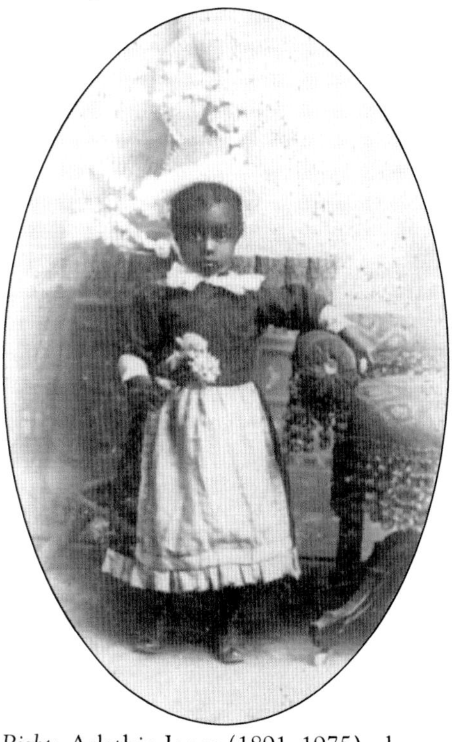

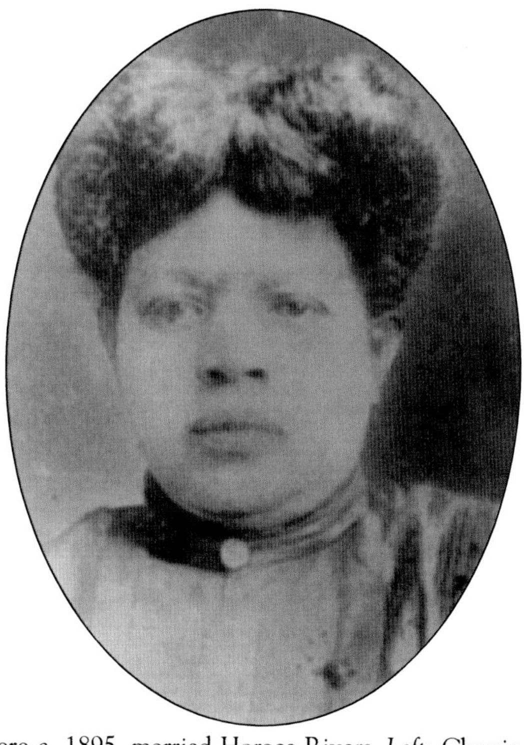

Right: Arlethia Jones (1891–1975), shown here c. 1895, married Horace Rivers. *Left:* Chanie Maxwell Rivers (1867–1927) was Horace's mother.

Elijah Griffin (1854–1941) and his son Augustus, along with Will Crenshaw, Duncan McCoy, Parker Shepard and others, owned a cotton gin on Nail's Creek. It burned down in about 1920.

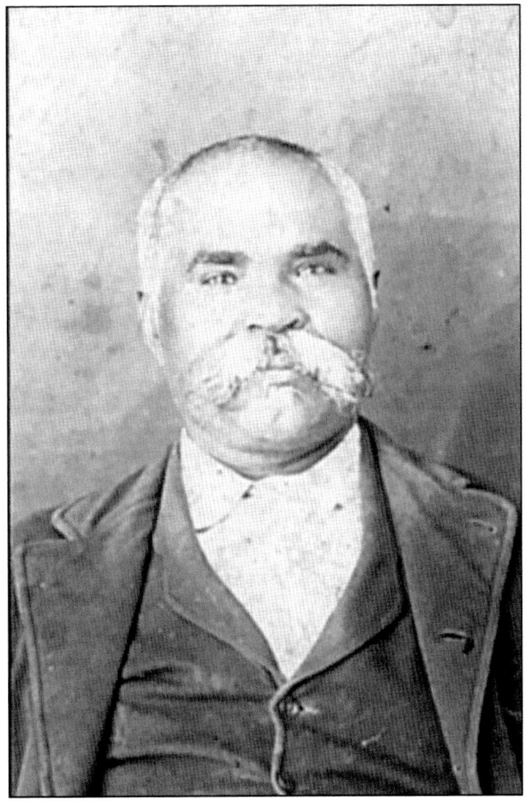

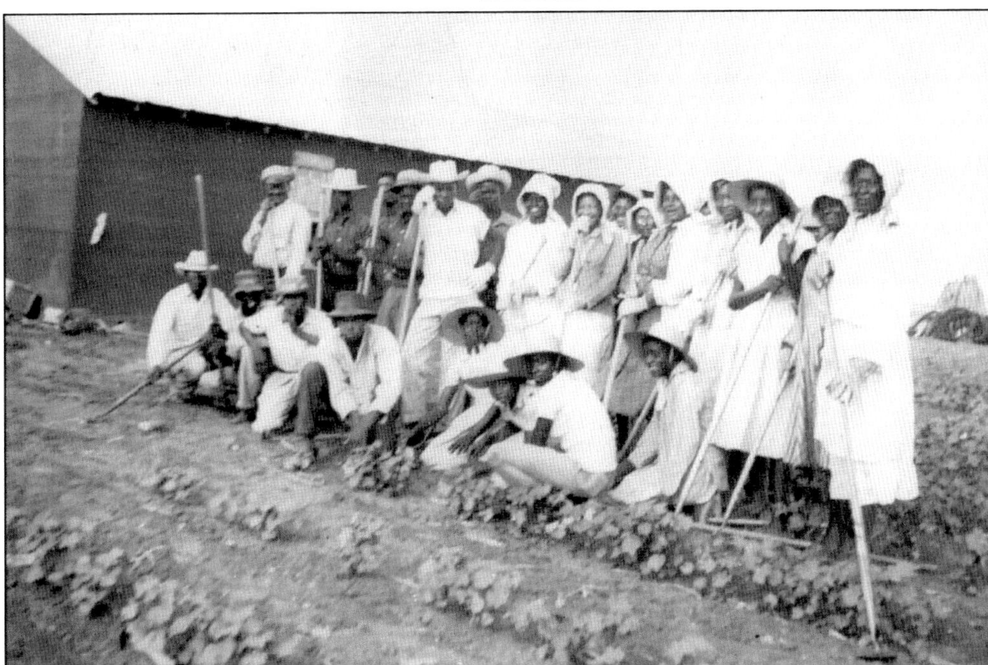

Among the workers chopping cotton *c.* 1930 in Beat Five are Frankie Jackson (third from the right), Roy Garcia (on the left), and Irene Huff (kneeling on the right).

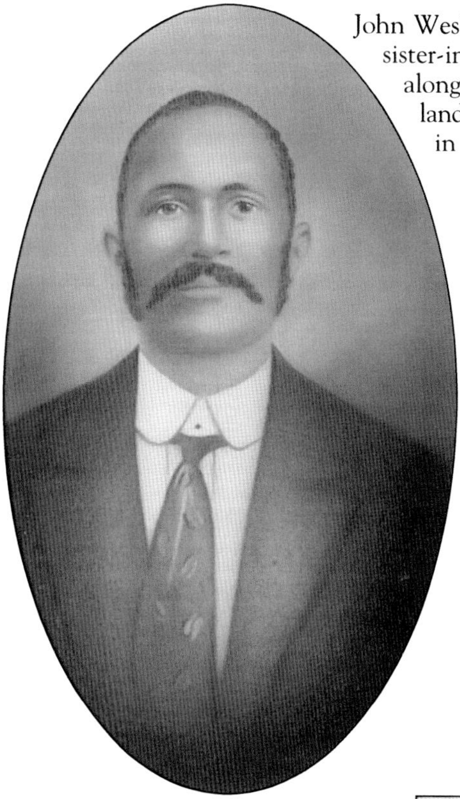

John Wesley Taylor (1866–1918) married Katie Rivers, the sister-in-law of Chanie Rivers. His father, Wesley Taylor, along with Dock Jones and Henry Francis, donated the land for the Sweet Home Missionary Baptist Church in 1890.

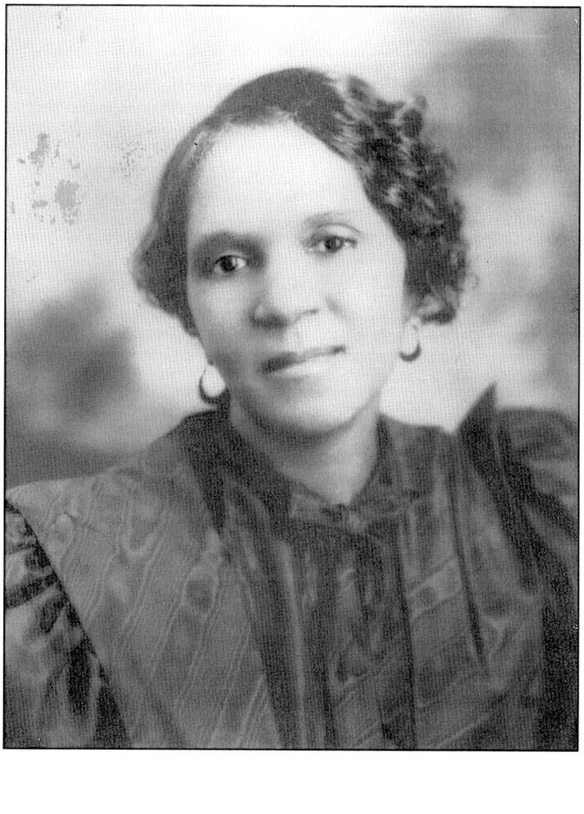

Mattie Taylor (1894–1988) was the daughter of John Wesley Taylor.

Wales Clemons (1896–1960) was the son of Tom and Caroline Baker Clemons, and was the grandson and namesake of Wales Clemons. His wife, Sarah (1838–1901), gave the land for the Shady Point Cemetery near Dime Box about 1895.

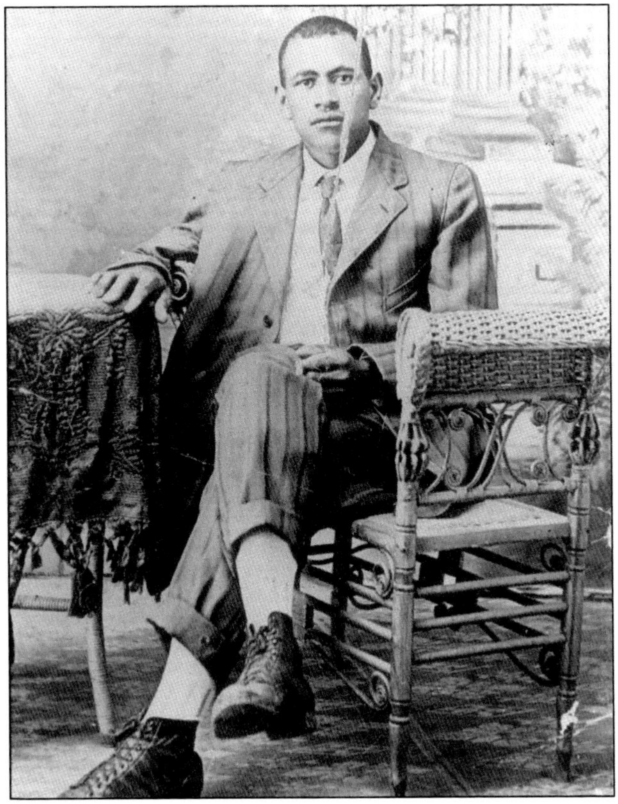

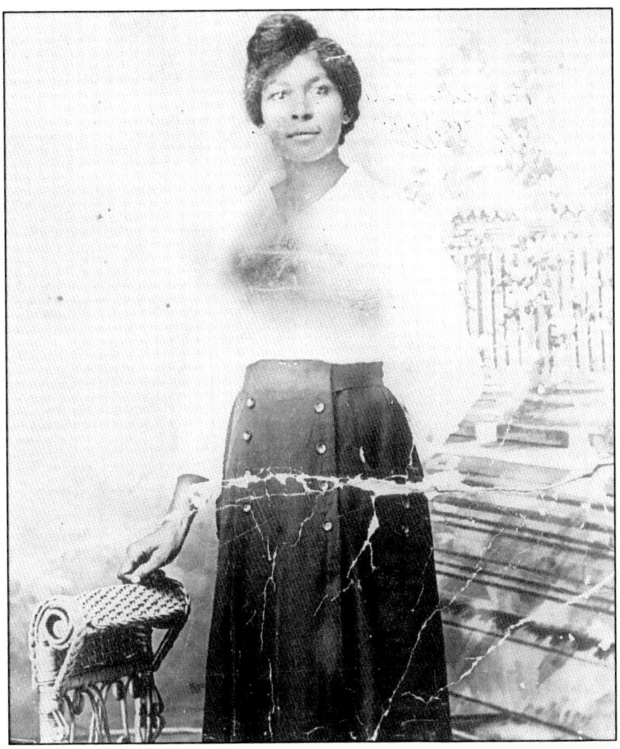

Eliza Shepherd Clemons (1878–1967) was the daughter-in-law of the first Wales Clemons. Her family also lived at Shady Point.

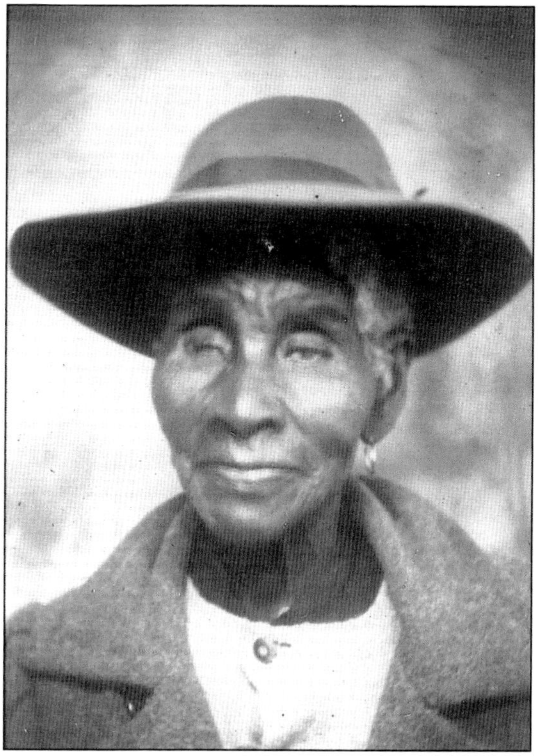

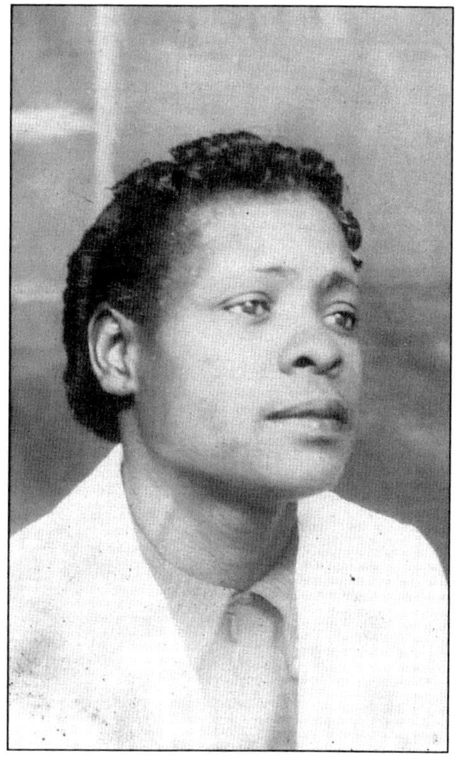

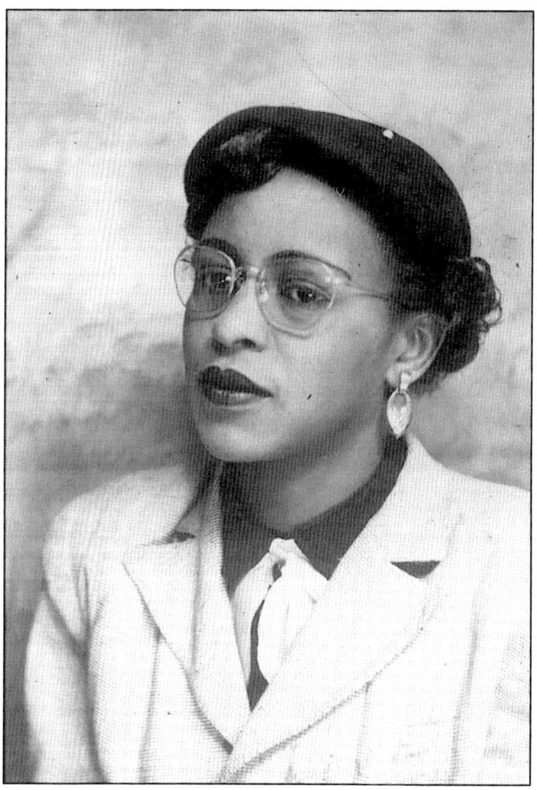

Three generations of women in one family are pictured here: Edna Lewis Alford (above left), who with her husband, Knight, purchased a 110-acre farm near Dime Box; her daughter, Emma Alford Mills (above right); and Edna's granddaughter, Linnell Ruth Malone (left). Knight Alford was an organizer and deacon of the St. Mary Baptist church in about 1900. Linnell Ruth Malone, whose daughter, Emma Jackson Wisdom, attended Post Oak School, recalls, "it was in rural Lee County that I learned that one cannot ride a hog as one might a horse, that a sow will attack if there is a threat to her newborn piglets, that turkeys are dumb, and that a city night is no comparison to a black night in the country, [but] there is no freedom like what one can feel in the wide spaces of rural living."

Mariah Gentry Williams was born in the Gold Coast of Africa, captured, and sold into slavery. She lived near Sweet Home community until 1948.

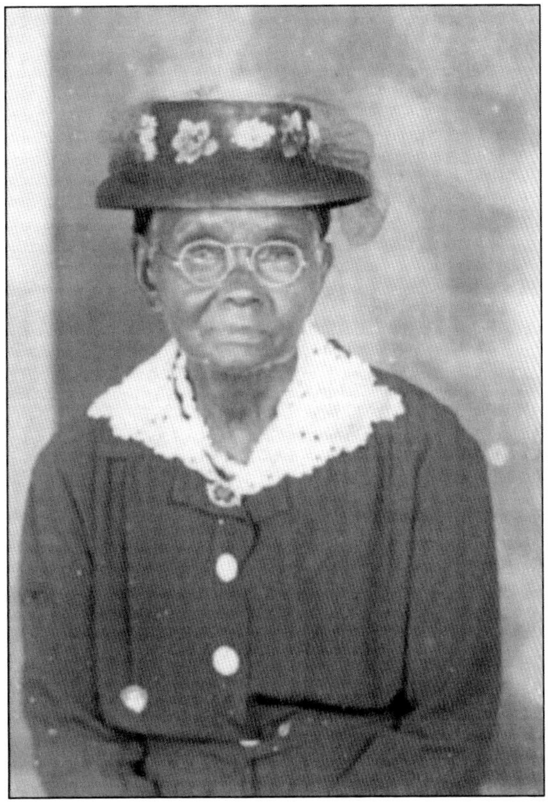

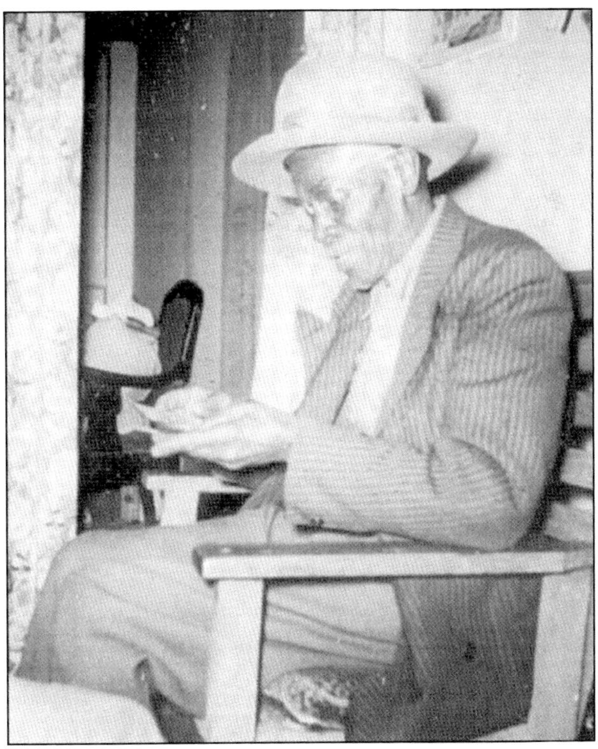

This photo of Sweet Home deacon Hortrude Booker (1877–1965) was taken in 1959 at the home of Rufus Washington. Six years later, when he was a fragile 87 and bundled up against the cold, Hortrude's clothes accidentally caught fire from his pipe. He died of his burns.

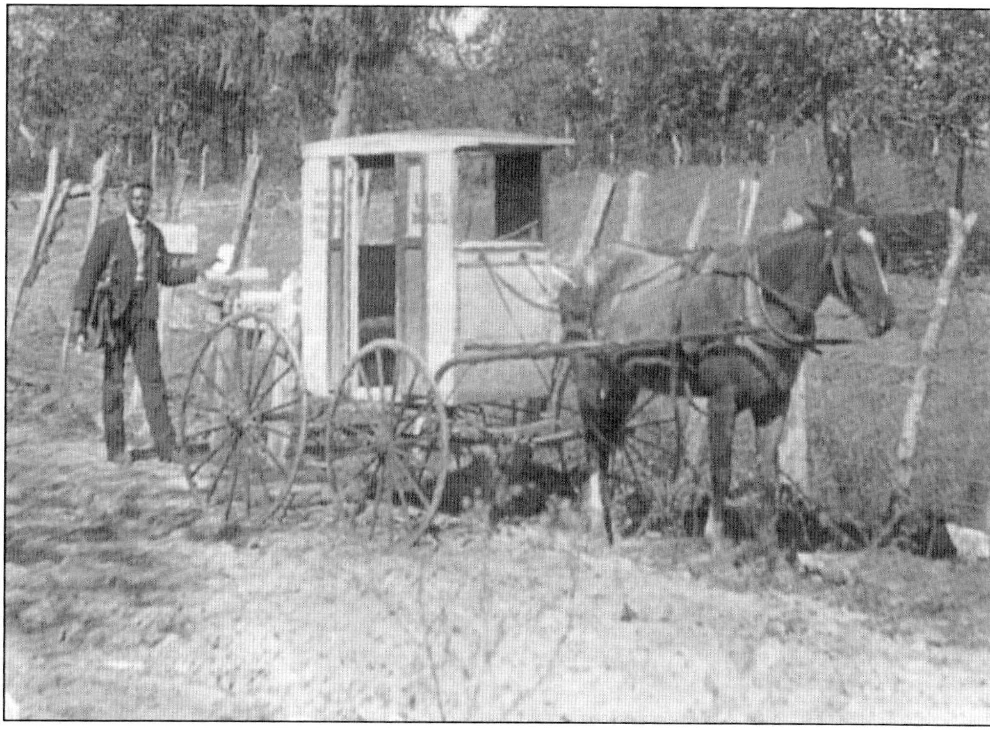

Elijah Campbell was the mailman on the Ledbetter route, which included Beat Five in Lee County, in about 1910.

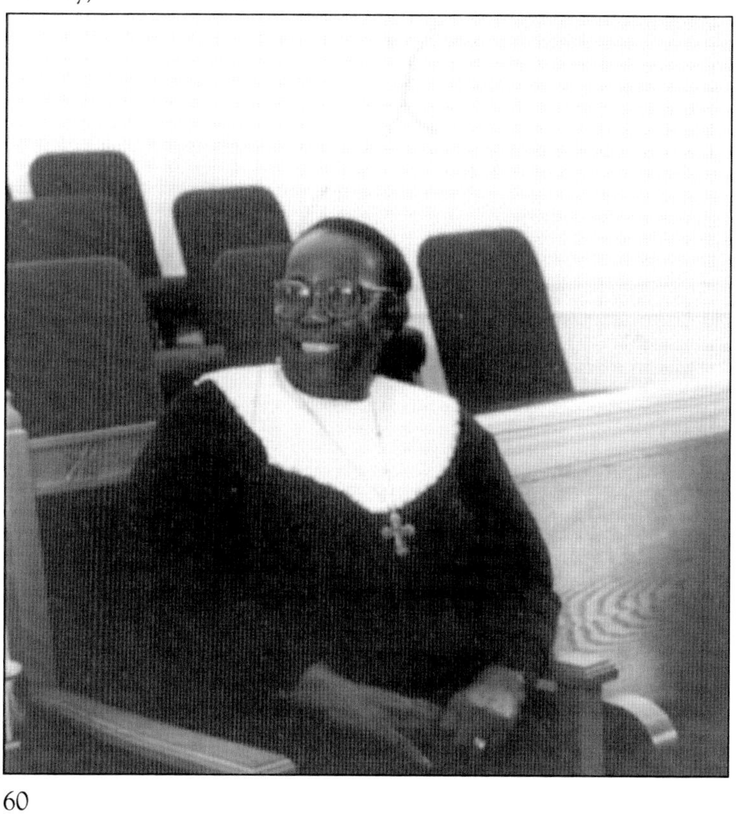

Julia Francis Ferguson was the first woman elder at Brenham District, A.M.E.

Three

Czechs of Dime Box

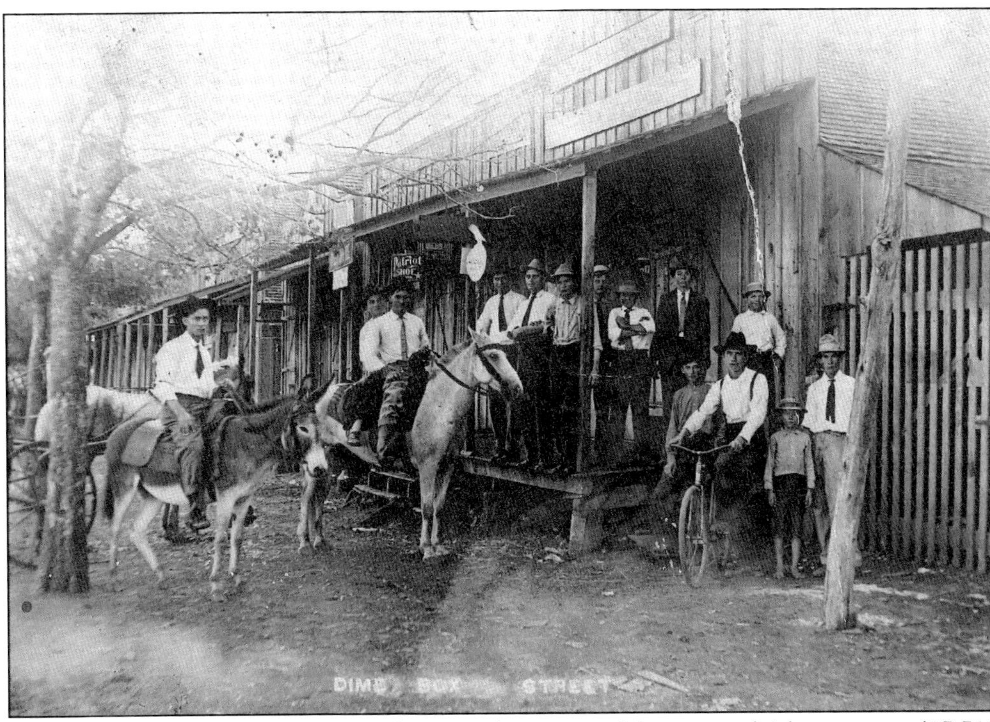

The Slavic community of Dime Box lies near the center of the personal 4-league grant (17,712 acres) given to Stephen F. Austin by the Mexican government in 1831 as a reward for having settled the first 300 Anglo families in Texas. The name seems to have referred to a box in which it was customary to either place an order or to pay for goods by putting a dime in a box for the mail carrier, who was expected to return with the order. The rich black prairie land of the area, the plentiful wood and water, and the relatively low prices for the land appealed to Czech and Moravian immigrants, who in 1881 had already come as far as Fayette County, located immediately to the west of the future Lee County. This peaceful Sunday afternoon scene contrasts with the customary lively Saturday night parties that no doubt preceded it.

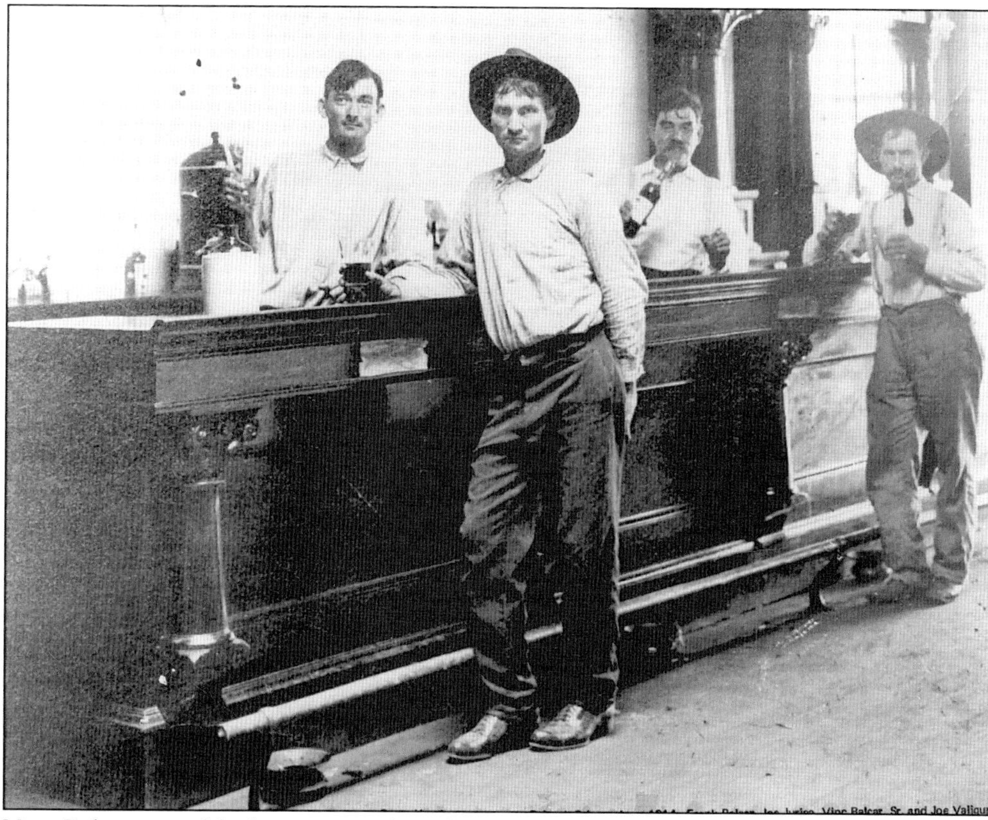

Vinc Balcar owned both a store and a saloon near the old San Antonio Road and later in New Dime Box. It was his policy that neither the store nor the saloon were open on Sunday, his day of rest and time for church. Also, no children were ever permitted to enter the saloon. Vinc's children, who brought him lunch each day, had to hand it in at the door. The dancing platform associated with the Balcar saloon was used for weekly dances and comedian shows. On occasion the parties got a little rough. At one such affair, two men—Bob Stanley and Joe Jurica—got their throats cut before Deputy Will Scarborough placed his hand over the pistol, just as someone pulled the trigger, and the hammer pierced the skin between his thumb and forefinger, stopping the firing of a shot.

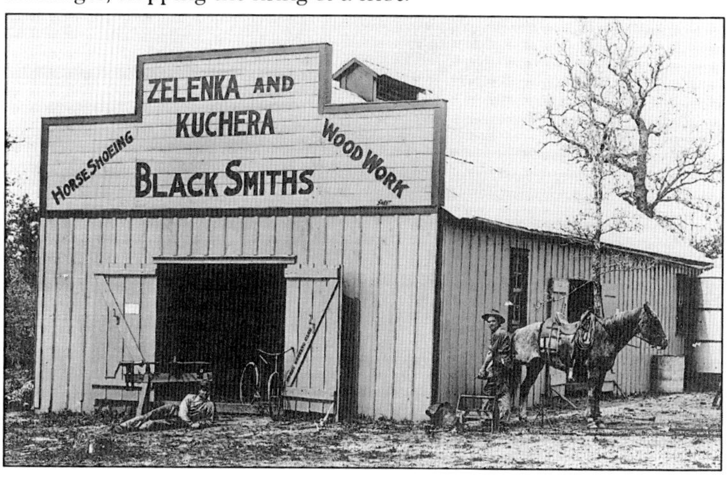

Frank Zelenka operated a blacksmith shop alongside the Balcar saloon and bar.

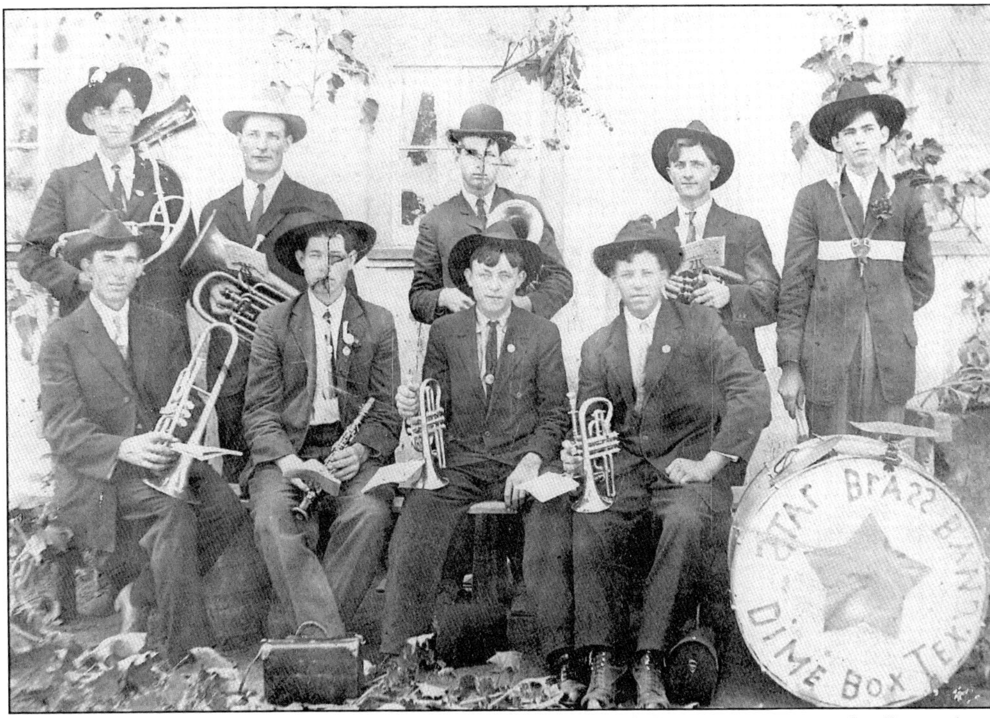

The Star Band became the Balcar Brass Band about 1915. Dances were social affairs where young and old could mix to celebrate and perhaps drink a little beer. They danced polkas, waltzes (including the garden waltz variation in which one man danced with two women, twirling first one then the other), schottisches, pekiky ("Little Joe"), and varsovienne ("Put-Your-Little-Foot").

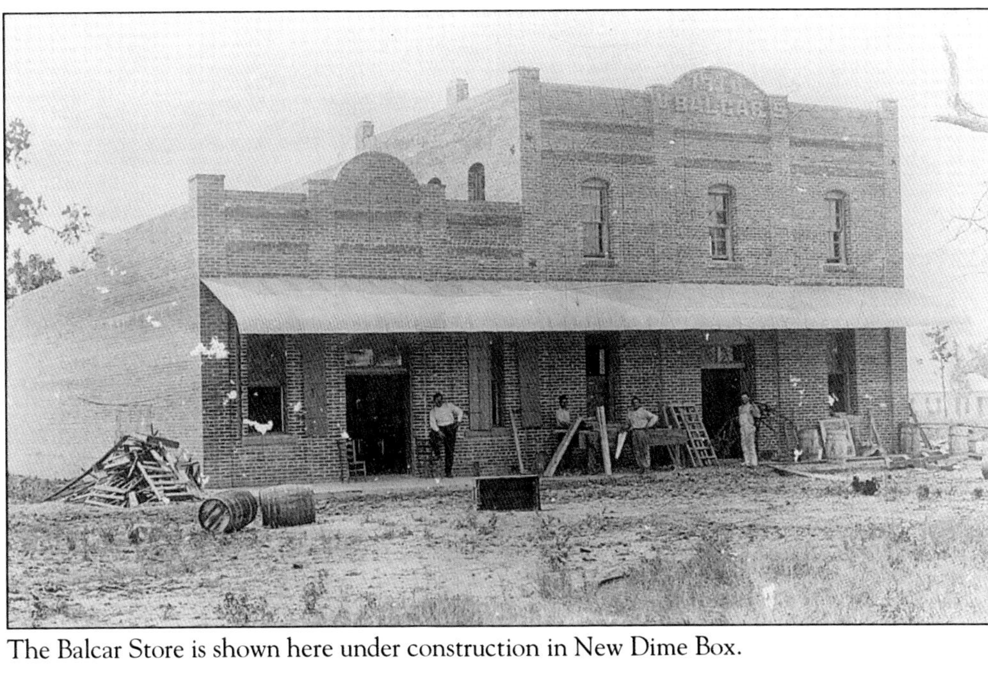
The Balcar Store is shown here under construction in New Dime Box.

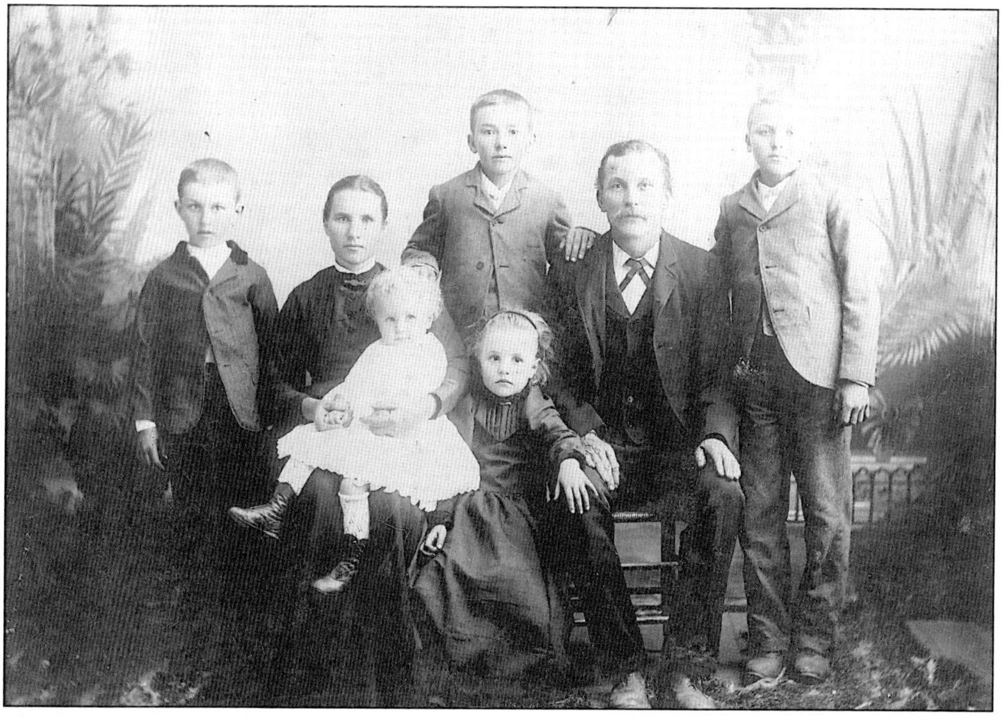

The family of Jan and Katerina (Jurica) Kocurek emigrated from "the poorest corner of poor Moravia" to Texas in about 1858. Their son Thomas was born in Texas and settled on a 260-acre farm near Dime Box in 1885. Thomas and his sister Francisca married Anna and Joseph Krupa, also sister and brother, and there are many descendents of both in central Texas today.

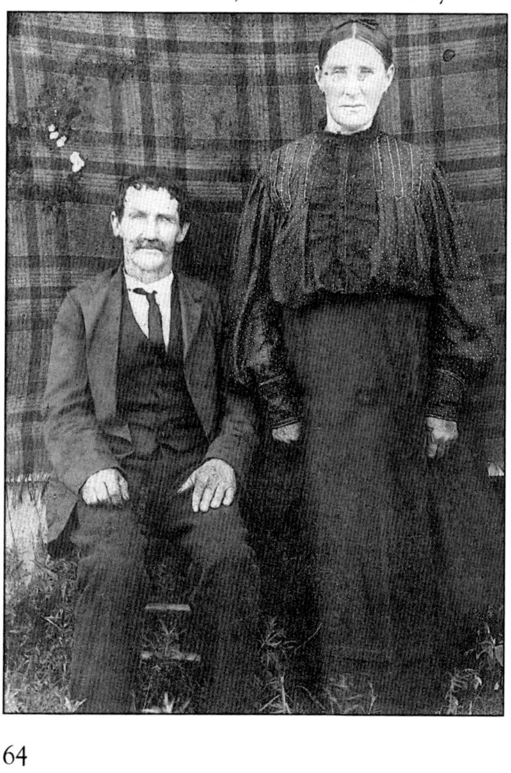

In 1873, Josef Blaha and his wife, Rosina, emigrated through New Orleans and Galveston. They came from the same small Moravian village as the Kocureks, following Tom Kocurek from Fayette County to the all-Czech community of Hranice (Ran-ice) near Dime Box. Josef gathered a sample of the black dirt to show his wife some of the Zaslibena zem (promised land). Josef had a molasses mill, a threshing machine, a hay baler, blacksmith equipment, and he made his own charcoal and lime. He also pulled teeth with grapplers for those who could stand it. His grandson, Albert Blaha, became the historian of the Hranice community. He wrote that his grandfather never became rich, but loved friends, land, horses, whiskey, and freedom in the new land. He never learned to speak English, nor could he write Czech.

Josef Krajcicek died in 1888, leaving a wife and six children. Within six months, his wife, Ludmilla, was murdered, strangled at night in a weedy gully. Some of the orphaned children shown here were taken in by the newly married Jan Simeks, others by the Kocureks.

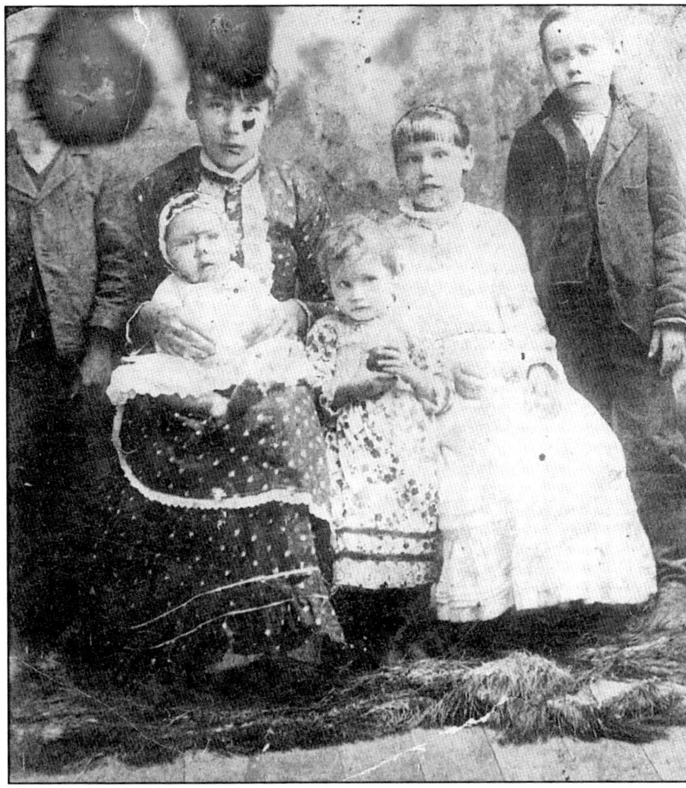

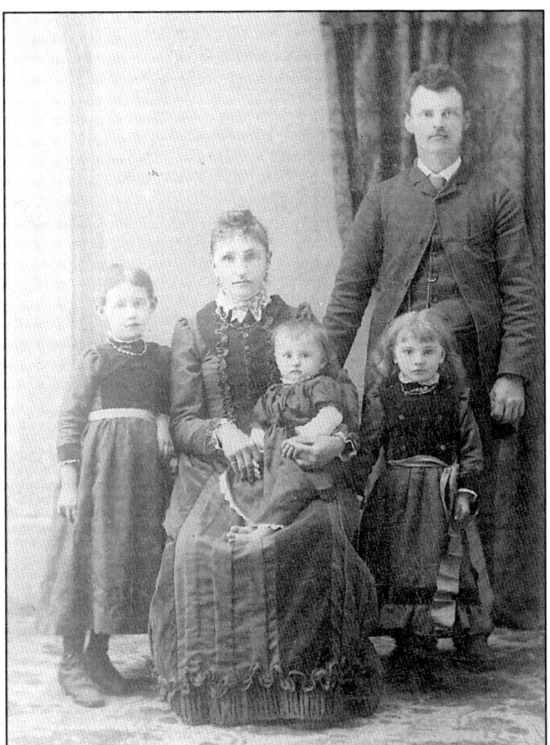

Jan Simek and his young wife, Veronika (nee Blaha), pose here with their children, including Frances Krajcicek (on the left). Within a decade, both Simeks were dead; their children and the two Krajcicek children were taken in by the Blahas.

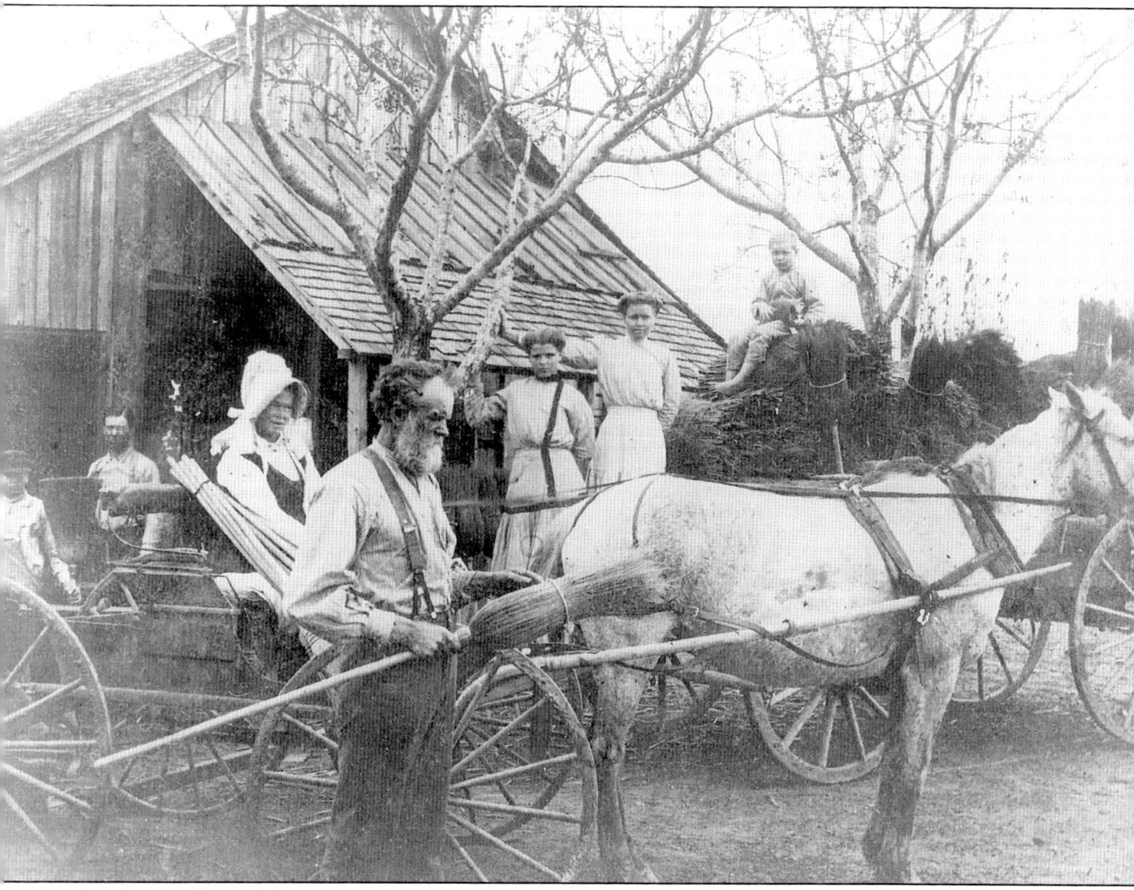

Frank Svach and his wife, Teresa, are pictured here *c*. 1910. Behind the wagon is a broom factory, which housed a "broom machine" for making brooms out of broom corn. This successful venture was established by Frank in 1901 in Katy with the help of his old neighbors in Dime Box. Svach had lost everything in the 1900 hurricane. He later sold the business to the Sealy Broom Company. Frank was an educated and enterprising man who had studied for the priesthood before emigrating from Moravia. He also owned a cane press, molasses cooking pans, and a hay baler in Hranice.

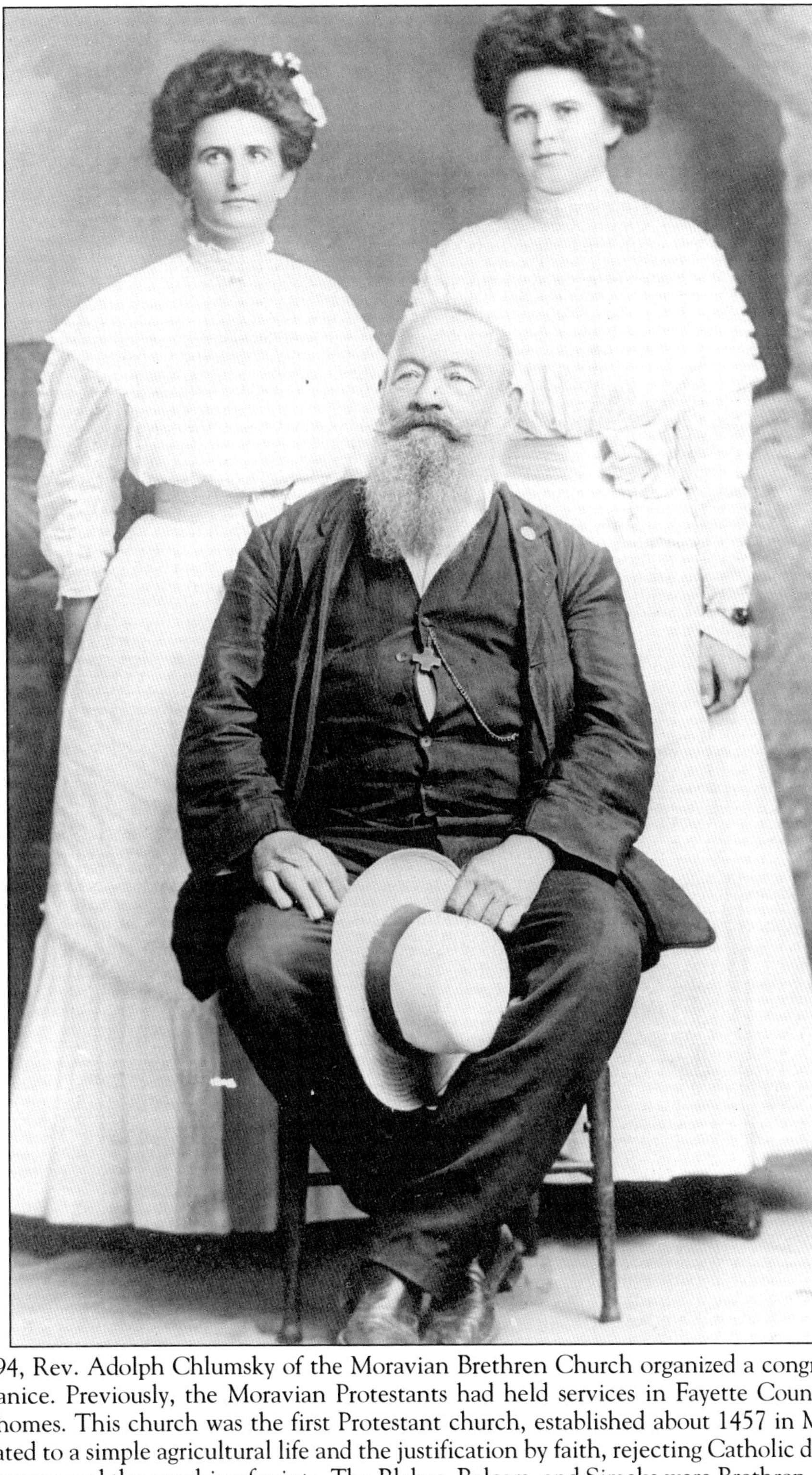

In 1894, Rev. Adolph Chlumsky of the Moravian Brethren Church organized a congregation at Hranice. Previously, the Moravian Protestants had held services in Fayette County or in their homes. This church was the first Protestant church, established about 1457 in Moravia, dedicated to a simple agricultural life and the justification by faith, rejecting Catholic doctrines of purgatory and the worship of saints. The Blahas, Balcars, and Simeks were Brethren.

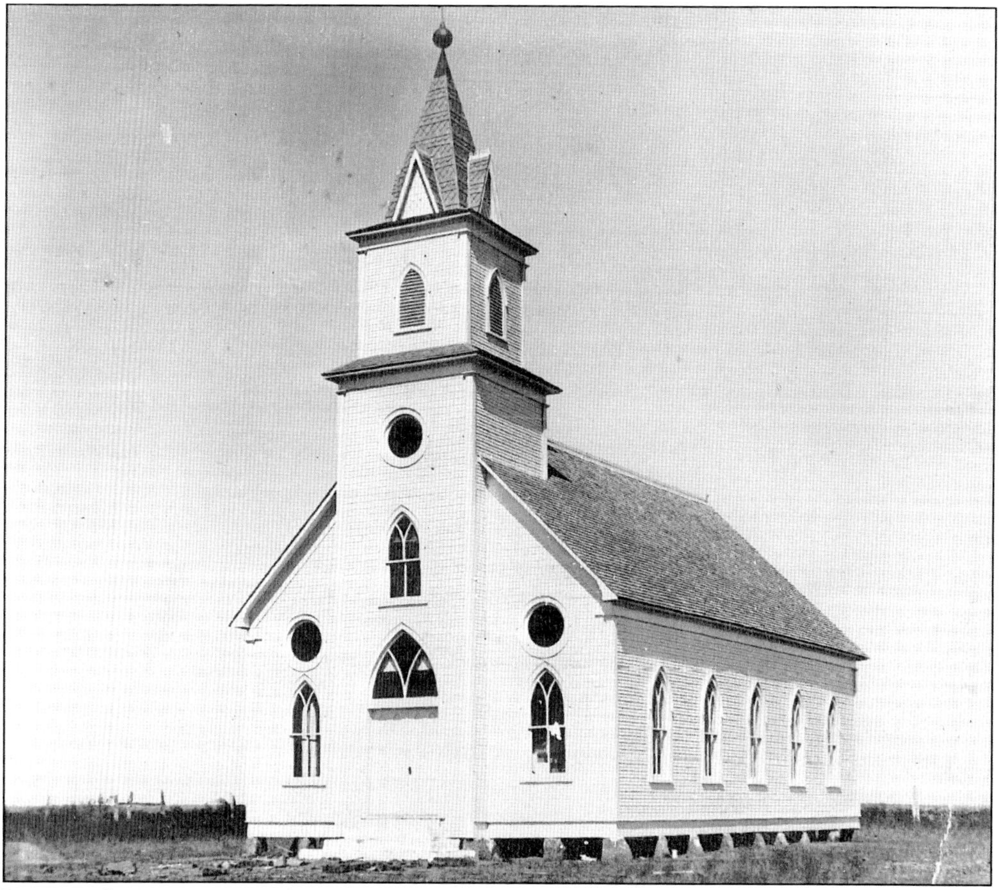

In 1911, the Moravian Brethren congregation dedicated their new church.

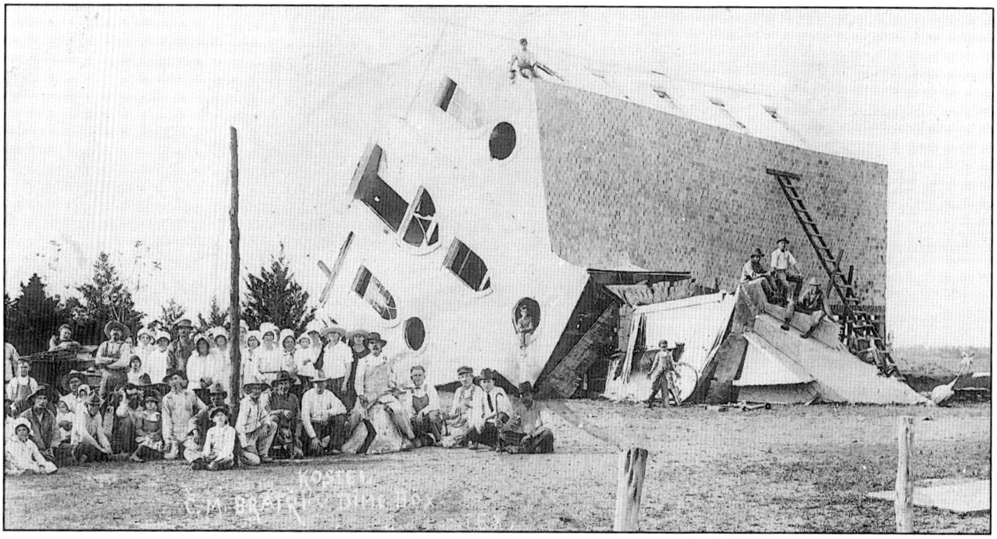

In April of 1922, a tornado overturned the building and destroyed it. The second church, which was completed in 1924, was struck by lightning in 1954 and destroyed by fire. The third church still stands.

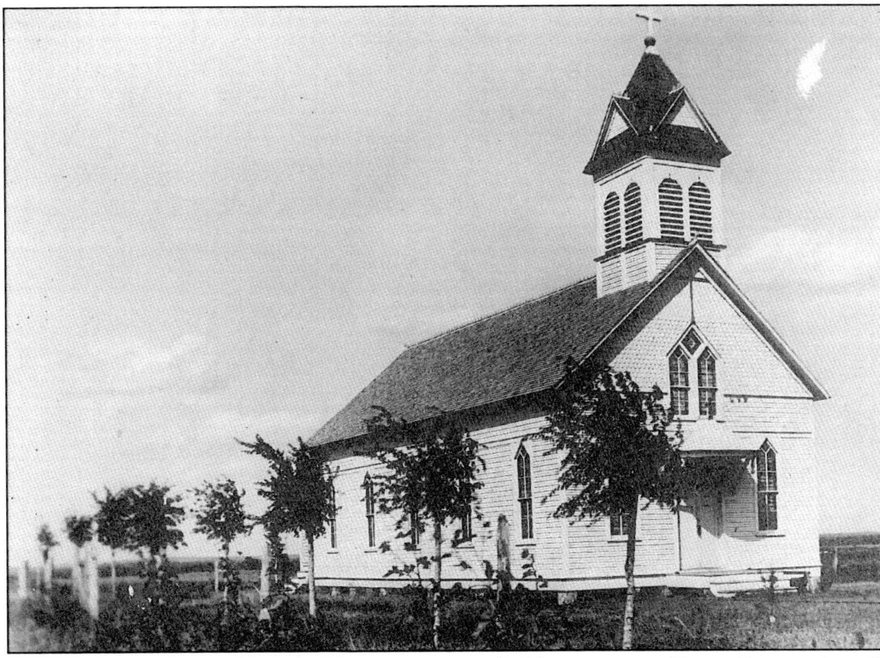

At first, the Catholic families of Slavic extraction held services in Dime Box in their homes. Then, starting about 1886, they held them in the schoolhouse. This church was completed in 1909.

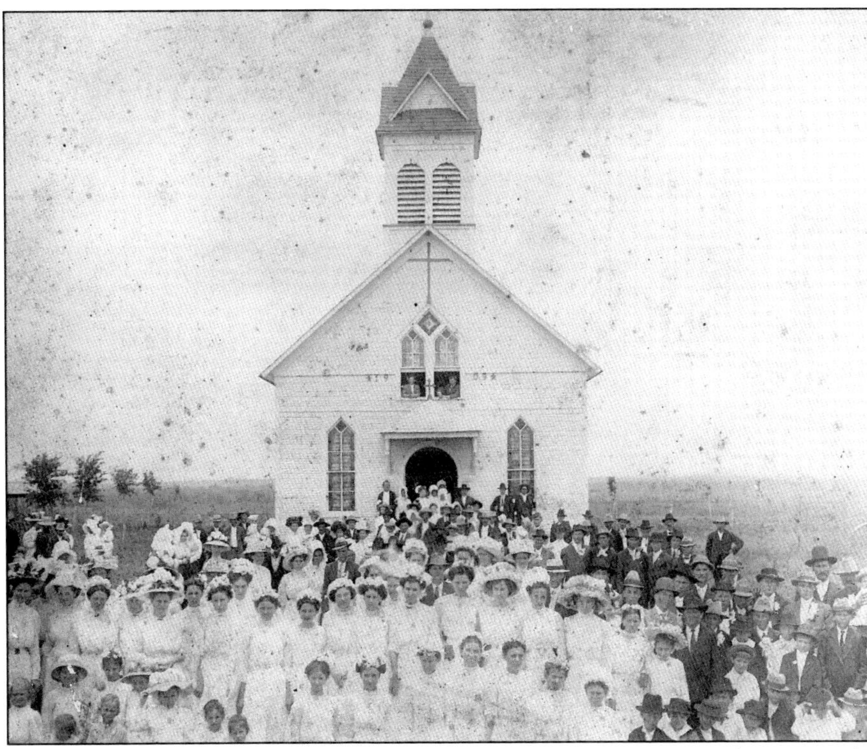

The Kocureks and Krupas, among others, were Catholic. The first confirmation class was assembled in 1911.

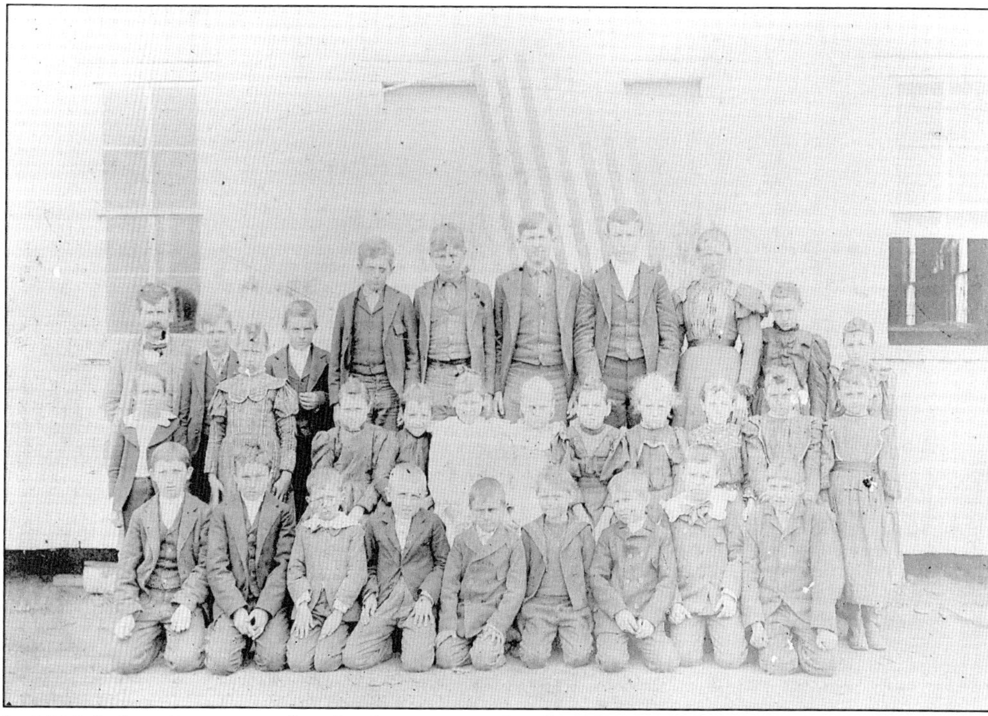

In 1886, before there was a church, there was a school at Hranice. That year, the school received contributions totaling $184 from 31 sources. Expenses were nearly $300, but $148 of that was a note.

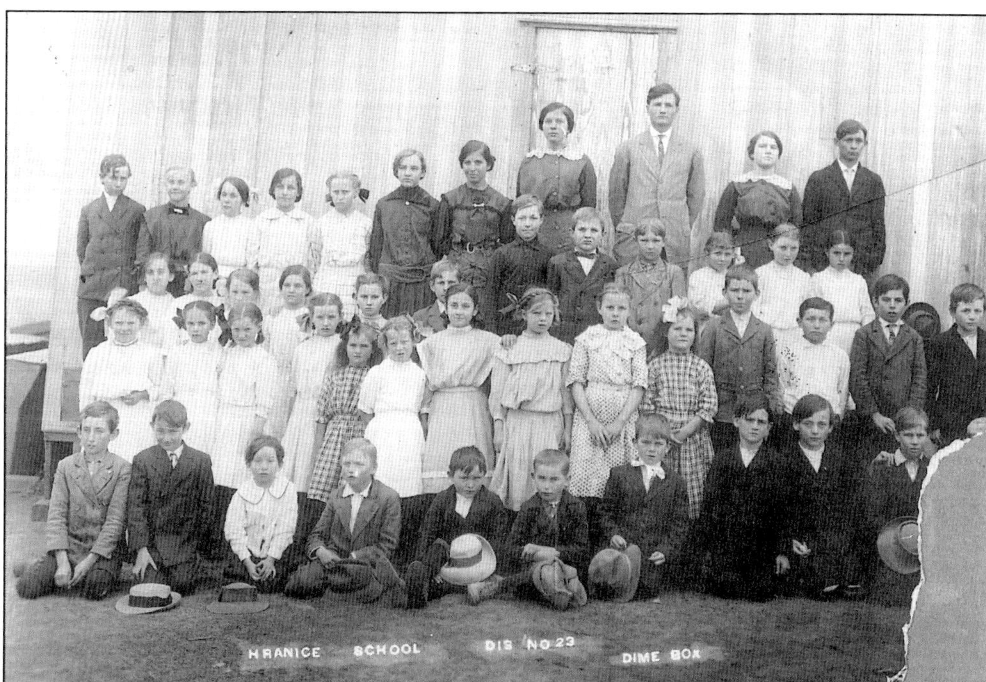

Hranice School was still a one-room schoolhouse in about 1912.

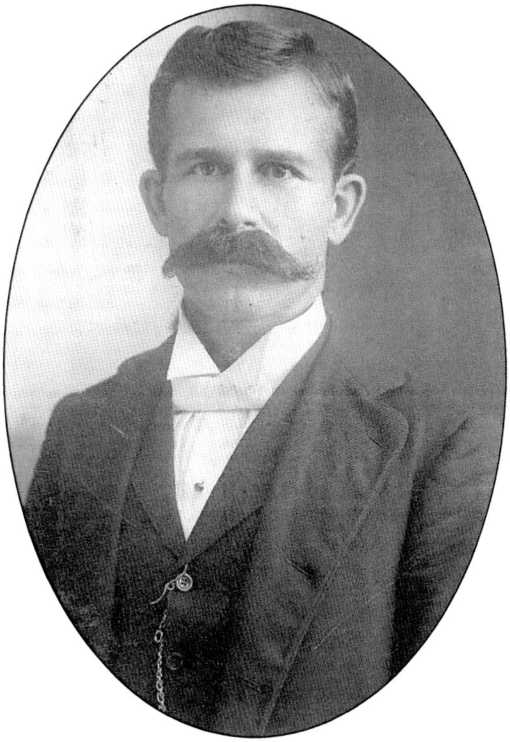 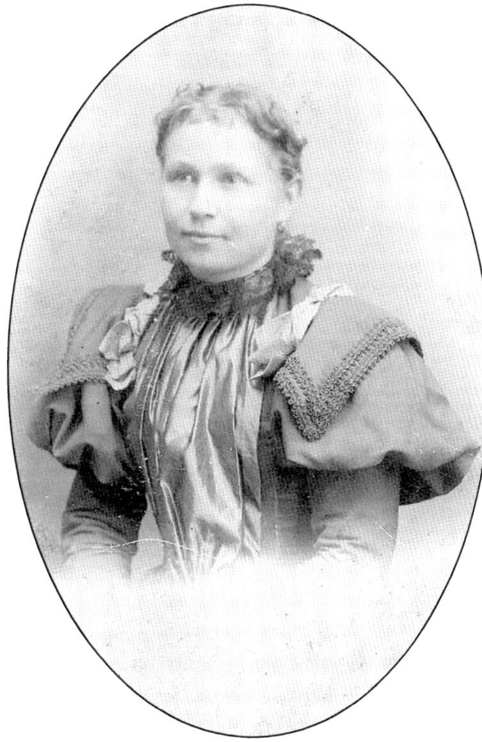

Many of the teachers had local ties. Frank Kadanka (left), who married a local girl, Albina Krenek (right), was a teacher from 1894 to 1900. Sadly, Albina died within a month of the wedding.

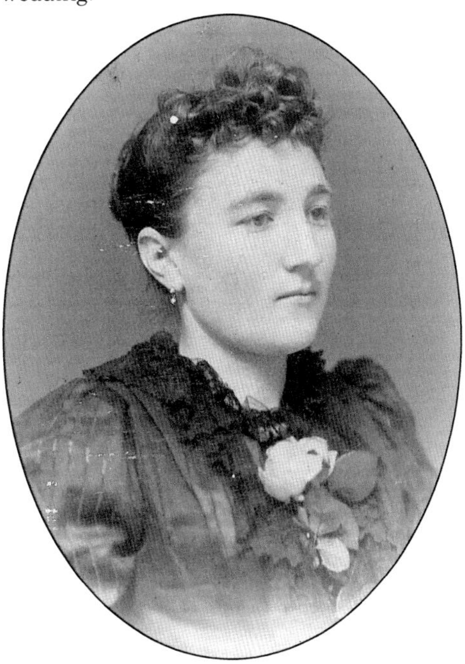 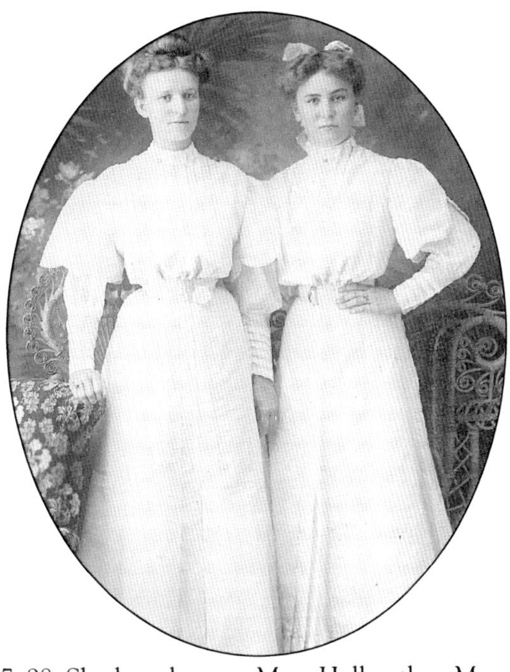

Left: Mary (Krupa) Muesse taught during 1897–98. She later became Mary Hollas, then Mary Cole. *Right:* Mary and her sister, Albina Krupa Kocurek, pose side by side.

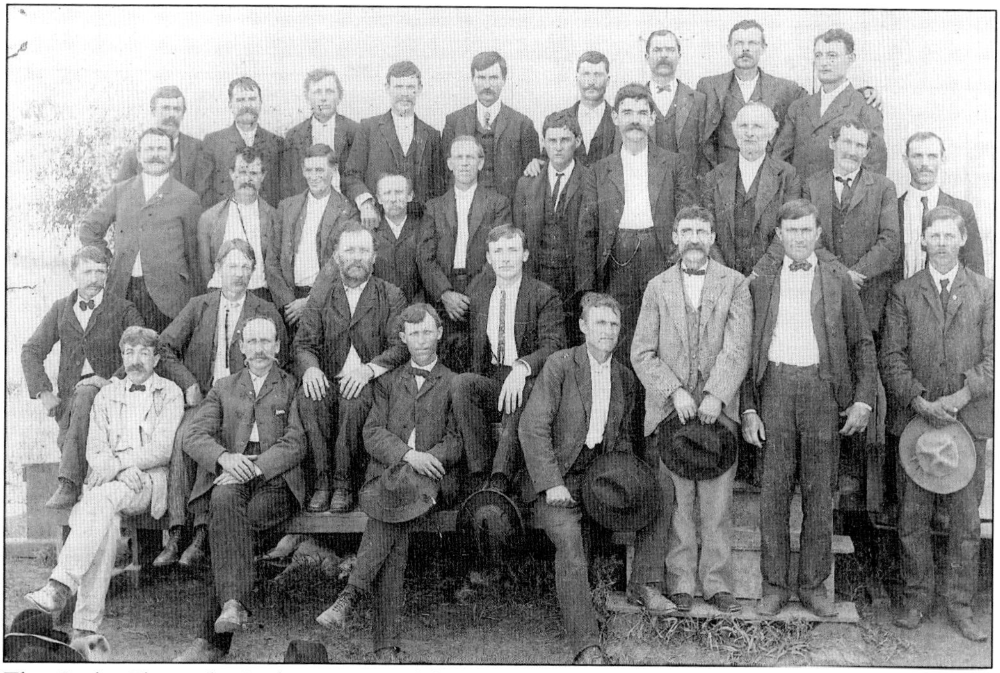

The Cesko-Slovensky Podporujici Spolek (CSPS) was founded in 1854 in St. Louis and in 1897, when the Hranice lodge was established, there were 15 lodges in Texas. In a disagreement about dues, the Texas lodges withdrew from the national association and formed their own lodge, the Slovanska Podporujici Jednota Ststu Texas (SPJST). The SPJST was a mutual aid society that offered insurance policies and held social events such as barbecues, dances, and meetings. The male and female members are shown here in separate photographs.

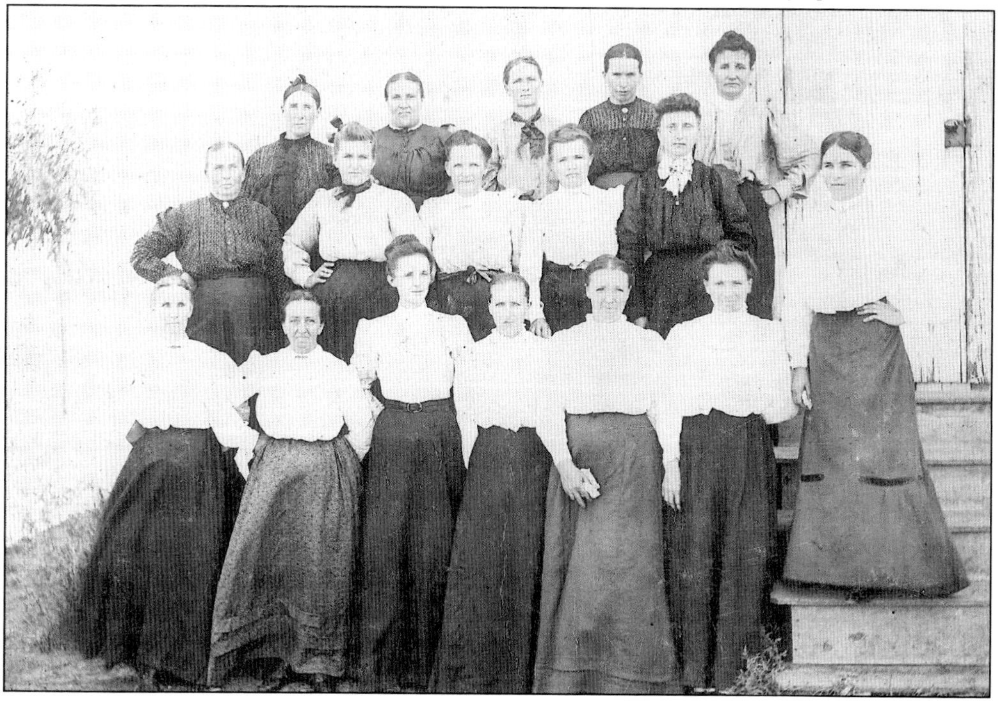

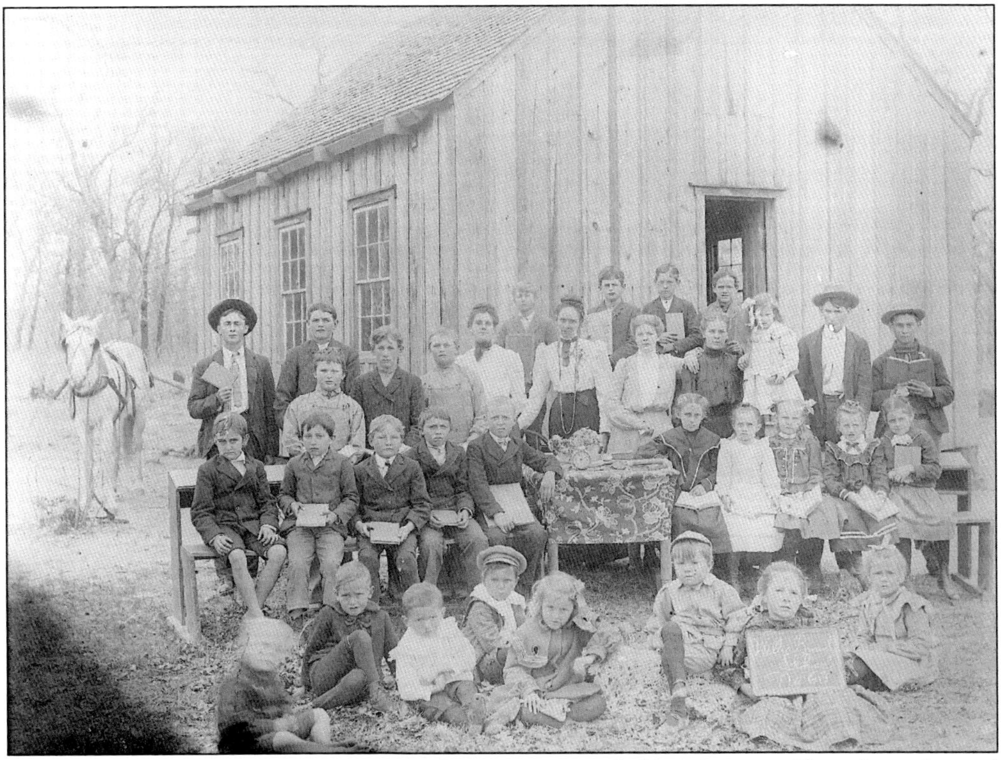

Willy Branch was the other community of Lee County settled by Moravian Slavs. It was located a little south of Dime Box.

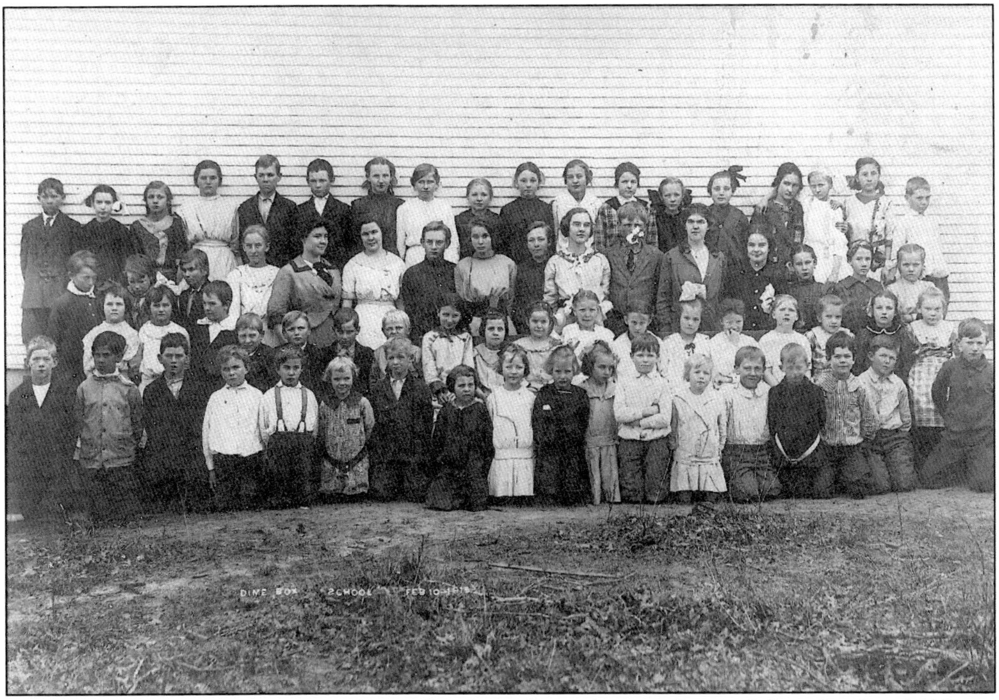

The students of the Dime Box Public School are shown here in front of the school in 1915.

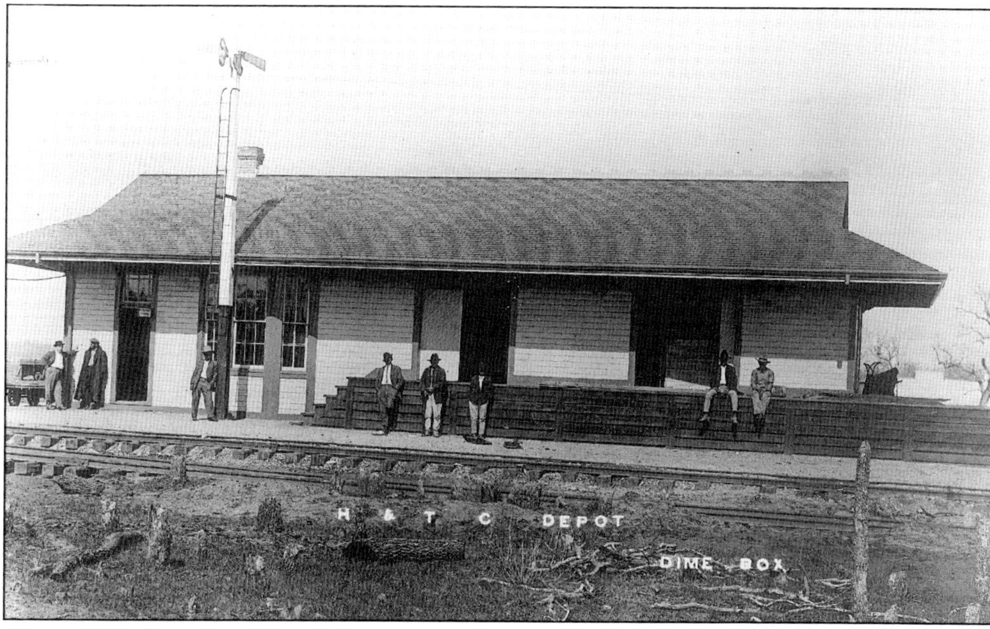

About 1910, the railroad decided on a route that would not pass through Old Dime Box, and a "New" Dime Box was established. "Numerous groups of surveyors [for the railroad] went through the area, and the last survey made was right across our garden and over the front yard. Well, this place was rather isolated and we were glad to know it soon wouldn't be so isolated. Lawyers for the railroad company got busy buying land on which the tracks would be laid; even if you didn't want to sell they could take it anyway. It cut the Moses farm in two. Soon a big camp for laborers was set up just below the hill in the Moses farm pasture. The people living in the tents wanted to buy all the country produce they could, so I sold them all my surplus vegetables, milk, butter and eggs, making it profitable for me." —Ada Moses memoir.

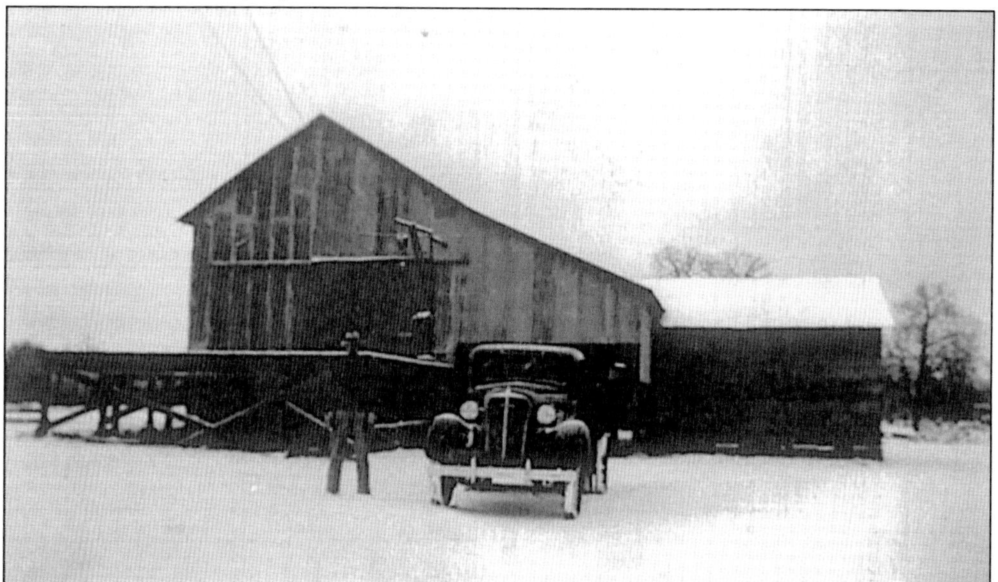

The Hannes Gin in Dime Box is shown here in the 1950s after a snowstorm, which was the occasion for the photograph. The image is the only one of the gin known to exist.

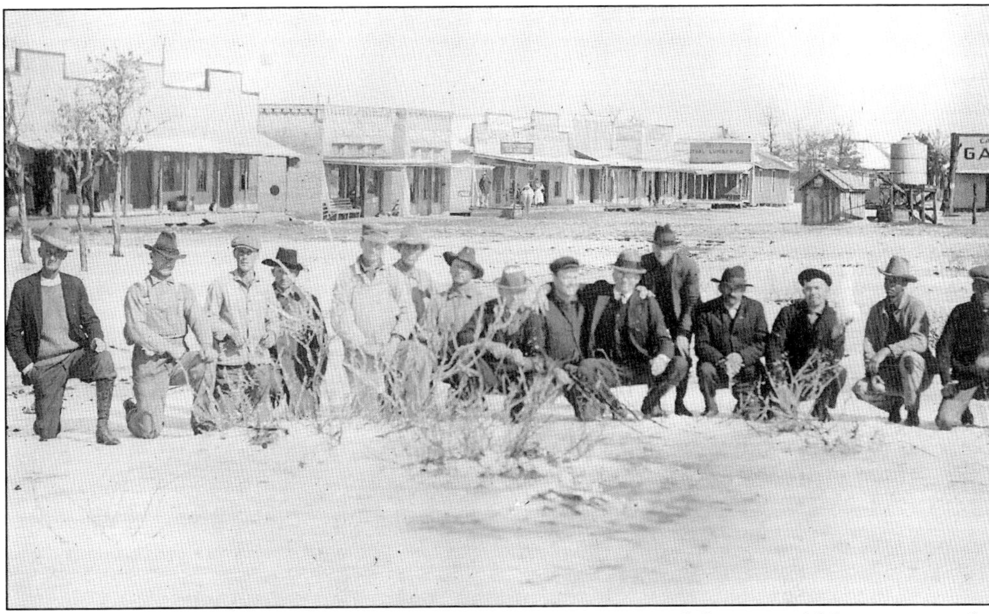

New Dime Box is pictured here in 1913. The town was moved from its old location on the Old San Antonio Road to the right-of-way of the new railroad. Not everyone wanted to move, so there came to be both an Old and a New Dime Box. One can make out some of the signs on the buildings. From left to right are Noah Albers' drug store, [Bowers] First State Bank, a drug and general merchandise store [Kocurek], a lumber company, and, on the right, Carl Bridges' Garage.

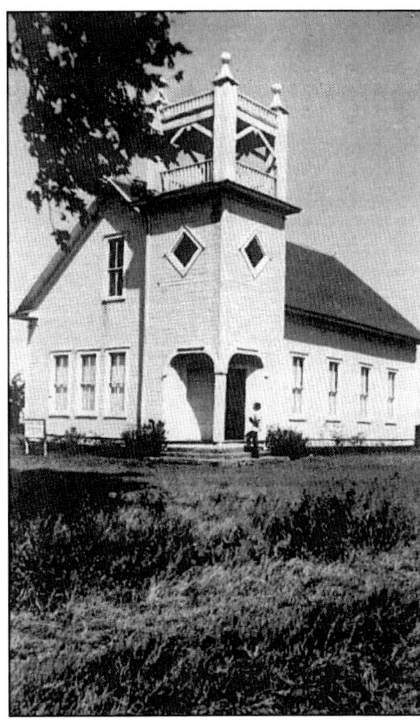

This is the Trinity Lutheran Church in Dime Box.

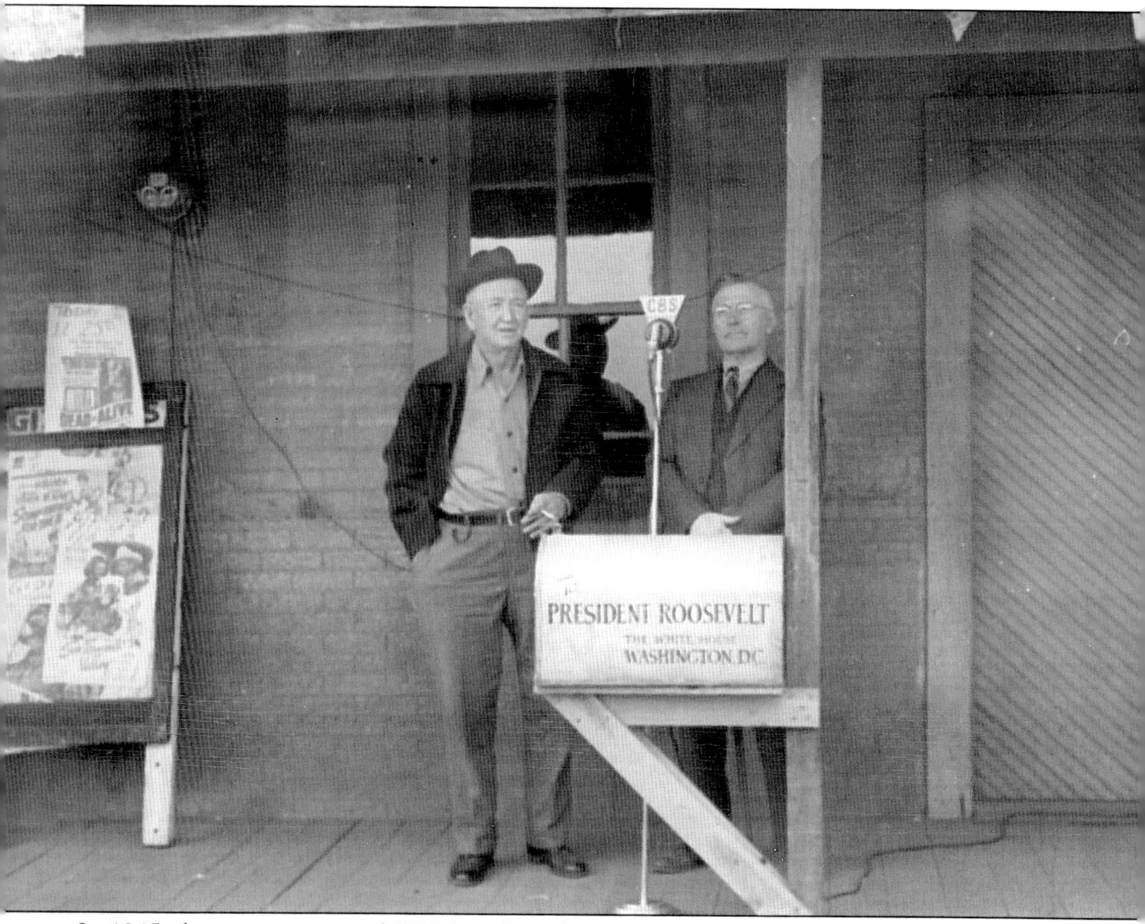

In 1945, there was a national CBS broadcast from Dime Box to kick off the March of Dimes. Mildred Kocurek, a local victim of the disease, was poster child of the year. Postmaster D.F. Stamps sent this post box to President Roosevelt addressed as shown and it was returned to Dime Box via the return address painted on the front.

Four

WENDS OF SERBIN

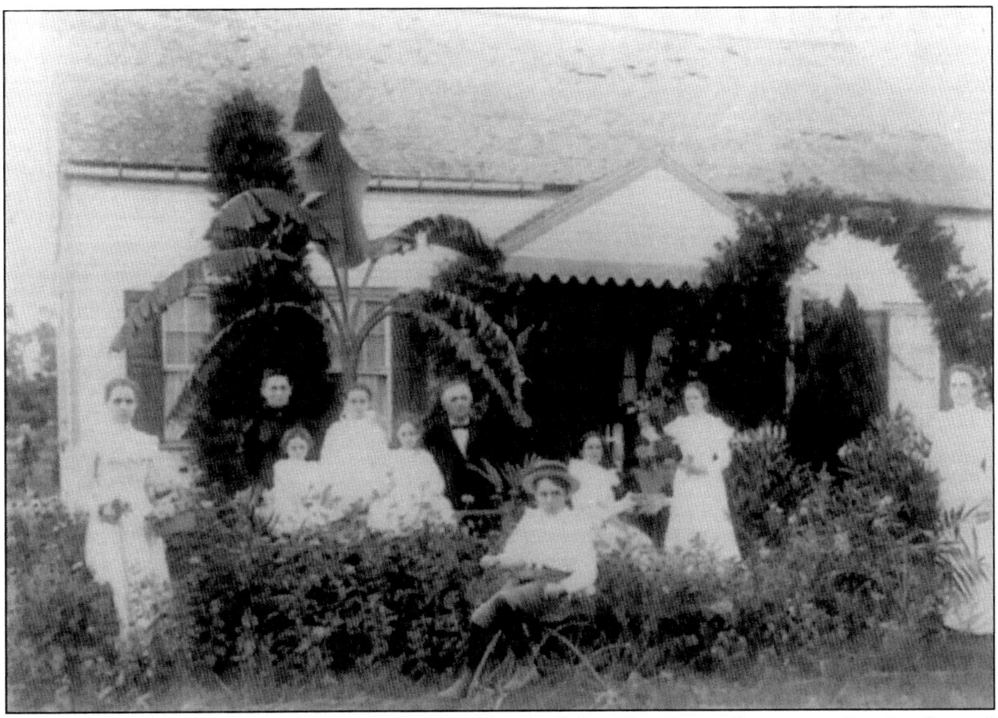

The town of Serbin was named for the homeland of the Wends, a Slavic people who formed a small population within Germany. A hundred years ago, the Wends of Serbin and the Slavic Czechs of Dime Box had cousin languages that allowed them at least elementary communication in their two native tongues. This is the family of Gerhardt Kilian, a teacher at St. Paul Serbin, posing in front of their home, the Teacherage. From left to right are Amanda Kilian Stein, Anna Gersch Kilian, Marie Kilian Luecke, Esther Kilian Kasper, Louise Kilian, teacher Gerhard Kilian, Martin Kilian, Martha Kilian Wolf, Selma Kilian Fehr, and Clara Kilian Schultz. (Photo by Chas. A. Meyer; courtesy of the Texas Wendish Heritage Museum Archive.)

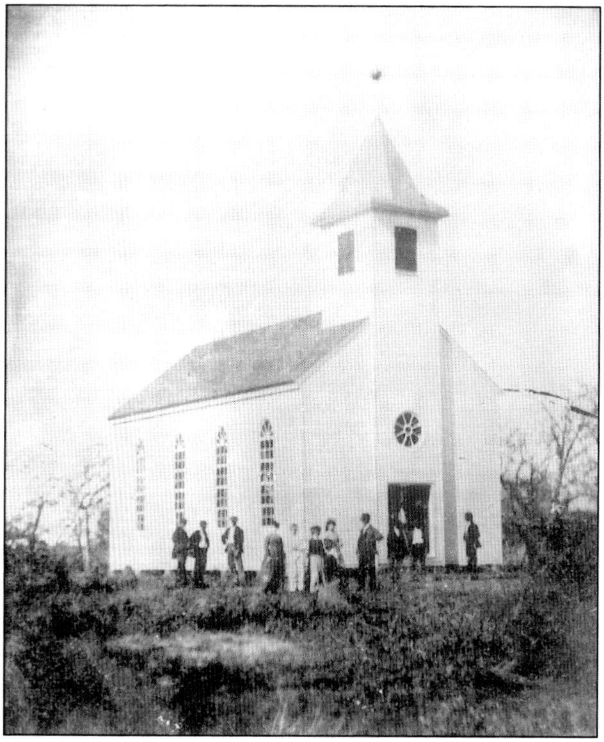

The Wends were Lutheran and followed Luther in insisting the Bible be taught in their native tongue, at first Wendish, later German. The second St. Paul's Lutheran Church in Serbin was dedicated December 25, 1859, and used until 1871. This picture was taken from an old tintype. (Ann Blasig Collection, Texas Wendish Heritage Museum Archive.)

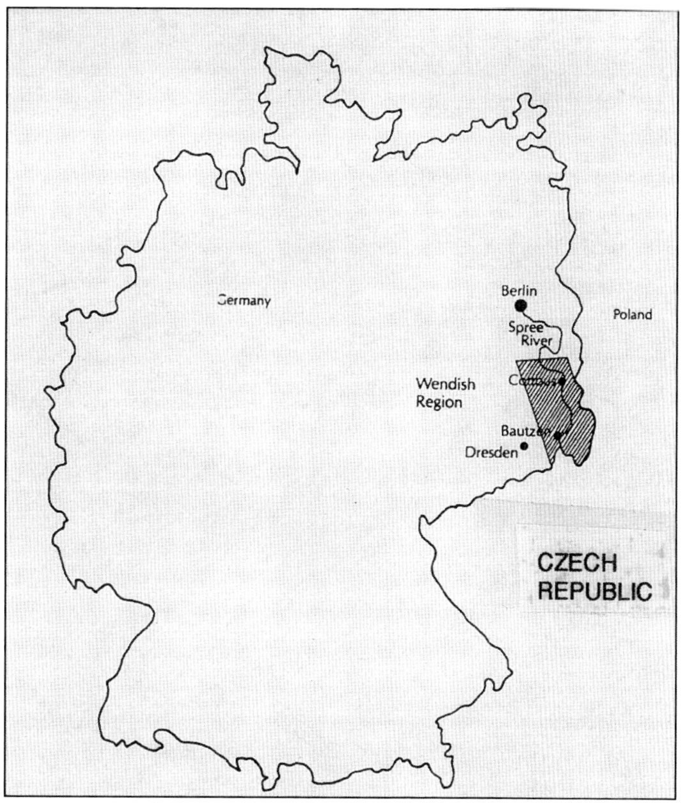

This map of modern Germany indicates the location of the Wendish homeland.

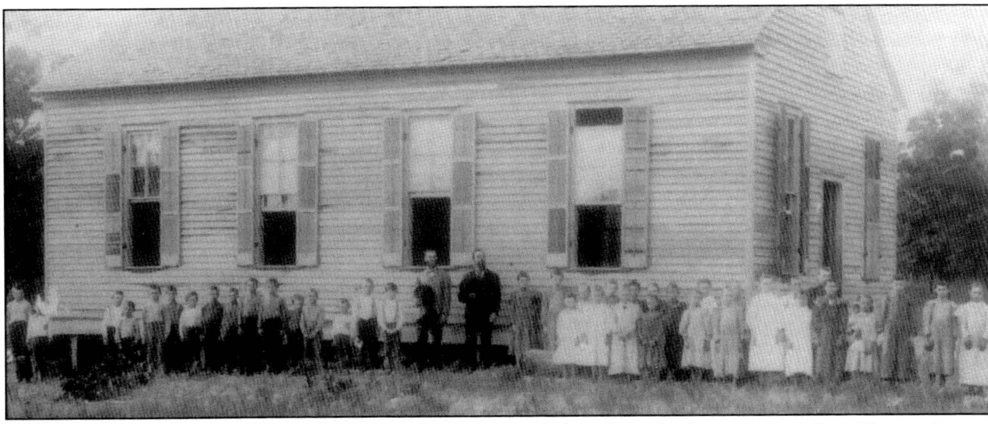

Posing with the children of St. Peter's Lutheran School in Serbin are teacher Ernst August Weise (left) and Pastor John Conrad Bernthal (right). (Carl August Weise Collection, Texas Wendish Heritage Museum Archive.)

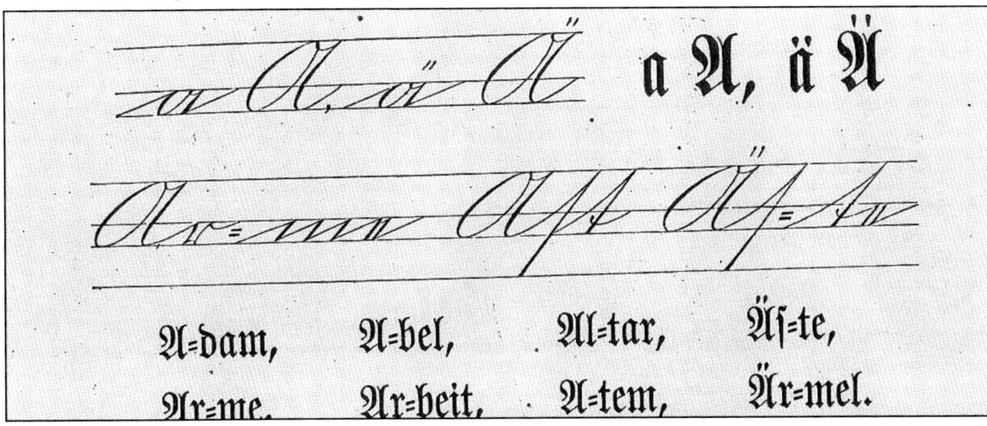

a A, ä Ä

A=dam, A=bel, Al=tar, Äſ=te,
Ar=me, Ar=beit, A=tem, Är=mel.

Like the sermons in church, c. 1900 school lessons were in German. This page from the writing and reading primer used in Lutheran Parochial Schools demonstrates that "A is for Adam." (*Schreiblesefibel fur den Unterricht den elementarklassen*, St. Louis, MO: Concordia Publishing House, 1904; courtesy Texas Wendish Heritage Museum Archive.)

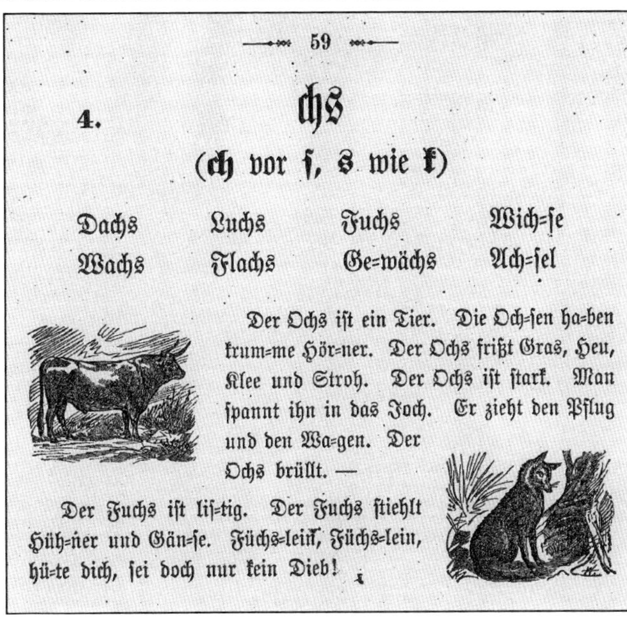

59

4. **chs**

(ch vor ſ, s wie k)

Dachs	Luchs	Fuchs	Wich=ſe
Wachs	Flachs	Ge=wächs	Ach=ſel

Der Ochs iſt ein Tier. Die Och=ſen ha=ben krum=me Hör=ner. Der Ochs frißt Gras, Heu, Klee und Stroh. Der Ochs iſt ſtark. Man ſpannt ihn in das Joch. Er zieht den Pflug und den Wa=gen. Der Ochs brüllt. —

Der Fuchs iſt liſ=tig. Der Fuchs ſtiehlt Hüh=ner und Gän=ſe. Füchs=lein, Füchs=lein, hü=te dich, ſei doch nur kein Dieb!

This page gives an example of "chs" as in ochs [ox] and fuchs [fox]. (Texas Wendish Heritage Museum Archive.)

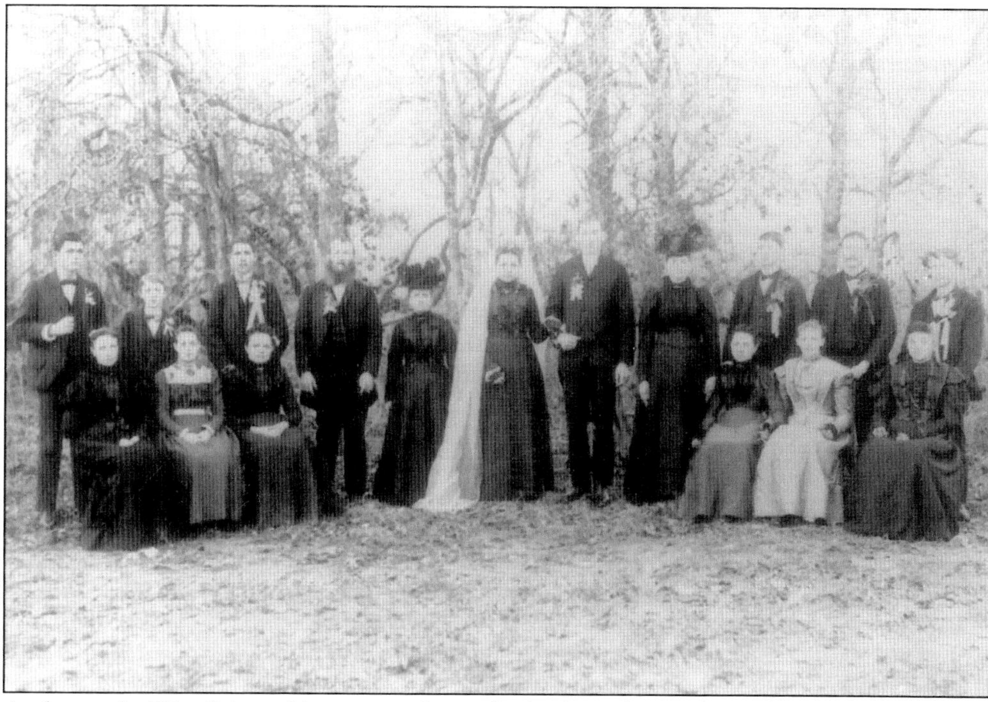

A photo of a Wendish wedding party shows the bride and attendants dressed in black. This custom of wearing black may simply have been a matter of practicality. Around 1900, the custom and costume changed and brides began to wear blue or gray, then later white. (Marie Kilian Luecke Collection, Texas Wendish Heritage Museum Archive.)

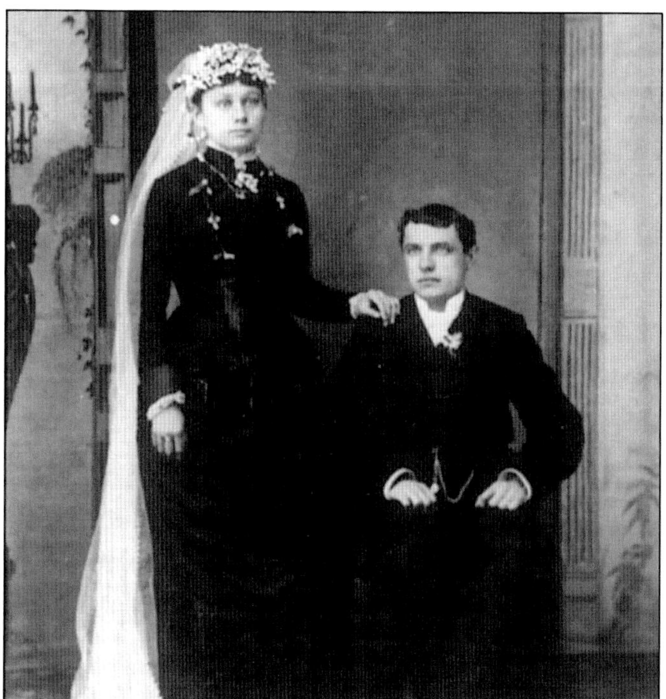

Bride and groom Marie Moerbe Kilian and Herman T. Kilian, the second pastor at St. Paul Lutheran Church in Serbin, pose in March 1886. Note the long veil and the traditional Wendish wreath braided of vines and flowers, with flowered pendants. (Photo by C. Peterson; courtesy of the Marie Kilian Luecke Collection, Texas Wendish Heritage Museum Archive.)

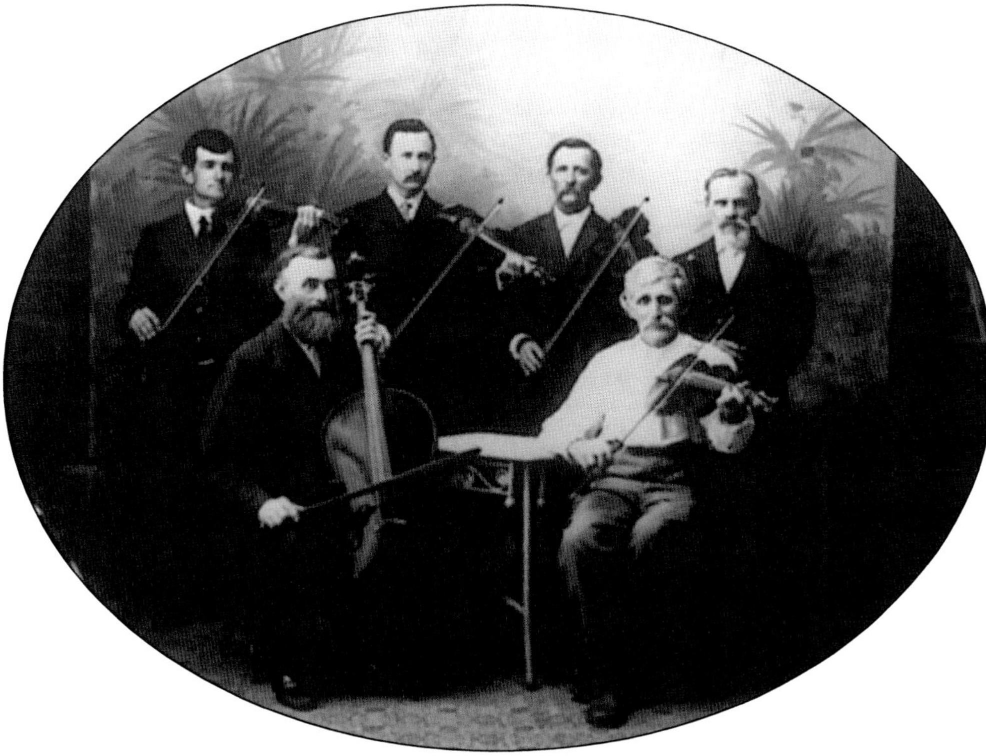

This Wendish fiddle band consisted of the following musicians, from left to right: (front) Johann Traugott Kriegel and August Wurm; (back) Henry Stuessy, P. Gerhard Hohle, Johann Hohle Jr., and Ernst Lorenz. (Texas Wendish Heritage Museum Archive.)

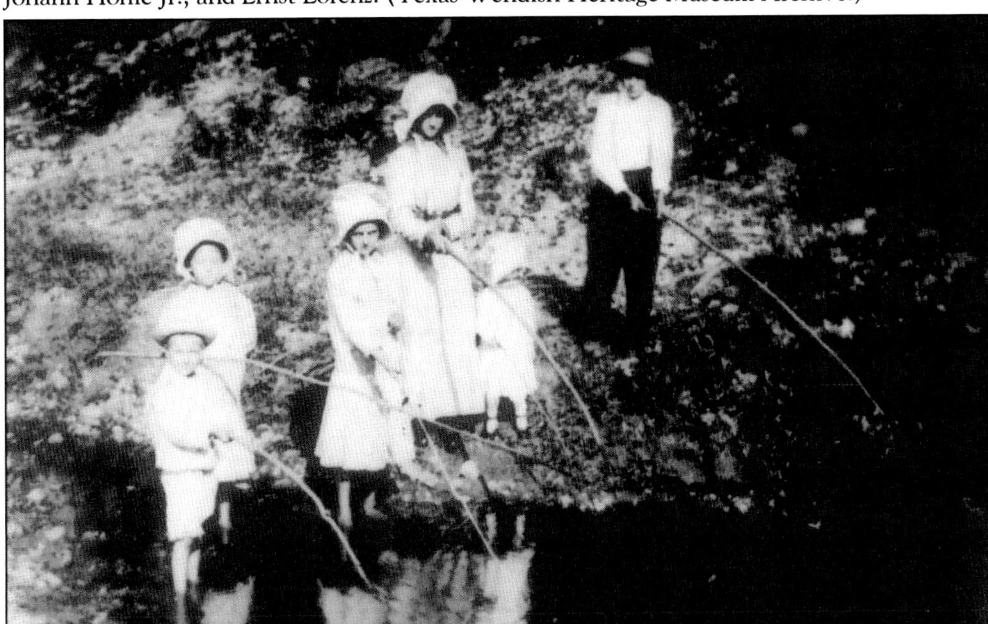

The August Mertink family fished in Pin Oak Creek on their farm. (Texas Wendish Heritage Museum Archive.)

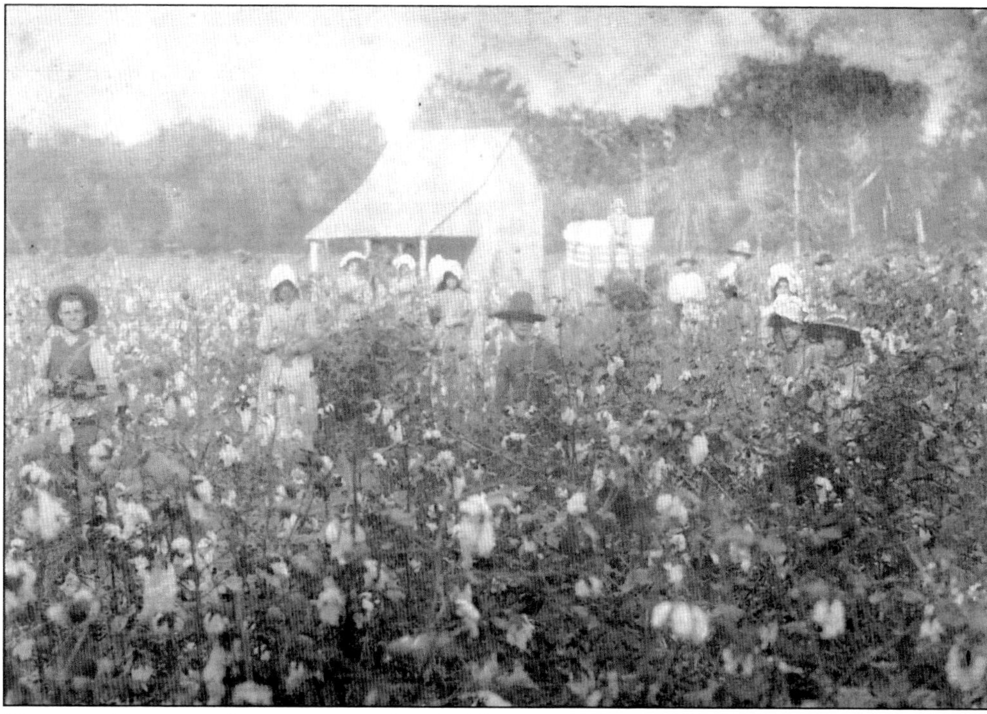

These workers are picking cotton at the Carl Benjamin Weise farm. (Texas Wendish Heritage Museum Archive.)

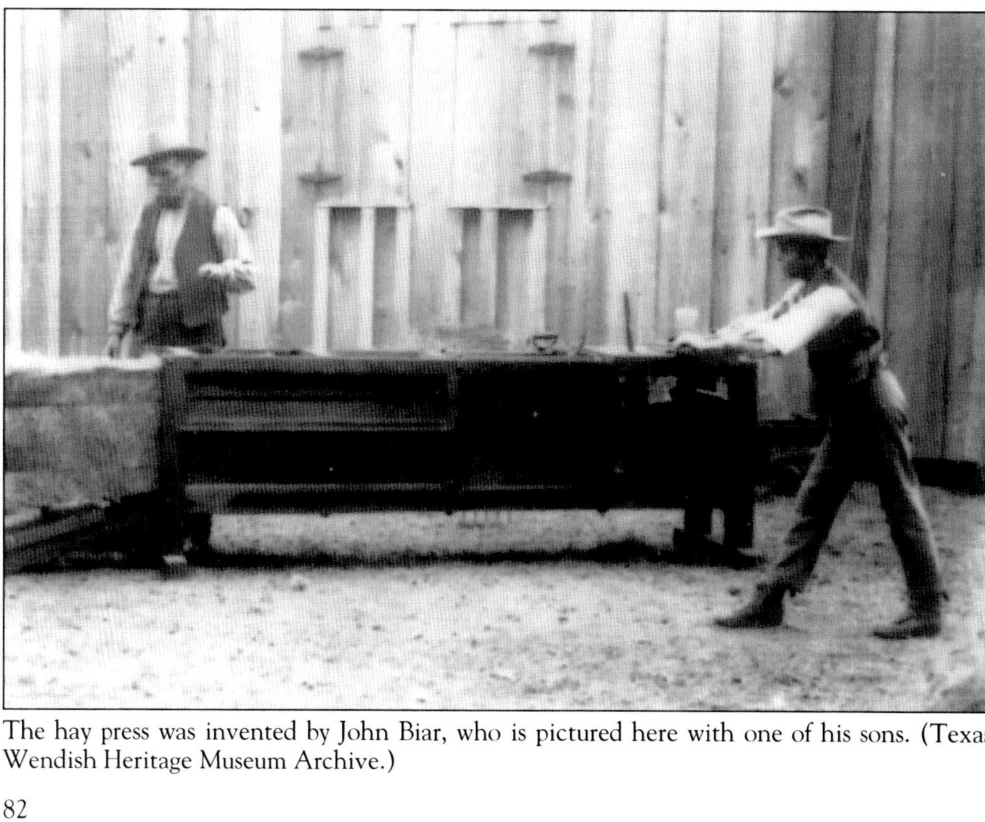

The hay press was invented by John Biar, who is pictured here with one of his sons. (Texas Wendish Heritage Museum Archive.)

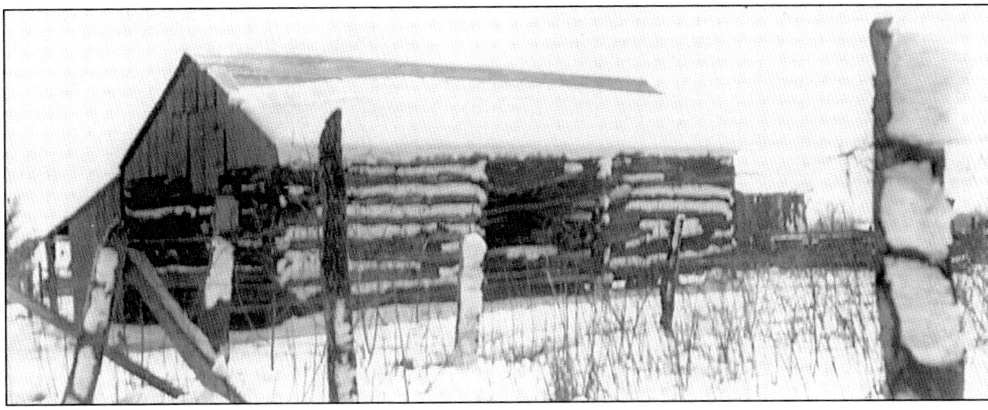

This very early log cabin still stands in the Serbin area.

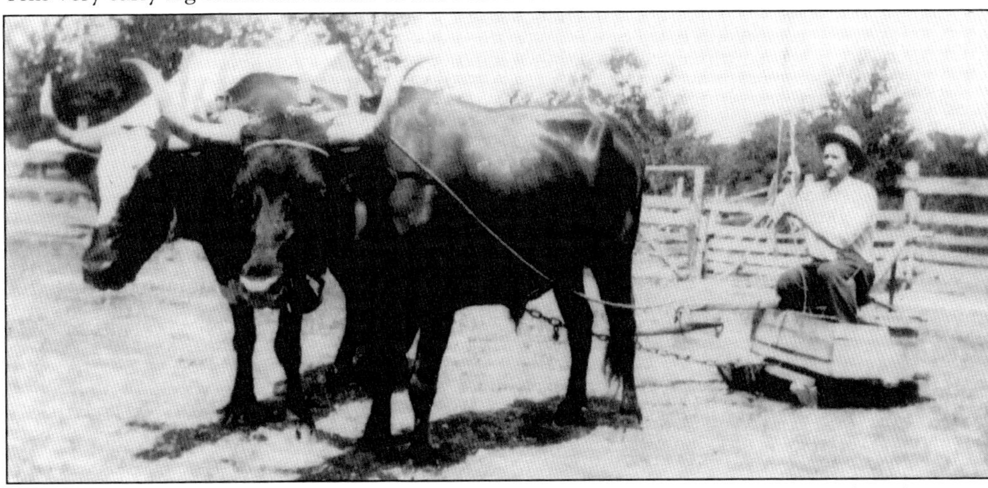

August Mertink appears here with oxen. (Texas Wendish Heritage Museum Archive.)

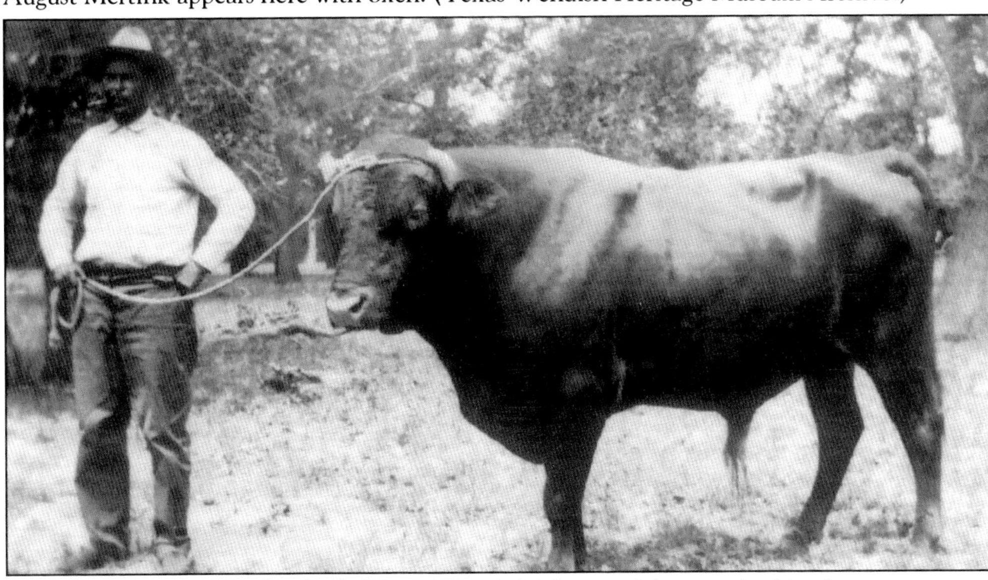

August Schultz poses with a bull. (Texas Wendish Heritage Museum Archive.)

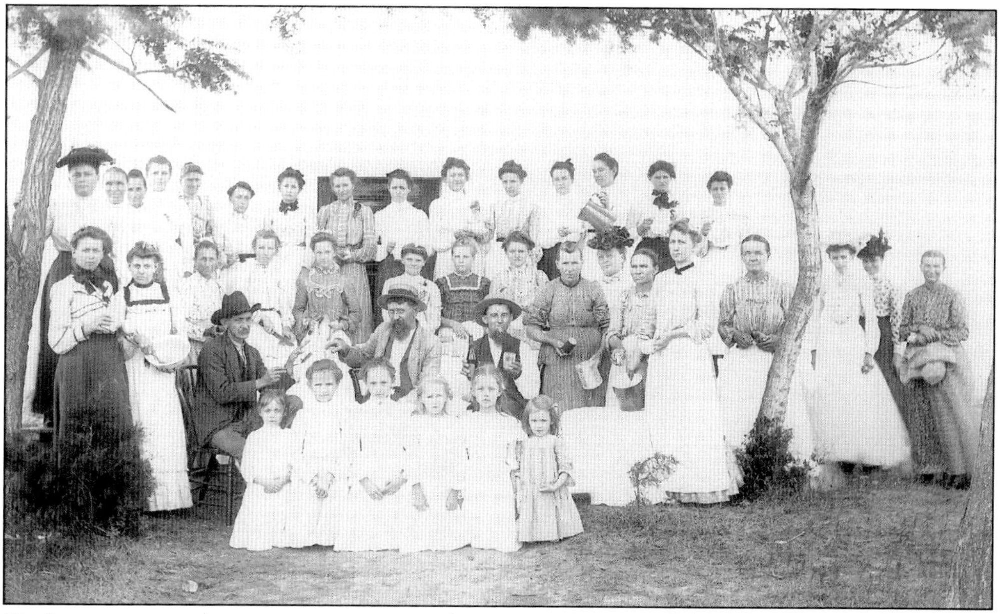

Cooks, servers, and managers are pictured at a convention of the Texas District, Lutheran Church-Missouri Synod in July 1918. Note the man at the middle left with an account sheet and pencil, the man next to the right with money, and the man on his right with a beer bottle and glass. The women have mixing pans, knives, potatoes, flour sifters, sausage, cups, saucers, pitchers, coffee pots, etc. (Courtesy Texas Wendish Heritage Museum Archive.)

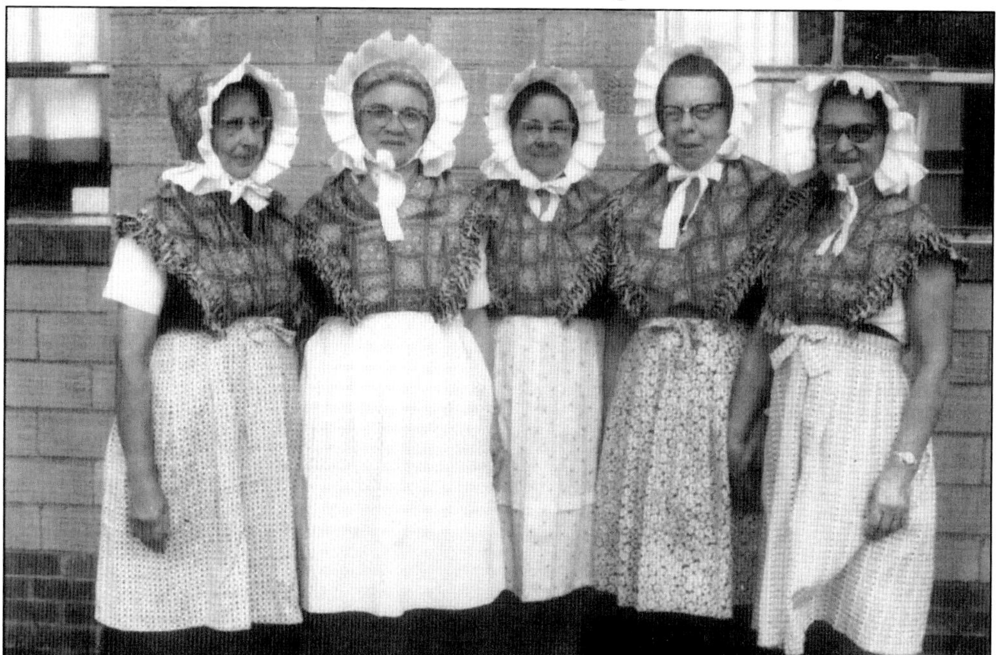

These charter members of the Wendish Culture Club, now called the Texas Wendish Heritage Society, are, from left to right, Frieda Wendland, Laura Moerbe Zoch, Lillie Moerbe Caldwell, Emma Dube Wuensche, and Gertrude Kasper Mitschke. (Photo c. 1976, courtesy of the Texas Wendish Heritage Museum Archive.)

Five

GIDDINGS

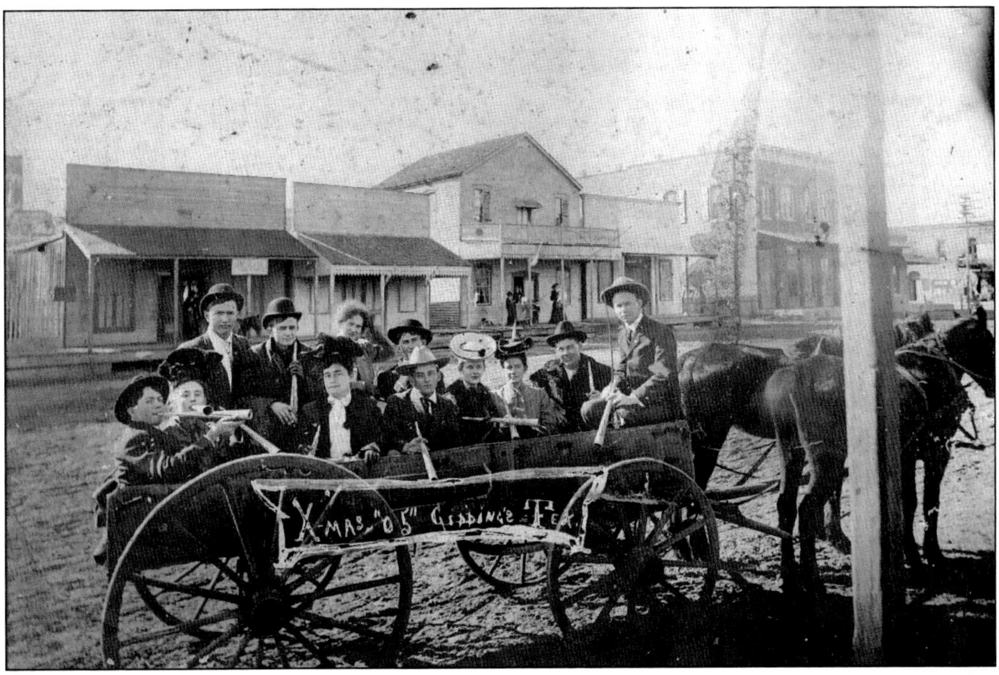

It is sometimes hard to tell the difference between Christmas and New Year's in Texas. This scene took place on Austin Street in front of the Grange, across from a grocery, barber, and millinery (note the women out front). There are still only wagons on the street—no cars, but the trains had arrived. A diary excerpt from December 25, 1905, reads, "Bright Christmas morning. Rubie seems so happy over her toys and presents. She got two dolls, gocart, tin & china dishes, chair, book, Buster Brown and Tige, some other little things, besides fire crackers, candy, nuts and fruit. Joe sent her a box of candy & Mr. R[ousseau] a box of cigars. Mr. R gave me 2 $5 gold pieces, gave Mr. R a glass dipper and socks. Rubie burnt her hand popping crackers." The Rousseaus had a fancier buggy. On August 7, 1893, the diary reads, "Whiskey $1.50. Mattie and Ellen washed, paid them $1.00. Got Blanche a third reader 70 cts. Put up a large jar of brandy peaches. Buggy cost $90.00. Little lumber and wheel prop $2.60. Got the horse from Mr. Carney, harness for the horse $12.50. Had a little ride in my new phaeton, rode up to Ma's and roamed about some." —Rousseau diaries.

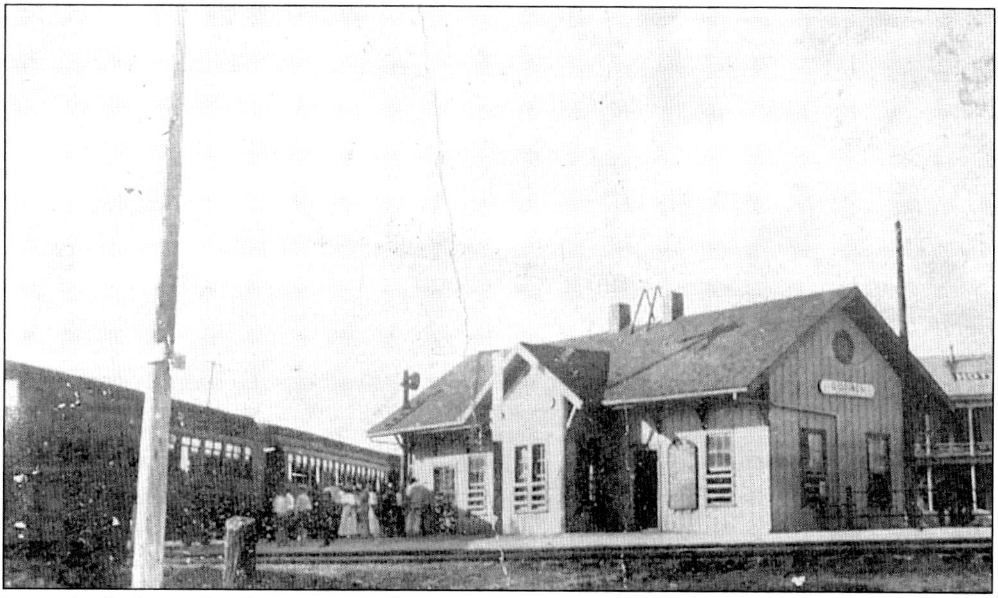

Instead of taking the shortest path from Brenham to Austin, which would cross the Yegua branches and require a number of bridges, the route selected in 1871 for the Houston & Texas Central RR followed the higher land of the divide between the Colorado and Brazos watersheds. Lexington and Lincoln were bypassed and Giddings grew to be the largest town in the county. In 1889 Giddings was also crossed by the San Antonio & Aransas Pass RR (SAAP), one of the many early Texas short lines.

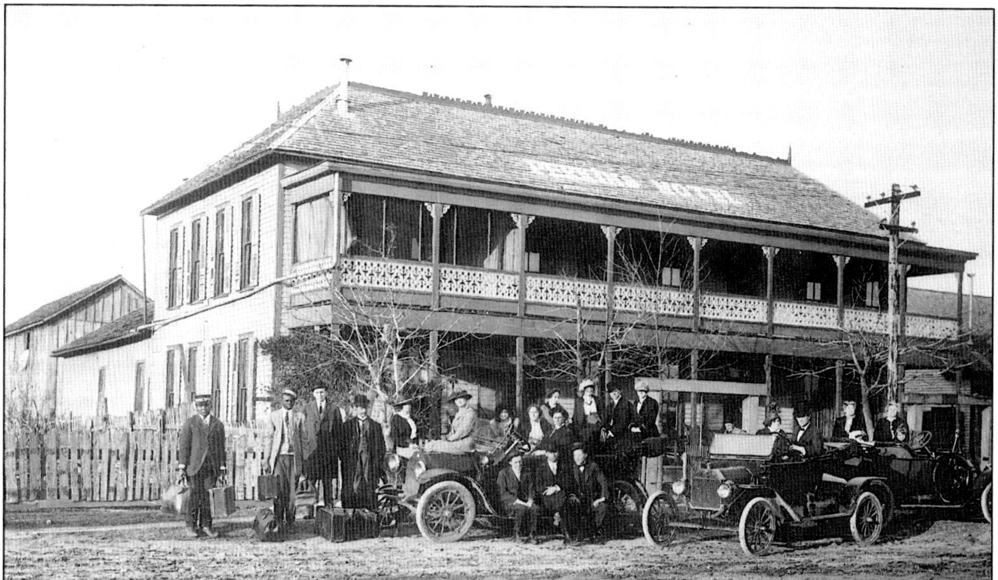

This photo of the Perkins Hotel is from about 1910. Like most of the hotels, the Perkins was adjacent to the railroad. In the 1890 City Business Directory, the Perkins Hotel's ad read, "First class accommodations $2/day," but the hotel was in business before then. On April 14, 1886, the diary read, "Commenced weaning Blanche. Mr. R ate with Mrs. Perkins 20 cts [also the next few days]." —Rousseau diaries.

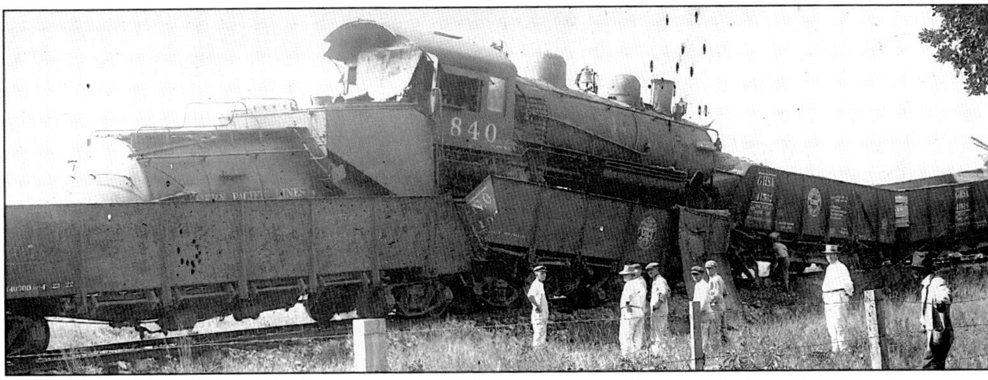

On May 31, 1900, Minnie Hester wrote, "There was a terrible wreck six miles from Lexington last night. The 12 o'clock train was wrecked and the engine was left standing on its head. The fireman was steamed almost to death and the engineer terribly burned. Both men lived until they were pulled from the wreck, but so great was their suffering they begged for someone to kill them. They did not live long. The fireman's eyes were burned out."

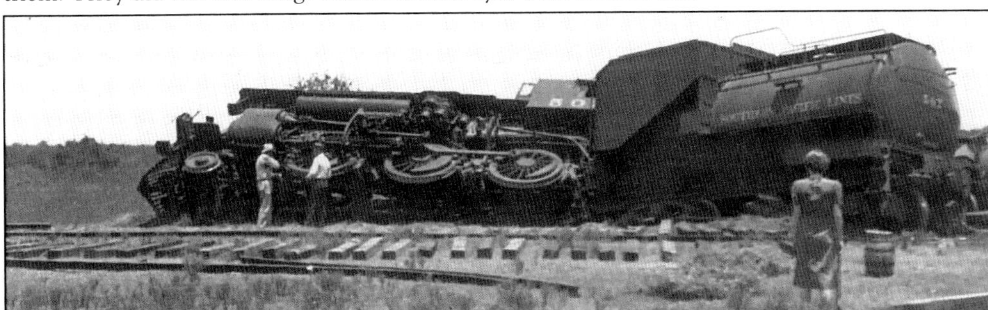

A young woman looks on in awe at another local railroad disaster.

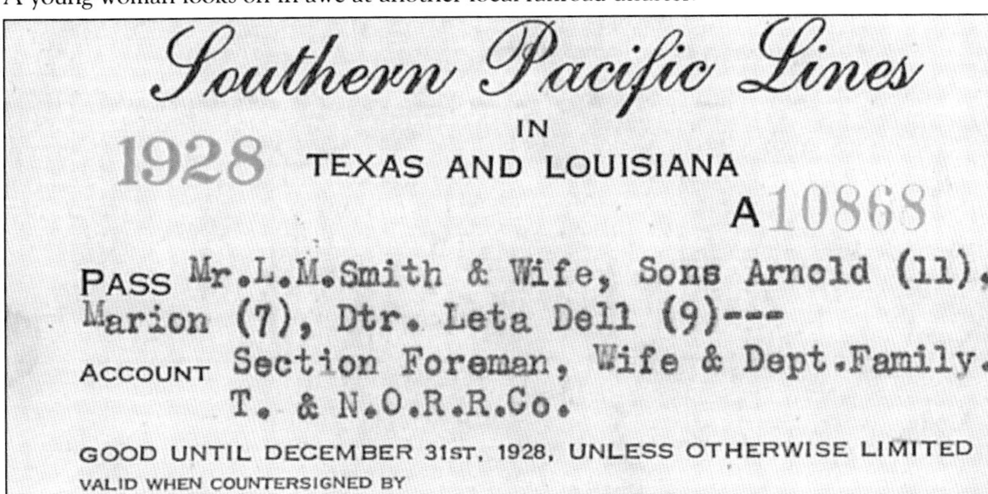

Southern Pacific Lines

IN

1928 TEXAS AND LOUISIANA

A10868

PASS Mr.L.M.Smith & Wife, Sons Arnold (11), Marion (7), Dtr. Leta Dell (9)---

ACCOUNT Section Foreman, Wife & Dept.Family. T. & N.O.R.R.Co.

GOOD UNTIL DECEMBER 31ST, 1928, UNLESS OTHERWISE LIMITED

VALID WHEN COUNTERSIGNED BY
P. C. MURRAY OR

H.M. Lull

L.M. Smith's railroad pass for 1928 was good for the entire family. His son Arnold followed him as a railroad man, and worked all his life for the Southern Pacific Lines, which took over the old Houston & texas Central.

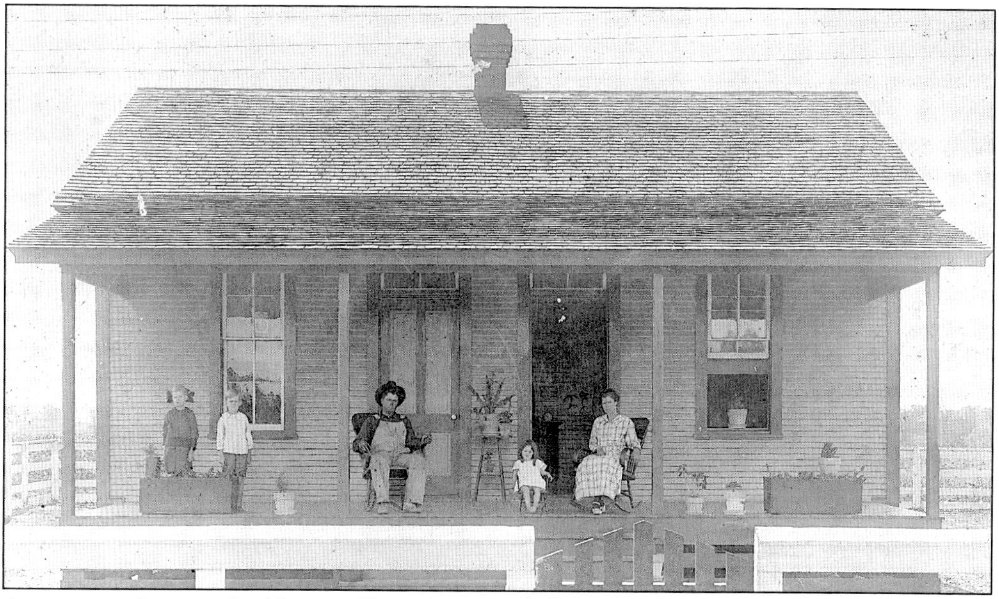

As a section foreman for 42 years, Henry Lee Smith (left center) was responsible for overseeing the condition of the rails, the switches, and the signal lights on his section of track. A section would be longer or shorter depending on the amount of work required. Sections in the yards of towns in which there were track intersections or in which there was heavy traffic would be short; those on rural stretches would be long. There were so many switches in Giddings that there was a man whose only duties were to oil them and keep the lanterns full of kerosene. The sturdily built section house was supplied by the railroad rent-free.

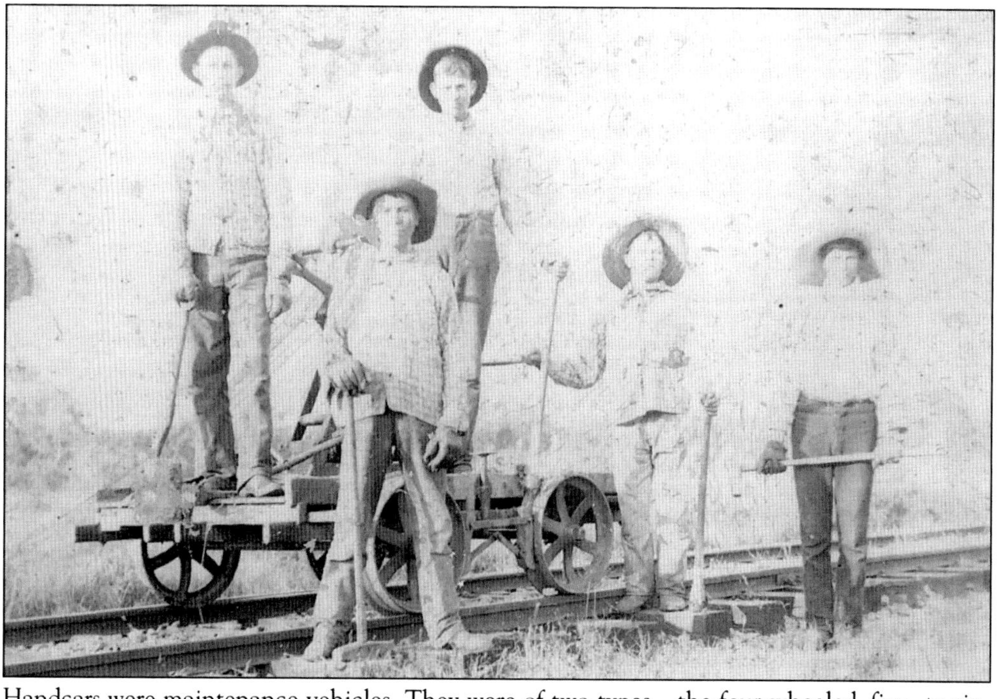

Handcars were maintenance vehicles. They were of two types—the four-wheeled, five- to six-man car shown here, and the smaller three-wheeler, operated by a single man.

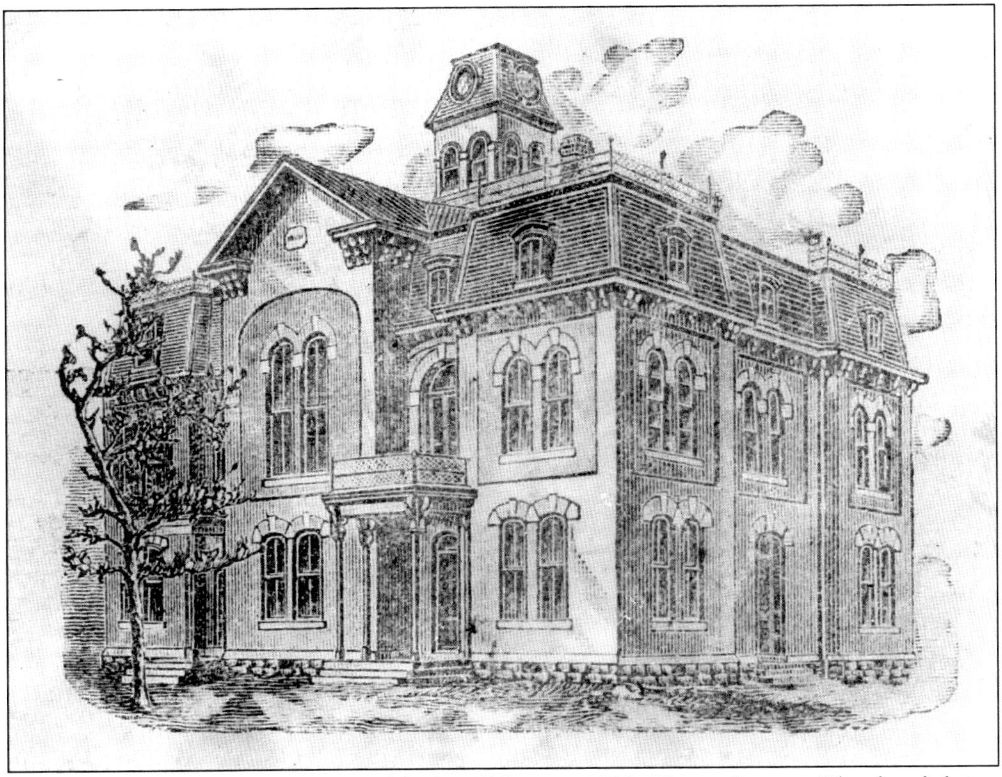

This is the old courthouse pictured before February 1898. Then, disaster. The fire fighting ladders were too short to reach the upper levels of the courthouse. A diary excerpt from February 11 reads, "While we were eating supper the fire bell rang, the courthouse was on fire, could not save, burned down in a few hours." —Rousseau diaries.

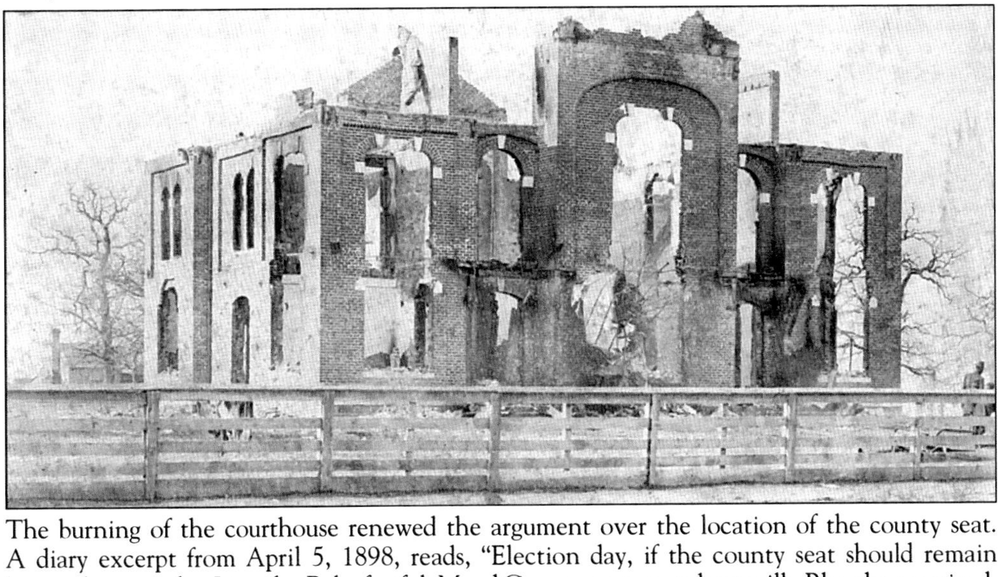

The burning of the courthouse renewed the argument over the location of the county seat. A diary excerpt from April 5, 1898, reads, "Election day, if the county seat should remain here or be moved to Lincoln. Baby fretful. Maud Carmean came and got milk. Blanche practiced, gathered peas for tomorrow." The entry for April 6, 1898, reads, "Giddings got the courthouse." —Rousseau diaries.

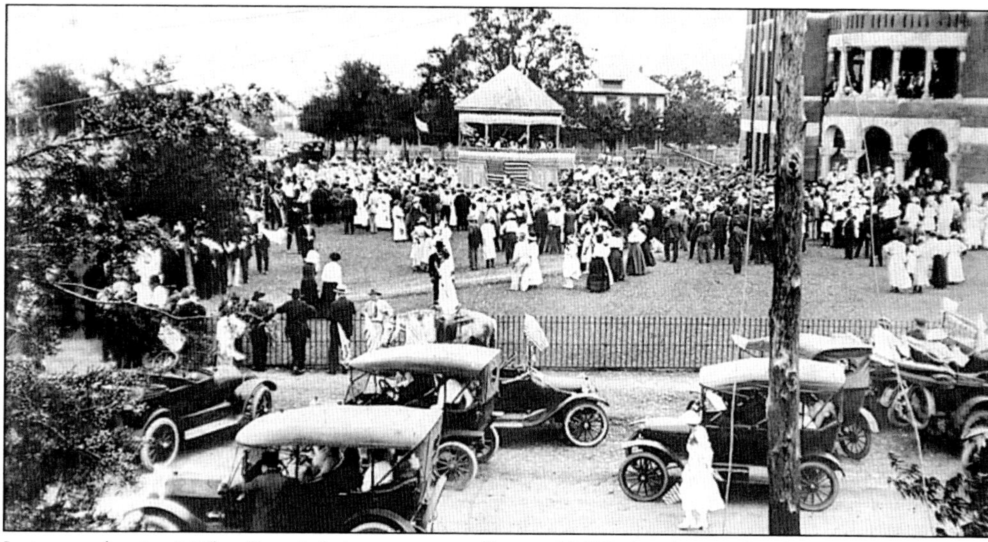

Is it an election? The Fourth? A patriotic rally in 1917? At the peak of Populism in 1896, Hige Turner wrote his father, Adam, "How did you vote! I did not go to the Election. I went to the cotton patch. I picked 217 pounds the election day. I sold my crop and went up on the prairie to pick cotton." —Turner letters. (Photo courtesy of the Texas Wendish Heritage Museum Archive.)

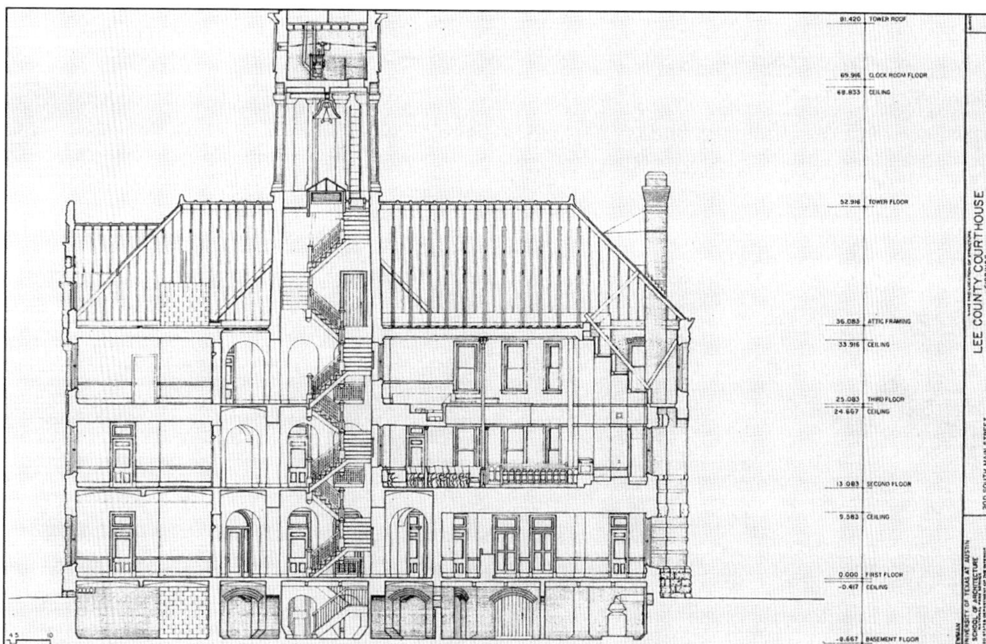

This image, and others to follow, are from set of detailed drawings that were awarded the Charles E. Peterson prize of the Historic American Buildings Survey. The drawings were made by students at the University of Texas School of Architecture in 1998. The courthouse architect, J.R. Gordon, designed a number of Texas courthouses. He prided himself that this was the ideal plan for a Texas courthouse—a welcoming entrance with porches on all four corners, courts on the second floor away from the crowds, and a central stairwell and clock tower to conduct the heat up and out of the building.

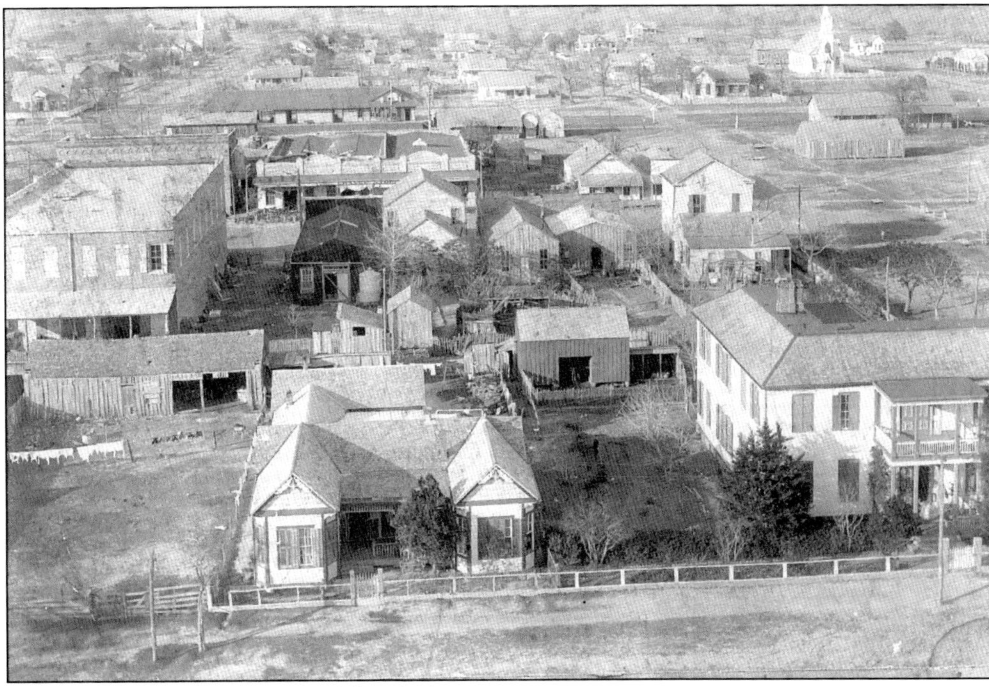

This view north from the top of the clock tower of the new courthouse was taken in about 1905. In Giddings, shops do not surround the courthouse square in the manner typical of most small county seats. The setting is a neighborhood of single-family dwellings. The house on the right is the Schubert-Fletcher house, which still stands. The next street over is Austin, the "main street" of Giddings. The lettering on the Grange store can almost be seen across Austin Street from the dark building to the left of the center of the picture. The stores facing the Grange are the same as those in the Christmas scene, now seen from the rear.

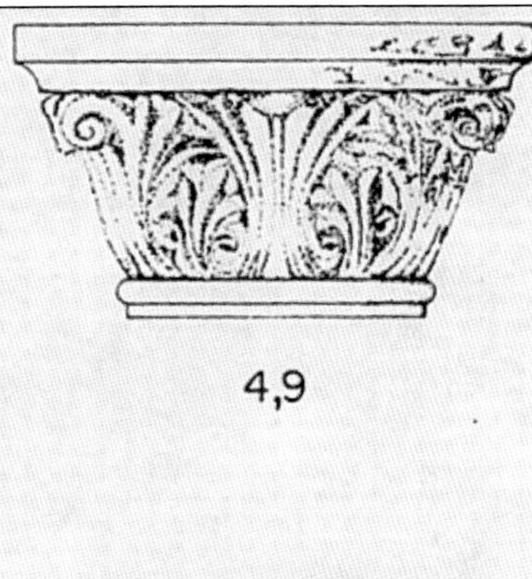

4,9

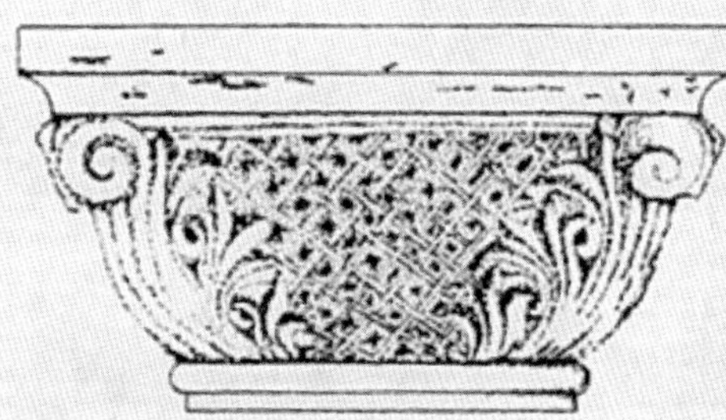

11

The column capitals are shown here in detailed sketches.

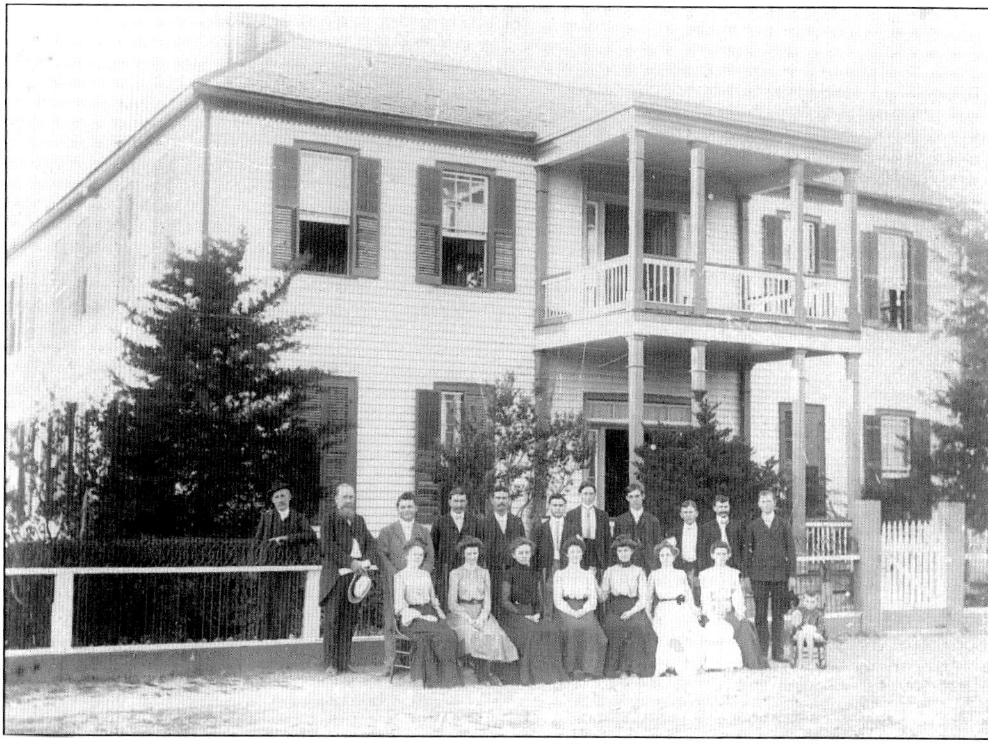

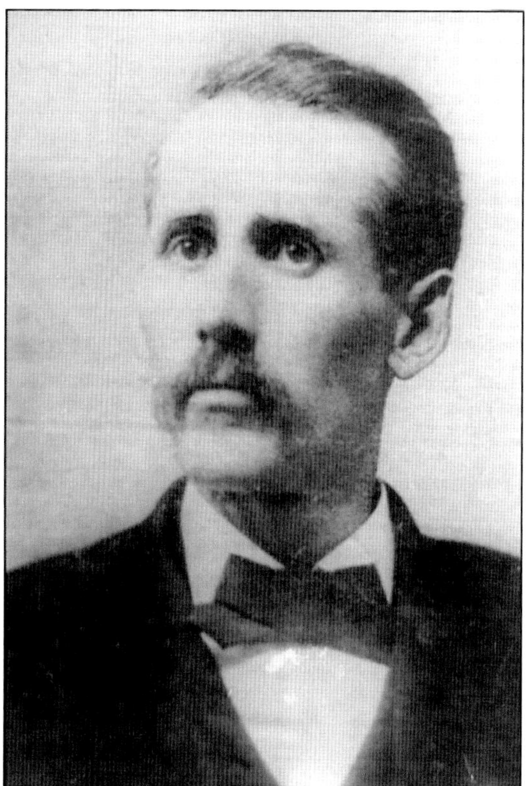

The Schubert family sold their house to the Lutheran Concordia College in 1890. In 1900 it was resold to Baylis Fletcher and his wife, Marie Hester Fletcher (1862–1956). The house stands today and is being restored by the Lee County Heritage Society.

Baylis Fletcher (1859–1912) was a trail driver, raconteur, storekeeper, politician, teacher, and historian.

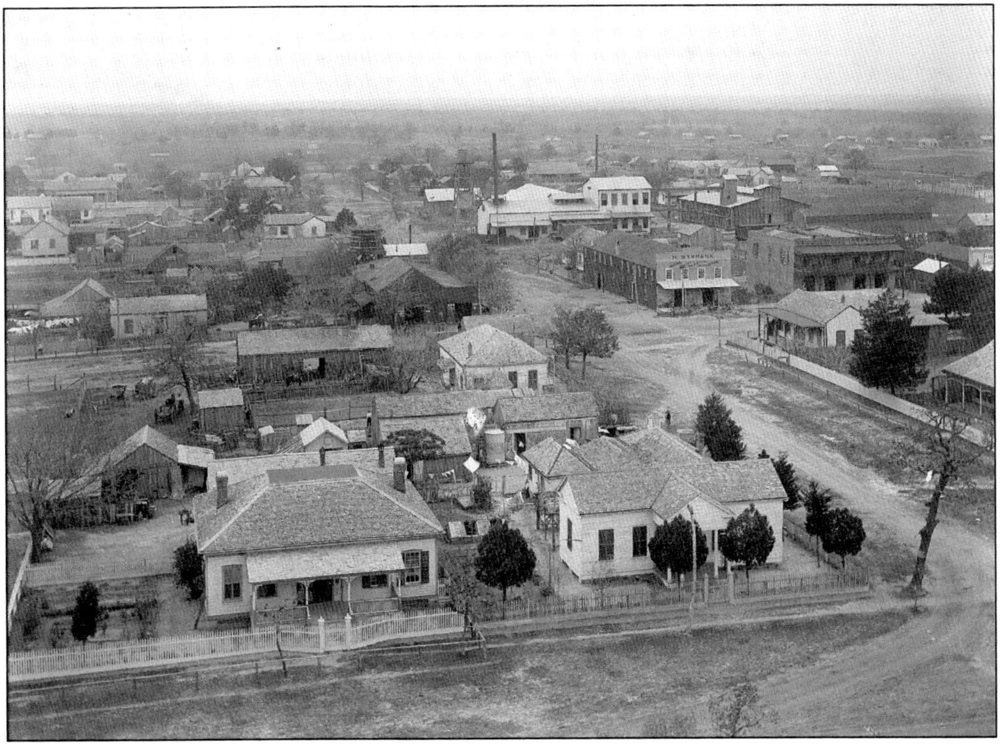

Around 1905, one of the houses across the street and to the west of the courthouse belonged to the Joekels. Later the Hillsbergs erected a two-story house on the corner lot. This house became the Placke's Traveler's Hotel. The two tall chimneys in rear center of the image mark the Cotton Oil Mill.

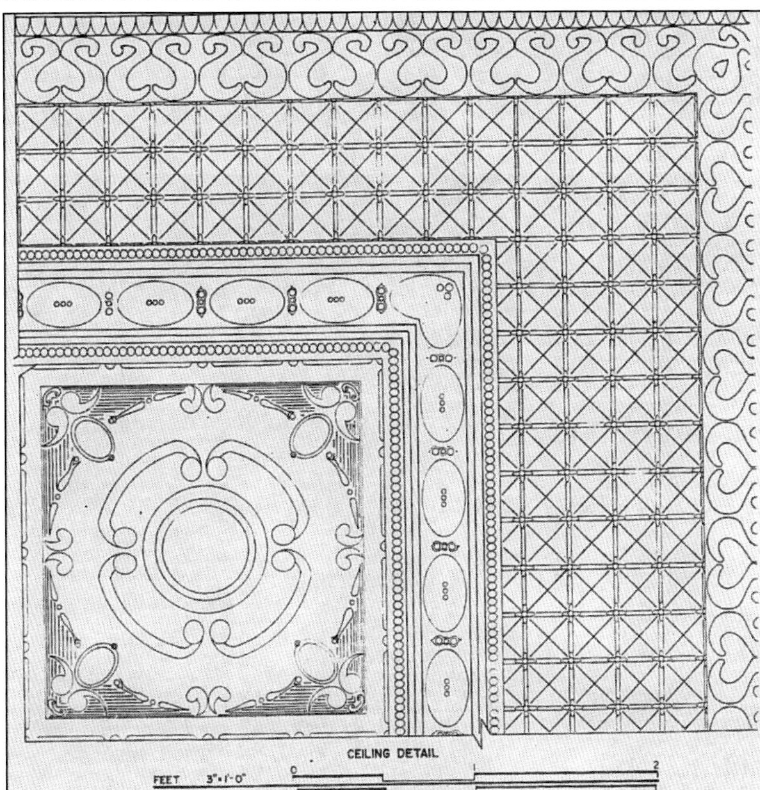

This detailed drawing shows the ceilings of the courthouse.

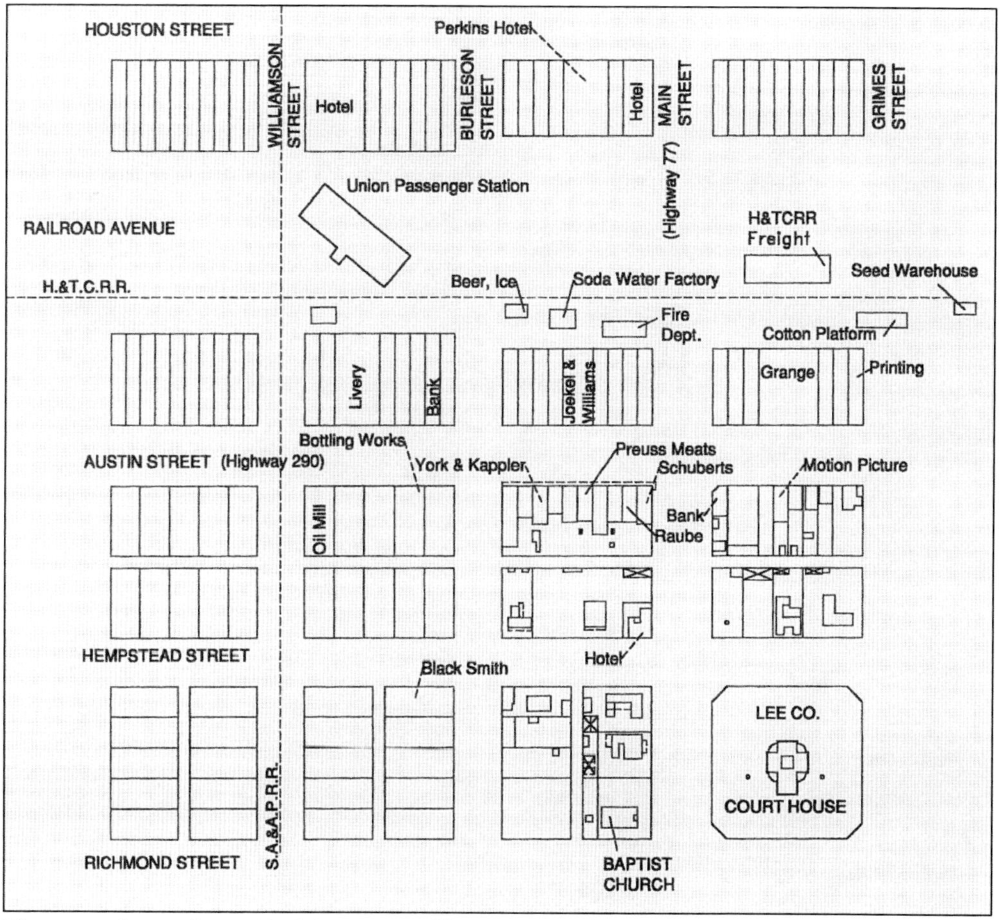

This view shows the *c.* 1910 locations of businesses and all the essentials for surviving Texas summers—an icehouse, beer storage, cotton storage, a soda bottling company, and a picture theatre.

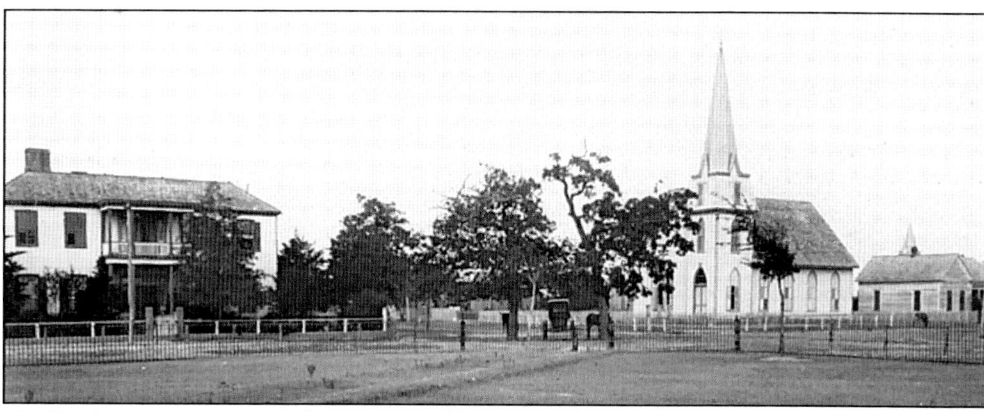

The Presbyterian church, built in 1885, still stands and is in use. It is located diagonally across the street northeast of the courthouse (just off the map). A diary excerpt from December 13, 1885, reads, "Mr. R attended the Presbyterian meeting in the new church this AM." —Rousseau diaries.

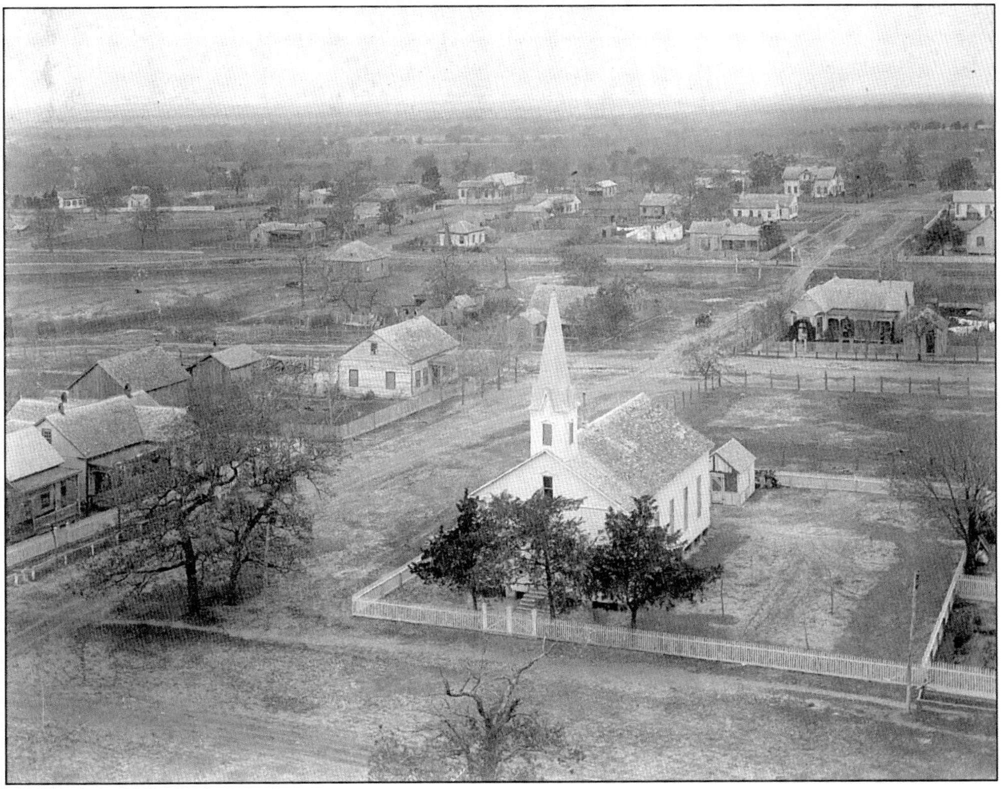

A Baptist congregation organized in 1872 and had a building constructed about 1880. It was rotated, then moved in about 1904 to a site visible to the left of the houses in this view west from the courthouse. It stood there unmoved until it was razed in 1959.

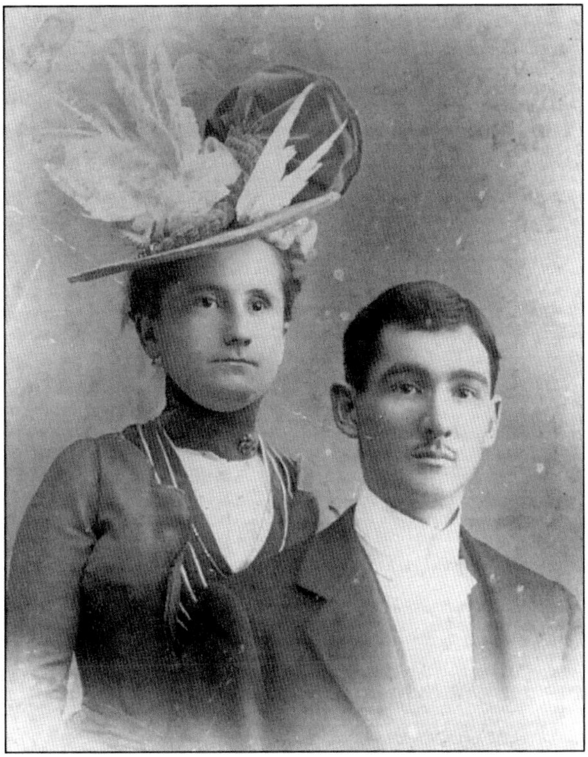

Fate (Lafayette) Fariss (1872–1954) married Alberta "Bert" Riggs of Lexington on November 25, 1899. Fate was a son of William Holmes Fariss and, like all the Farisses, a member of the Baptist Church. Fate and his brother, Ira, were associated with the Grange store.

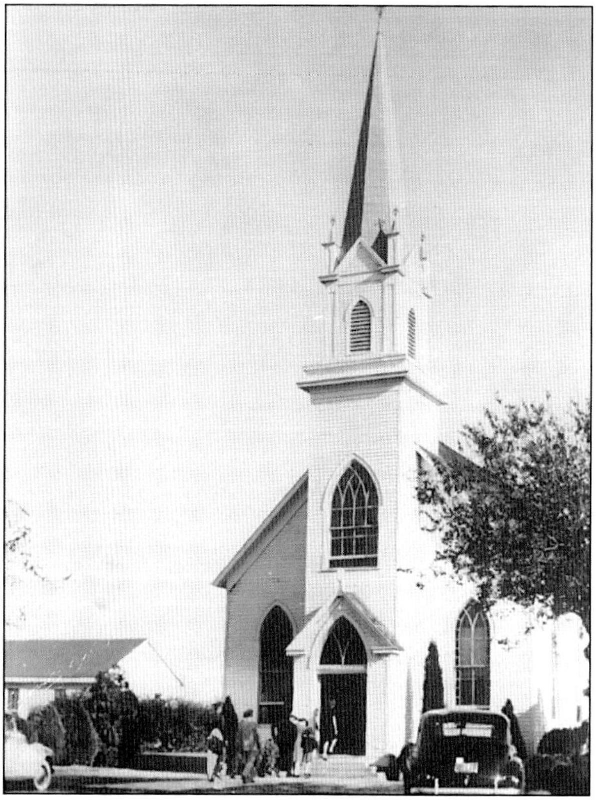

The Immanuel Lutheran Church can also be seen in the right of the background of the view north from the courthouse. It was torn down in 1959.

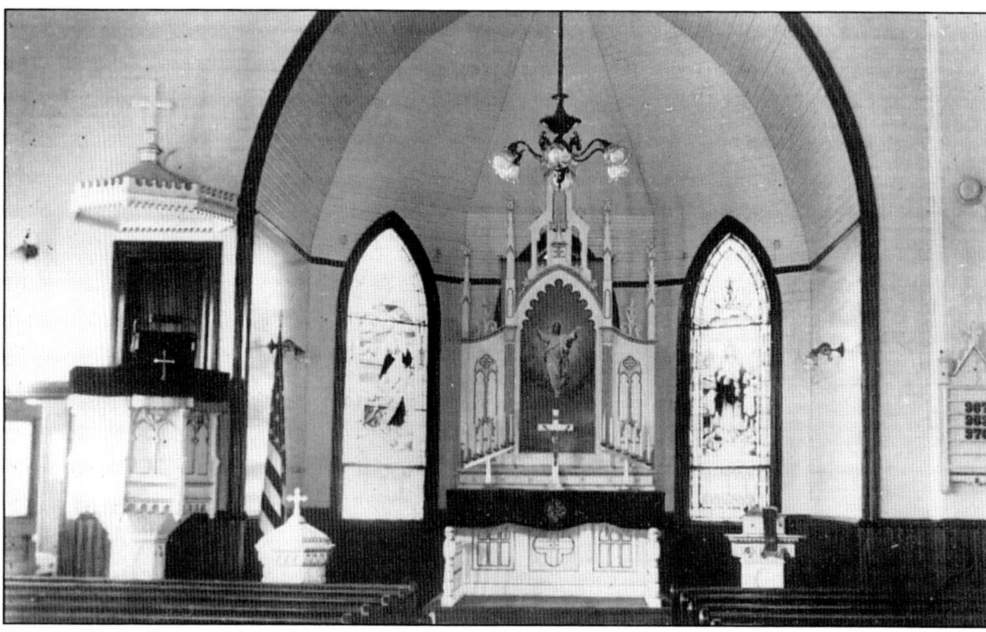

This is the interior of the Immanuel Lutheran Church.

This is the Gustave Lehman and Hermine Wirth wedding, which took place at Immanuel Lutheran.

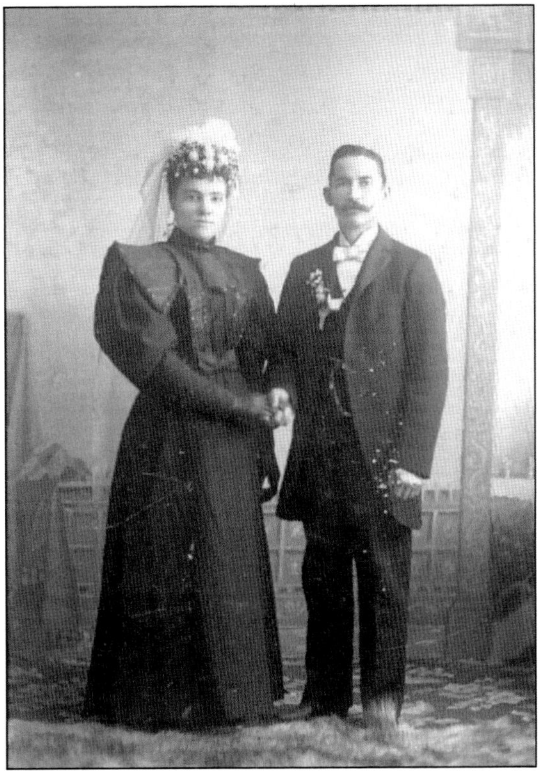

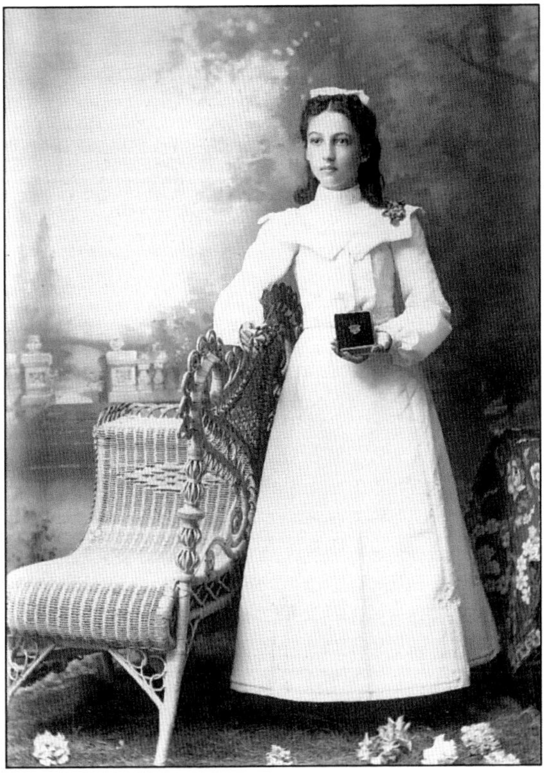

The Emily Luecke (Placke) confirmation was conducted at Immanuel Lutheran.

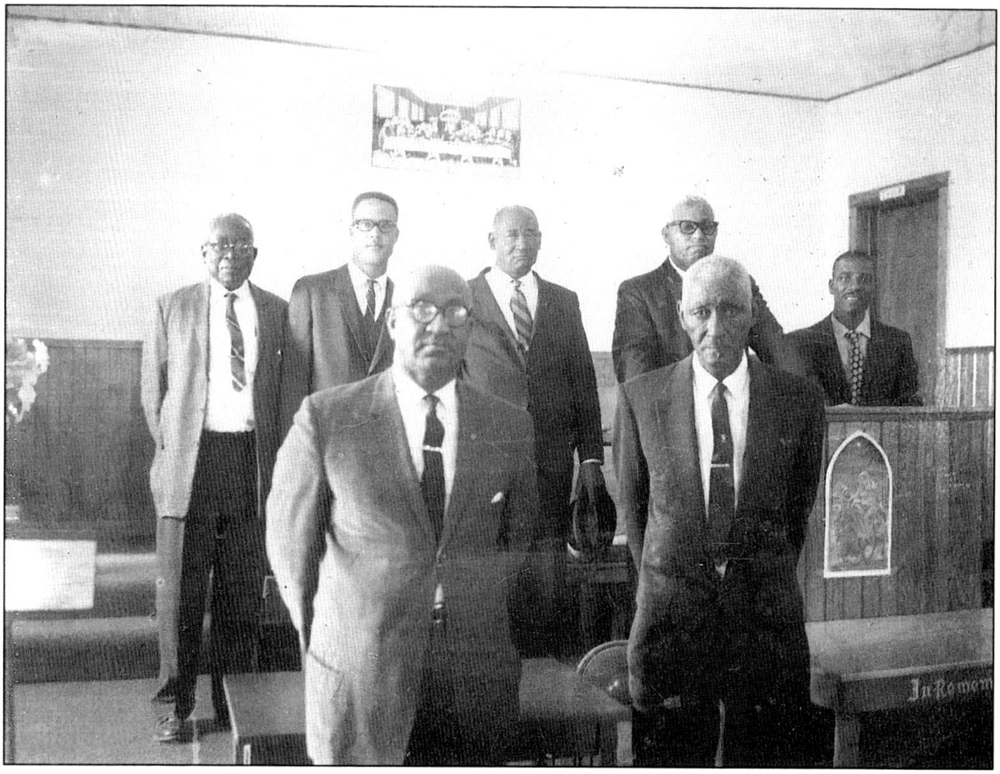

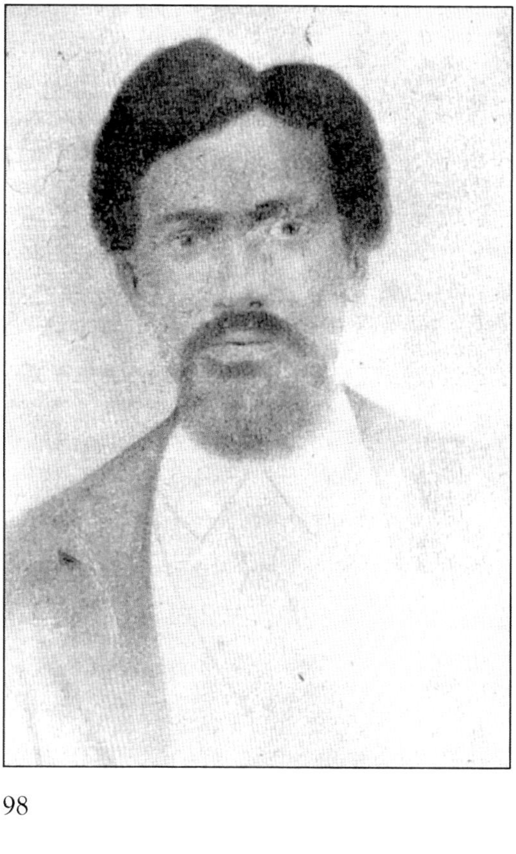

St. Paul Missionary Baptist Church, the oldest black church in Giddings (organized in 1870), joined with Willow Grove to form Bethel Union Church. The minister and deacon board are pictured from left to right as follows: (deacons in the front row) Lucian P. Thompson and Samuel Clinton; (ministers in the back row) Ollie Johnson, James Lane, an unknown visitor, E.E. Simpson, and R.E. Goins.

Matthew Gaines was a former slave, a minister affiliated with the Willow Grove Baptist Church, and a Texas state senator from Lee County for two sessions starting in 1869. He sponsored the legislation chartering Giddings as a city and was a spokesman for civil rights.

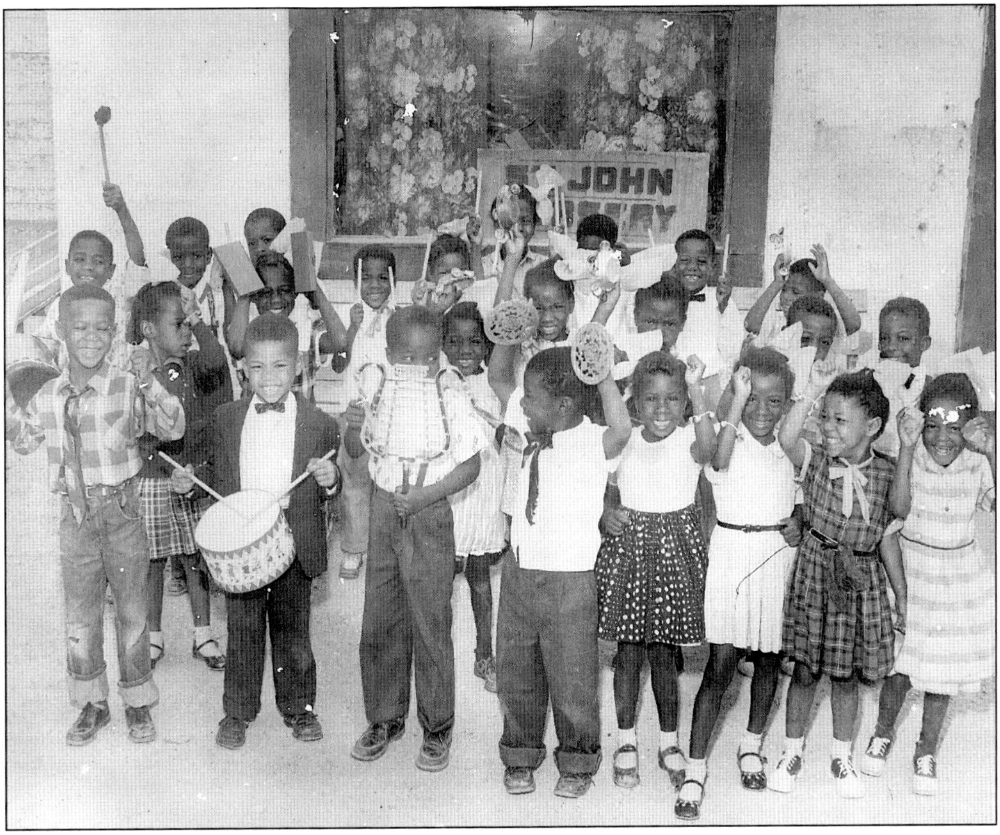

The St. John's Nursery Band is shown here c. 1950.

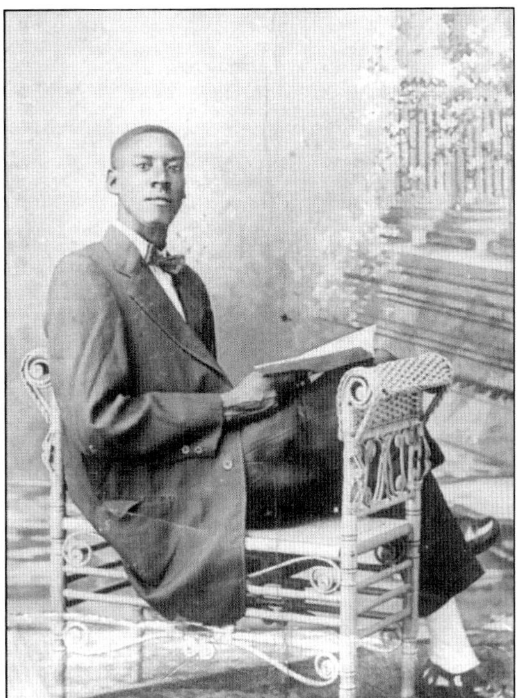

Walter R. Wormley, pictured as a young man, was a member of Willow Grove and Bethel Union Churches.

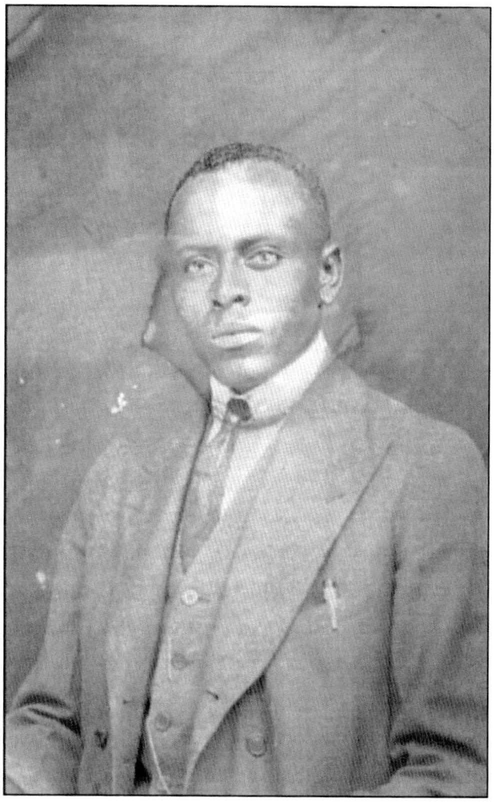

Professor Woodfork preached at Sweet Home and elsewhere. He married Maggie Betts, the daughter of Professor Betts.

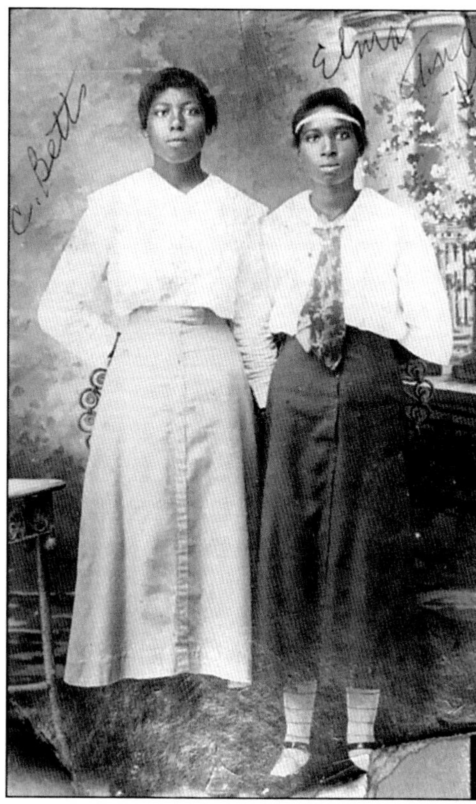

Calanthia Betts was the granddaughter of Abraham and Margeret Betts, and Elma Anderson was the daughter of Abraham Anderson, and the granddaughter of Rev. Anthony Anderson. Both grandsires were residents of Betts Chapel community and the Methodist Church since about 1880.

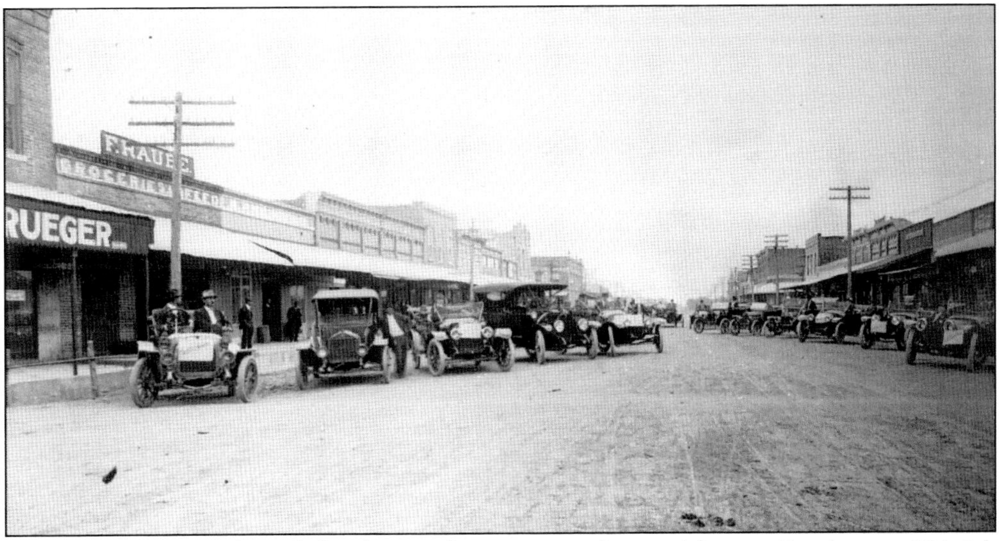

In 1903, Giddings had a soda bottling works, a carriage shop and factory, 2 icehouses, 18 brick stores, a lumber yard, 3 hotels, and a national bank with $50,000 capitol stock. There were 8 churches, 7 lawyers, 6 physicians, 5 cotton buyers, 4 milliners, 3 bakers, 2 dentists, and a new courthouse. Its telephone exchange had 100 subscribers. By 1910, Giddings also had automobiles. The F. Raube store on the left was one of the older stores. An ad in the 1890 City Business Directory read, "Raube & Neumann, Staple and Fancy Groceries, Fine Wines and Liquors, Fresh Beer always on Tap."

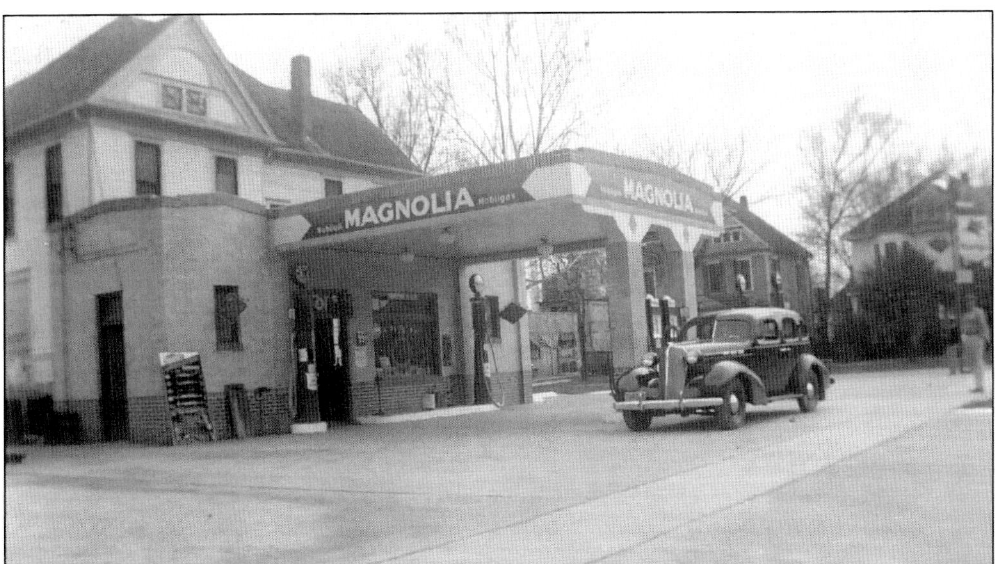

In later years, Magnolia gas stations came to dot central Texas. This one still stands in Giddings.

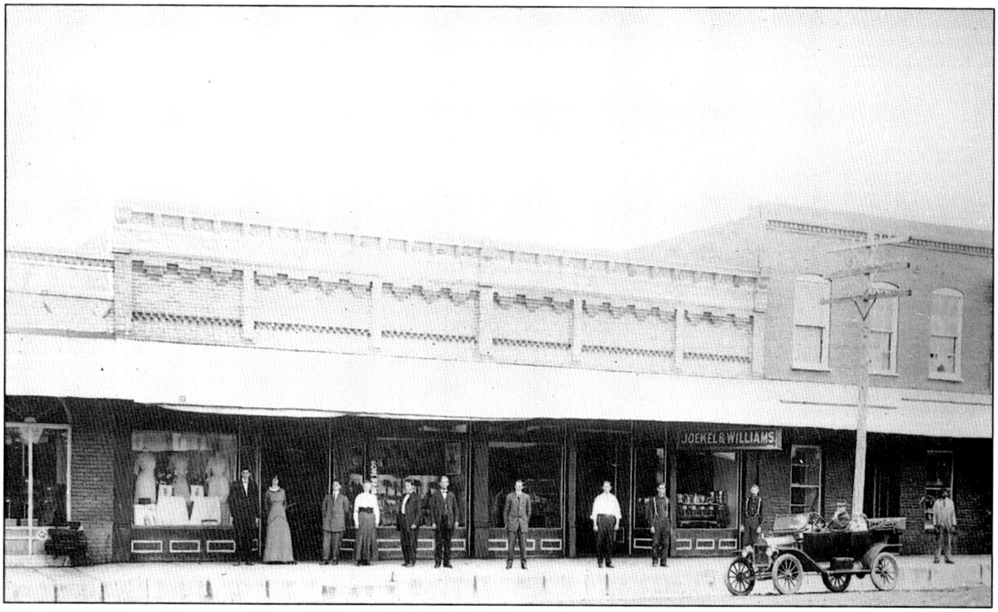

The 1890 City Business Directory also contained the following ads: "F. Joekel Candies. Fruits, Tobacco, Cigars, Fresh Bread and Cakes Always on Hand" and "Henry Joekel Saddlery and Harness, Boot and Shoe Maker. Repairing done with neatness and dispatch."

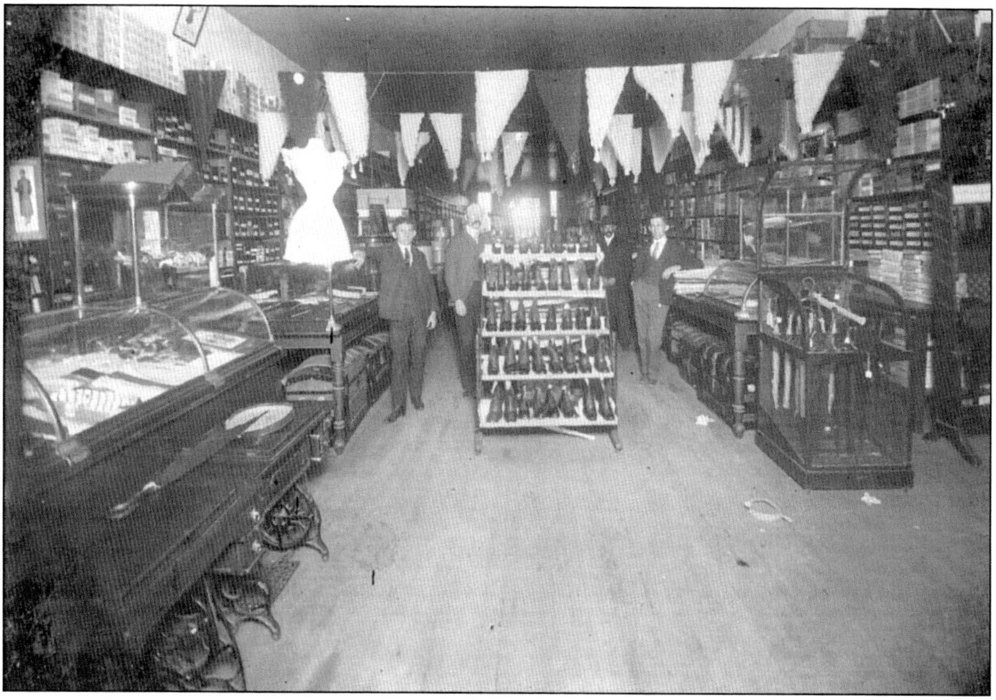

A 1903 ad states the Joekel firm was established in 1889 as "Dealers in General Merchandise—Eight Departments—Dry Goods and Notions, Clothing and Hats, Gents' Furnishing Goods, Boots and Shoes, Ladies' Ready to wear Garmt's, Furniture, Hardware, Glassware, Queensware, And Groceries. ** We also sell the Southland Chilled Plow Company's Farming Implements, and have the agency for the celebrated and world renowned Garland Stoves."

John George Hardmeyer, born in 1835 in Switzerland, emigrated to New York with his brother, Carl August, in 1857. In 1861 his sisters, (Anna) Marie and Emma Elizabeth, followed. The brothers had left the city before the girls arrived, but the girls found work as seamstresses. Marie married Fred Joekel, a baker who lived in the same tenement. After they saw an ad requesting information on the girls, the girls and Fred set off for Mississippi where they expected to find the brothers. But a Mississippi flood, during which the brothers had to be rescued from treetops, had forced the brothers to move on. The girls and Fred followed the trail to Brenham and finally to Giddings. Marie was so disappointed by what she found there that she returned to New York for a couple of years. The Hardemeyer brothers built the York house.

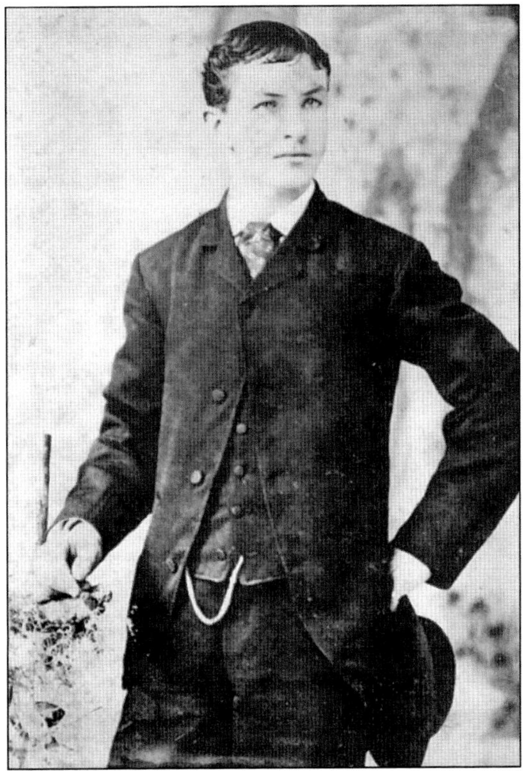

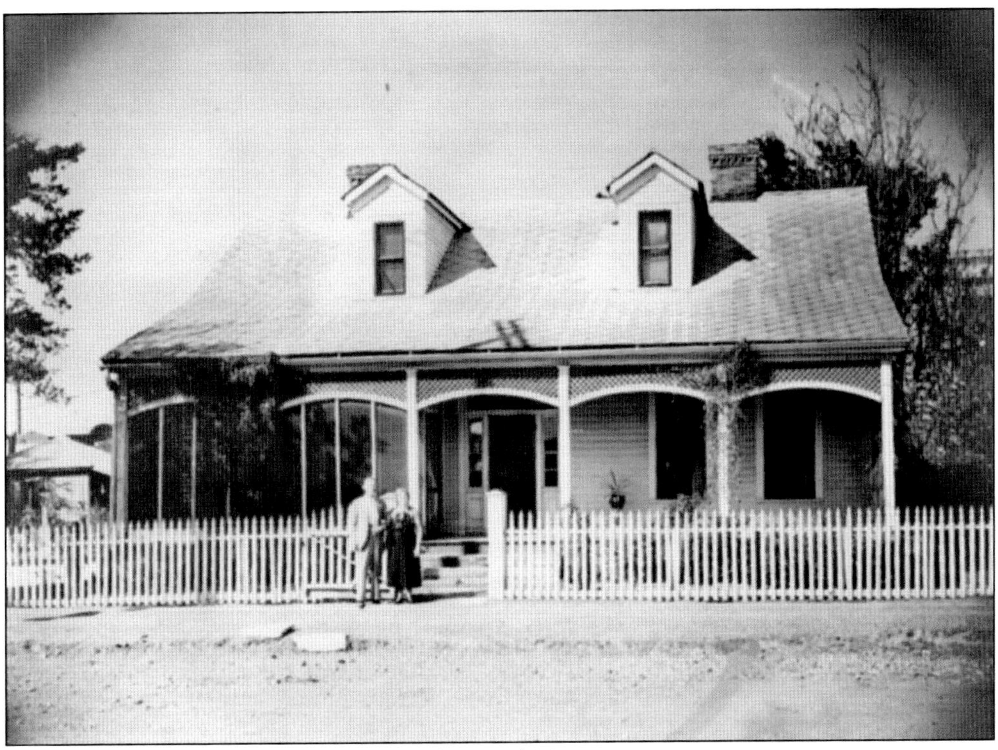

The York house is now the Lee County Historical Museum.

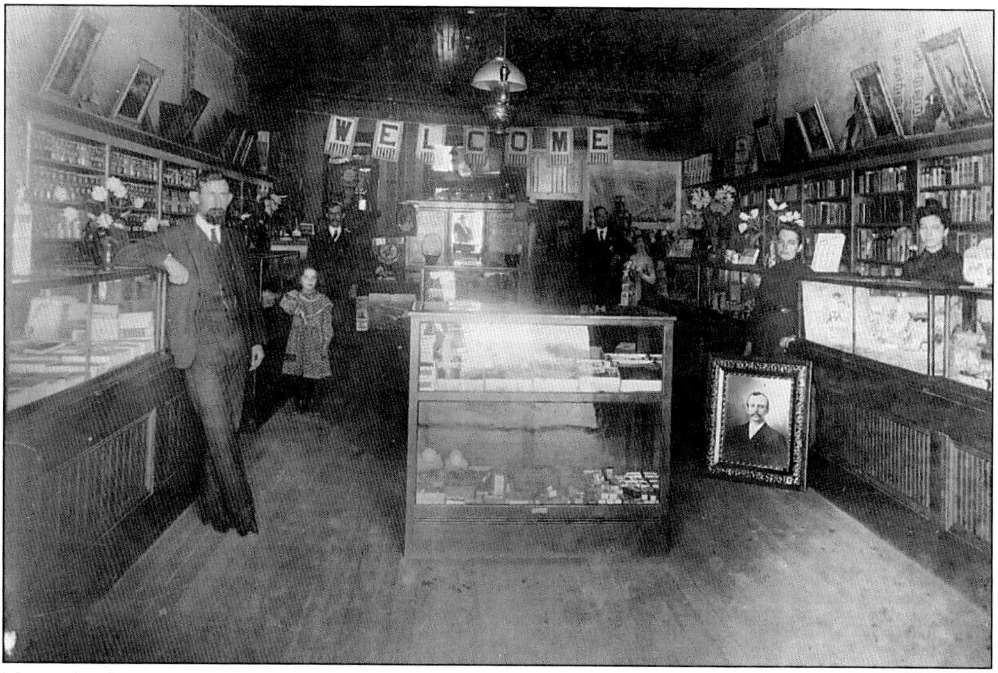

Note the kerosene lantern hanging in the center. Their ad read, "Dr W. E. York and H. C. Kappler The New Drug Store. Druggists and Stationers. We Handle a Complete Line of Patent Medicines, Toilet Articles, Sundries and Drugs. A Portion of your Patronage Would be Appreciated." The portrait on the floor is of the deceased Mr. Kappler. The young woman behind the counter is Emily Luecke. Herman Luecke and Erna Lehman are visible in the background behind Dr. W.E. York.

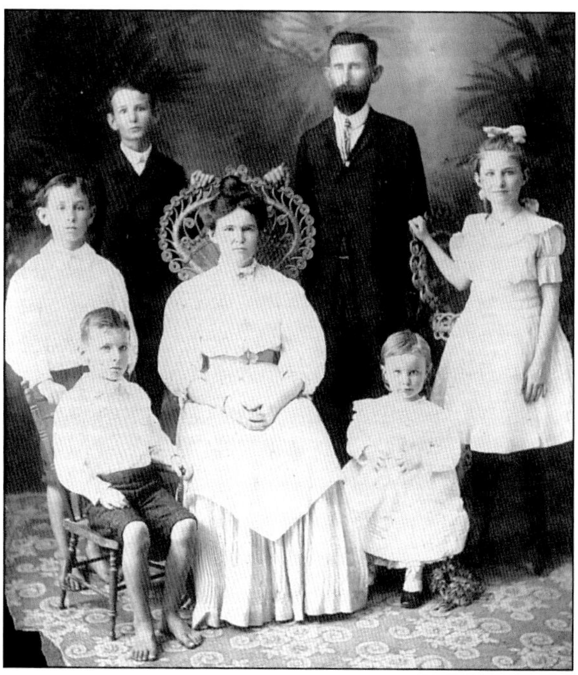

The York family surrounds Mrs. Annie Elizabeth (Patton) York in about 1907. From left to right they are as follows: Asa, Milton, Patton, Dr. York, Louise, and Alton. The York family had been in Texas since 1830 and in Old Evergreen in the early years. Dr. York had a medical degree from Tulane.

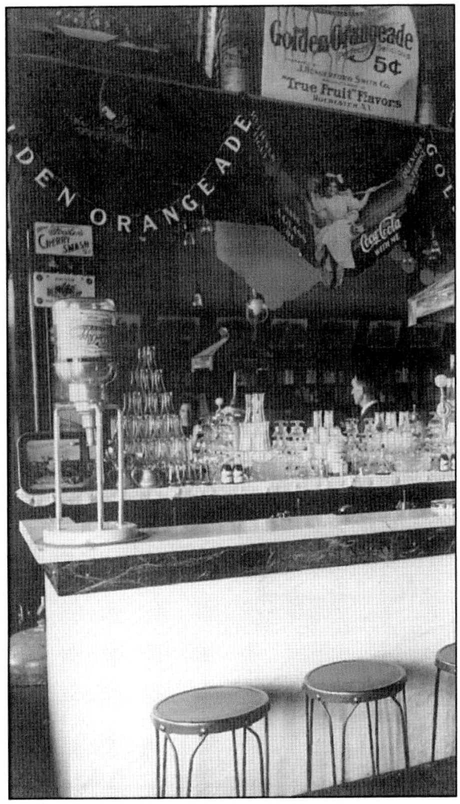

The York & Kappler pharmacy had a classic marble-topped soda fountain with wire chairs. Texas' favorite soda, Dr. Pepper, is dispensed from the large bottle on the left, Jersey Crème from the smaller jar on the right. Mrs H.C. Kappler's name is on the cash register just out of view on the right. The York pharmacy later moved to a new location. There, the telephone exchange was upstairs, as was Dr. Childress' dental office. In the 1930s they even had curb service for the soda fountain."

Sun Cholera Mixture.

Tincture of Opium,
Tincture of Capsicum,
Tincture of Rhubarb,
Spirit of Camphor,
Spirit of Peppermint, of each, 1 fl. oz
Mix. Dose, a teaspoonful in wate
after each evacuation of the bowels.

Compound Tincture of Opium.

(Squibb's Diarrhœa Mixture.)

Tincture of Opium,	1 fl. oz
Tincture of Capsicum,	1 fl. oz
Spirit of Camphor,	1 fl. oz
Purified Chloroform,	3 fl. dr
Alcohol, sufficient to make	5 fl. oz

Mix. Dose, from 30 to 60 minims.

Bateman's Pectoral Drops.

Opium,	120 gr.
Catechu,	120 gr.
Camphor,	120 gr.
Oil of Anise,	30 min.
Caramel,	1½ fl. oz
Diluted Alcohol,	64 fl. oz

Digest for ten days.

This is a sampling from the 1889 *Remington Practice of Pharmacy*, a standard reference. In those days, many medications included generous amounts of alcohol and often a little opium.

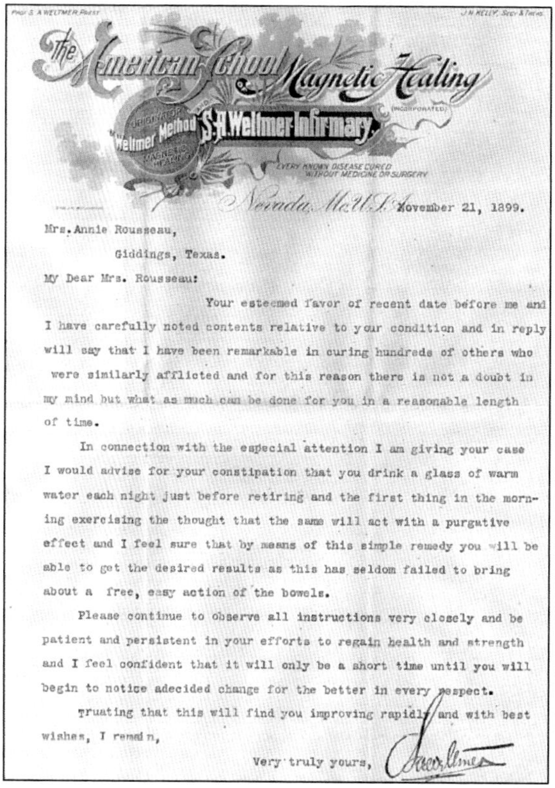

PROF. S. A. WELTMER, PRES'T. J. H. KELLY, SEC'Y & TREAS.

The American School of Magnetic Healing (INCORPORATED)

Originator Weltmer Method Magnetic Healing and S. A. Weltmer Infirmary.

EVERY KNOWN DISEASE CURED WITHOUT MEDICINE OR SURGERY

Nevada, Mo. U. S. A. November 21, 1899.

Mrs. Annie Rousseau,

Giddings, Texas.

My Dear Mrs. Rousseau:

Your esteemed favor of recent date before me and I have carefully noted contents relative to your condition and in reply will say that I have been remarkable in curing hundreds of others who were similarly afflicted and for this reason there is not a doubt in my mind but what as much can be done for you in a reasonable length of time.

In connection with the especial attention I am giving your case I would advise for your constipation that you drink a glass of warm water each night just before retiring and the first thing in the morning exercising the thought that the same will act with a purgative effect and I feel sure that by means of this simple remedy you will be able to get the desired results as this has seldom failed to bring about a free, easy action of the bowels.

Please continue to observe all instructions very closely and be patient and persistent in your efforts to regain health and strength and I feel confident that it will only be a short time until you will begin to notice adecided change for the better in every respect.

Trusting that this will find you improving rapidly and with best wishes, I remain,

Very truly yours,

Diarist Annie Rousseau ordered a number of magnetic healing treatments from Dr. Weltmer for unspecified ailments. She also recommended them to her stepmother. Weltmer's mail order business was so successful that the federal government had to raise the status of the post office of tiny Nevada, MO, to first class.

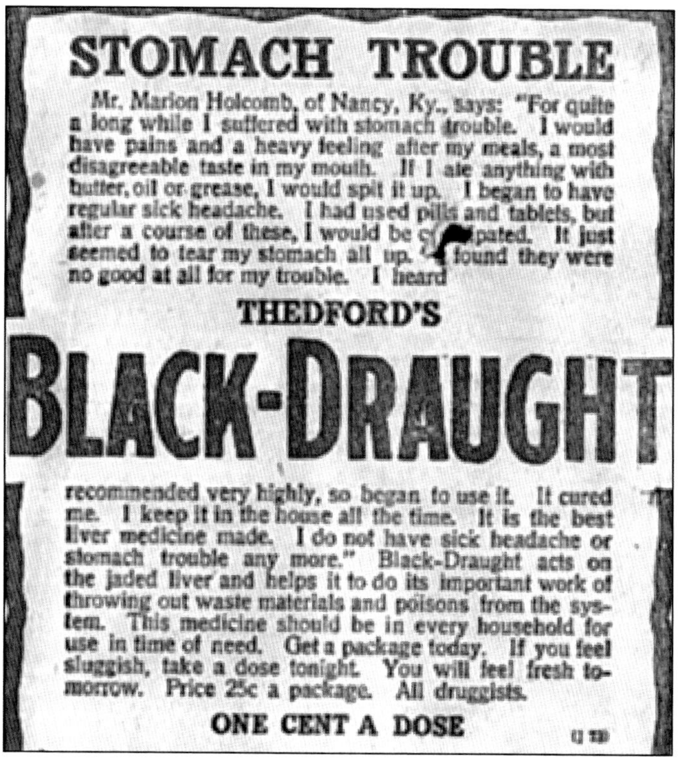

Black draught was a favorite (and dreaded) spring tonic, and the popular Kickapoo Indian Oil was boosted as a tonic by a traveling show in Giddings. On December 29, 1890, Annie Rousseau wrote, "After supper, went to the concert, the last night of the Kickapoo Indians. The proceed was given to the cemetery, paid 45 cts." —Rousseau diaries.

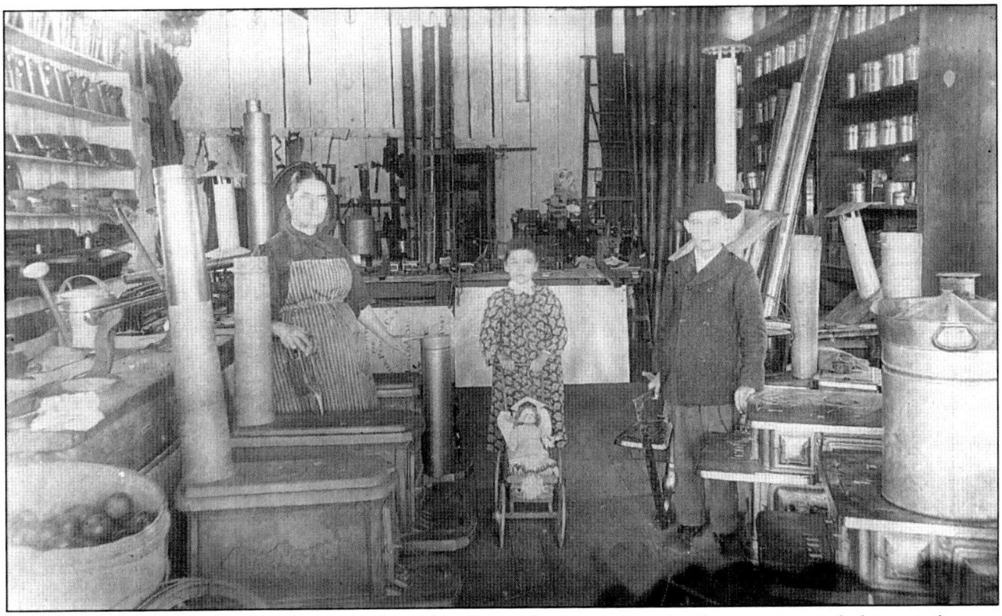

Both Mr. And Mrs. Luecke worked in their tin shop on Austin Street. From left to right are Amalie Lehmann Luecke, Emilie Luecke Placke, and Herman Luecke. "Everything was wide open and you might watch people working at their trade, and there seemed to be plenty of work to do, and the town was always crowded with country people selling their cotton and buying things needed." —*A History of Lee County, Texas.*

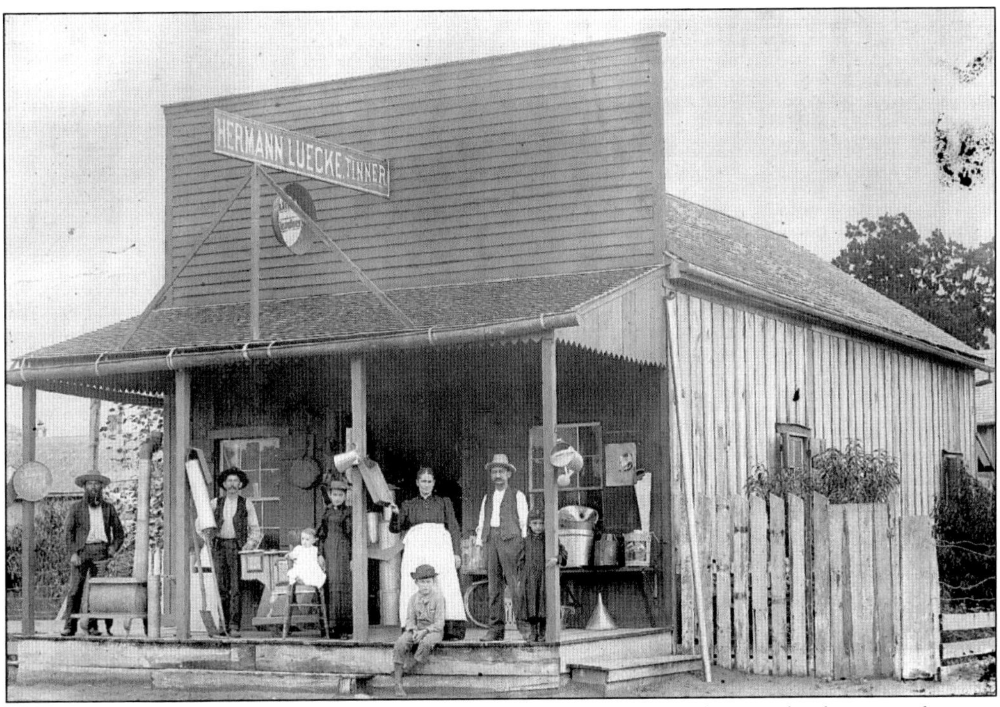

This picture of the Luecke Tin Shop shows the Lehmans and Lueckes on the front porch.

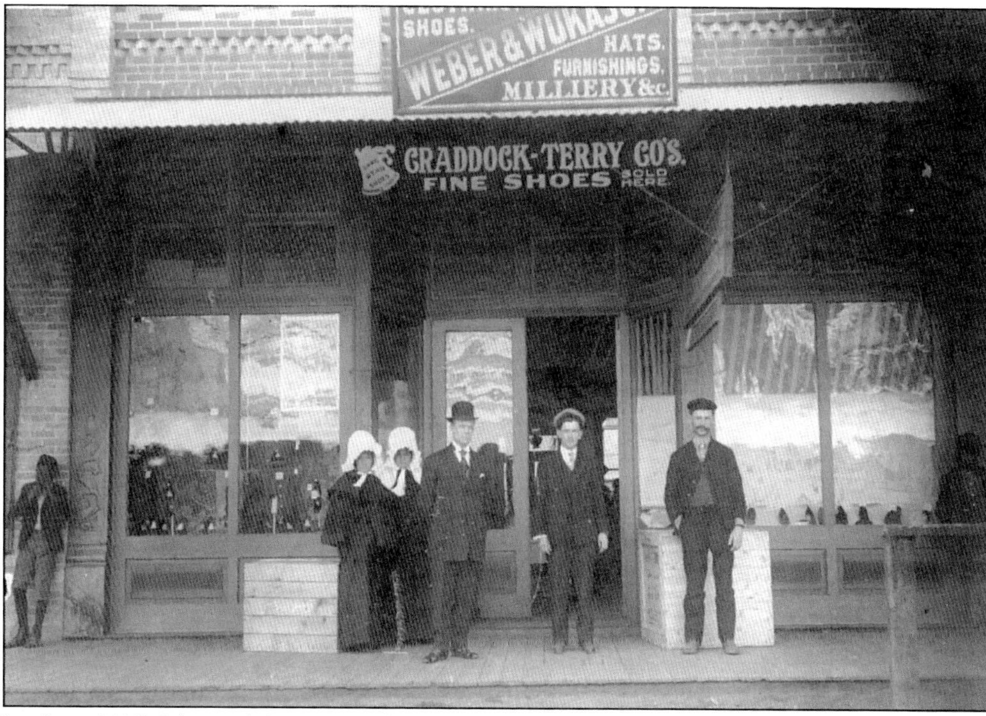

In about 1905, John and Augusta Weber were in partnership in a dry goods store with Wukasch. Augusta was a milliner. The two women outside the store seem to be modeling the hats displayed in the interior photograph below.

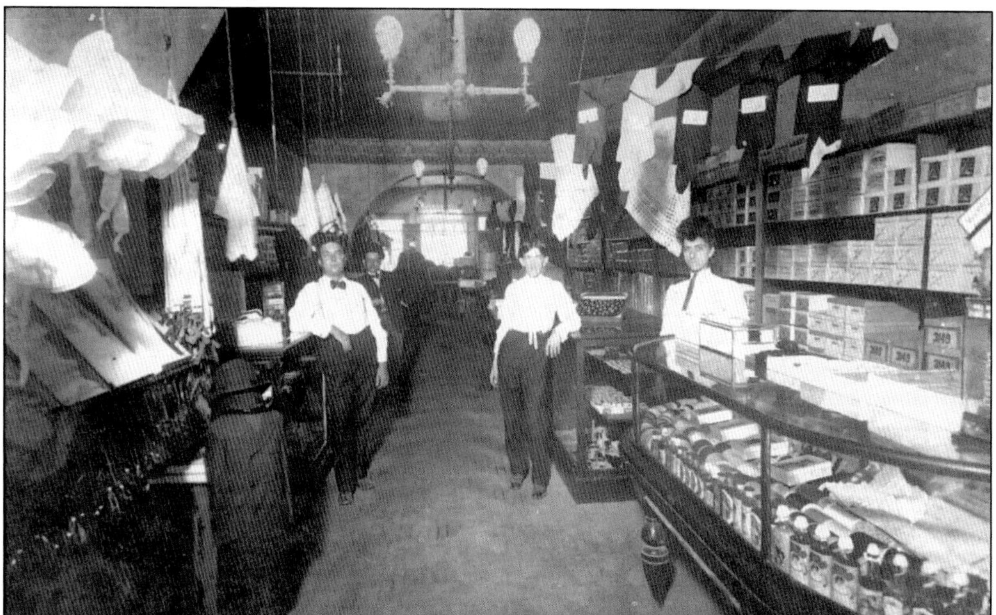

Augusta Wukasch's bonnets hang in the front of the store on the left. Note the gas light fixture hanging in the center of the store. The Webers lived in the house seen behind the Baptist church on p. 95.

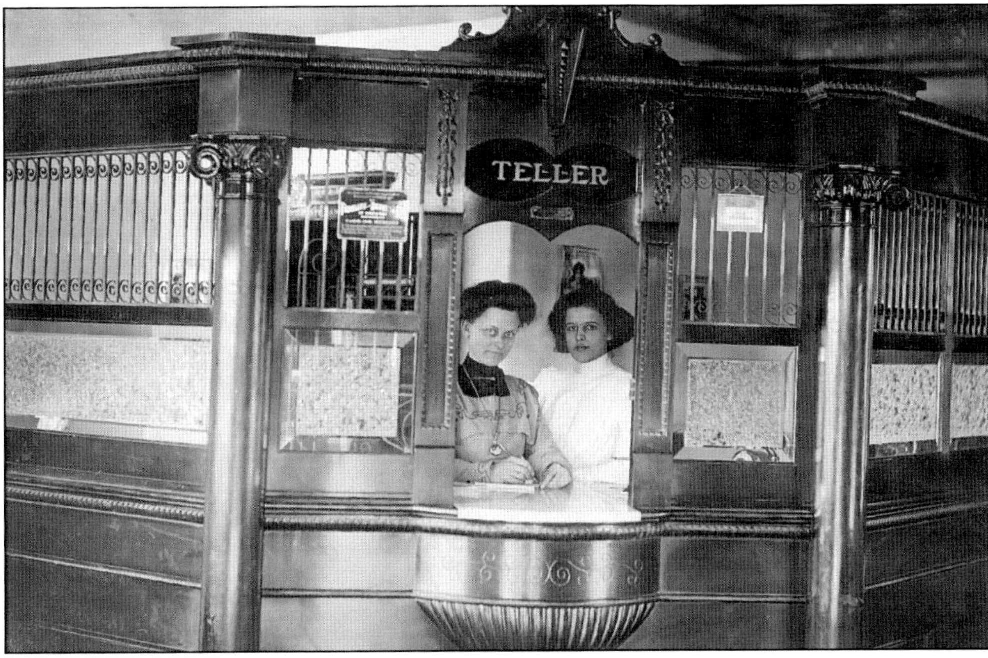

Two bank tellers pose for a photograph.

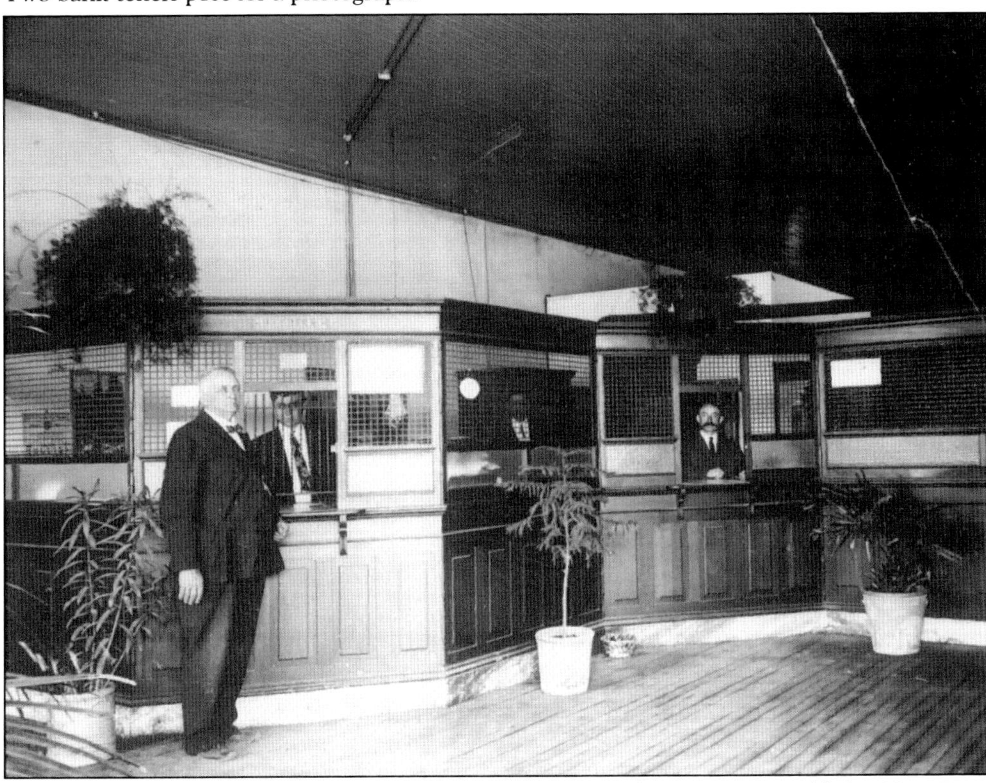

A 1903 ad for the First National Bank reads, "Dr J. A. Fields Pres., J. D. Fields Jr., Vice-Pres., I. J. Fariss Cashier (son of W. H. Fariss), A. J. Nisbet Asst. Cashier, Capital Stock $50,000 Surplus and undivided profits $25,000 >Accounts Solicited<."

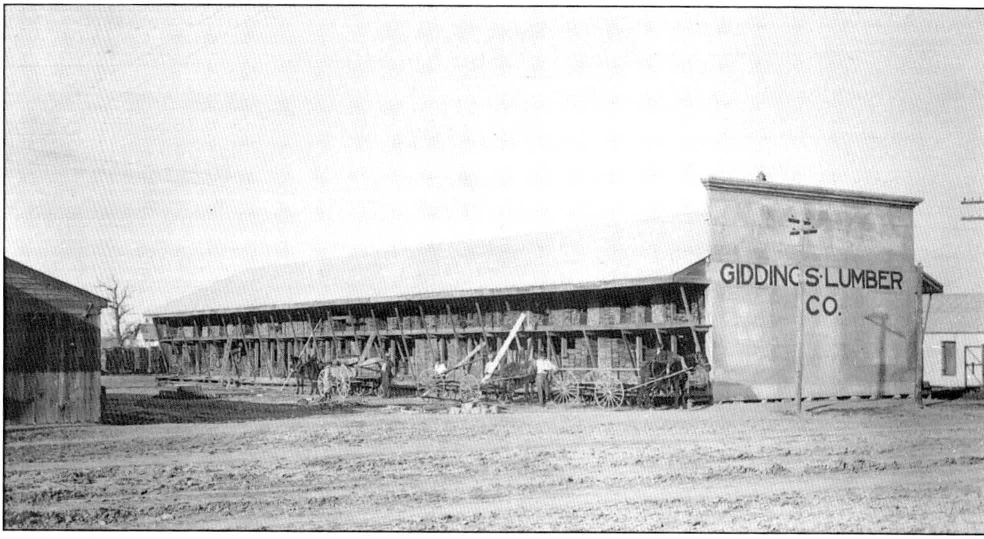

Under the name of the owner, the lumber yard's advertisement in 1890 was as follows: "J. C. Hillsman & Sons Lumber, Shingles, Coffins, Builder's Hardware, etc. etc. East and Austin St. Lumber And All Kinds of Building Material, Large Stock of fine High Grade and Also Cheap Buggies, Hacks and Carriages. Wagons. Also Coffins. We meet any competing prices on our Goods, for Cash, on same styles and qualities."

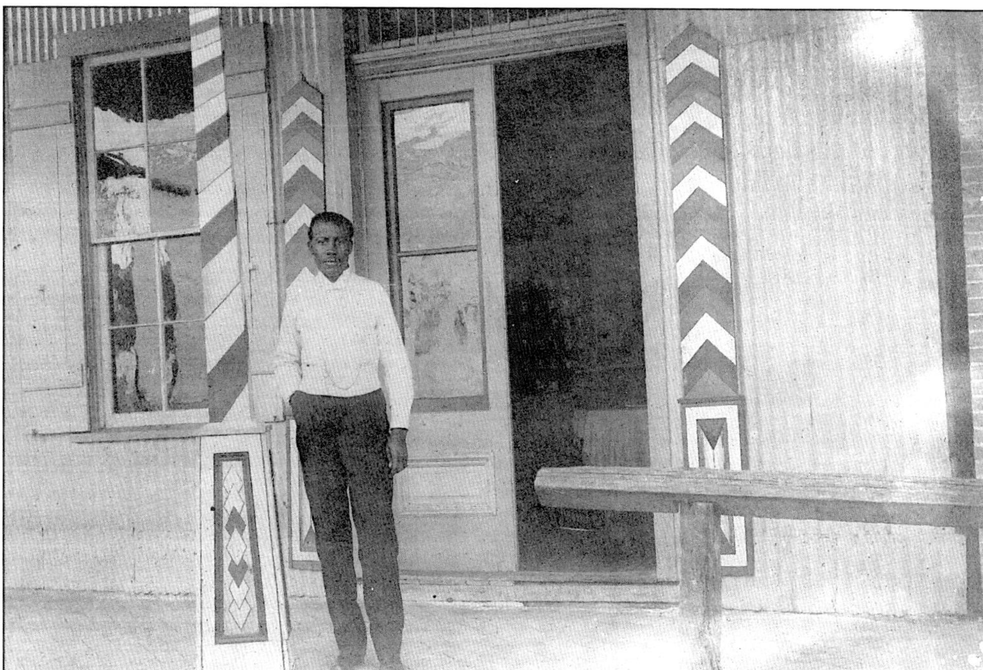

At the age of 14, John White was apprenticed to barber Bob Bennett. He was too young to handle a razor, according to his mother, so at first he used a pocket knife to shave the men. He learned the trade well and later bought the shop from Bennett, renamed the store, and continued as barber to the men of Giddings. The man in the picture is John's twin brother, Sam, outside the barber shop behind the First National Bank.

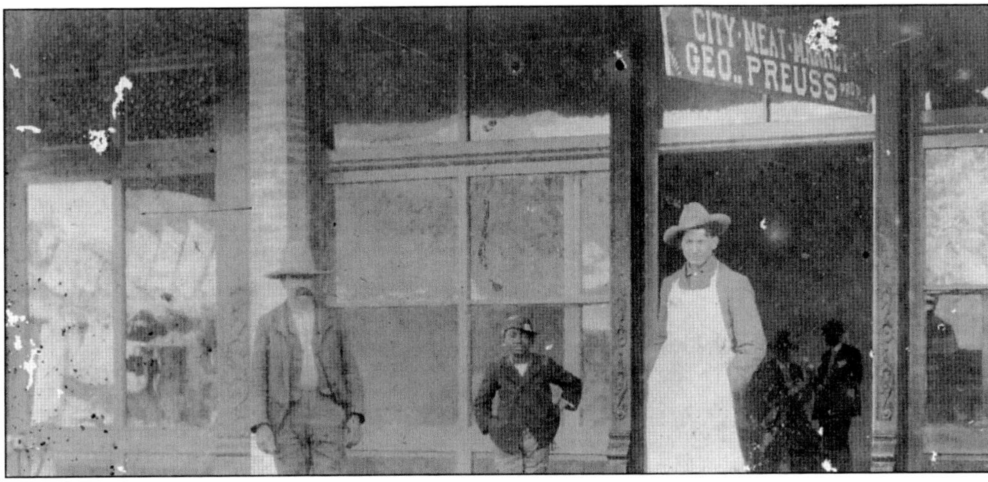

George Preuss's meat market was located on Austin Street in about 1904.

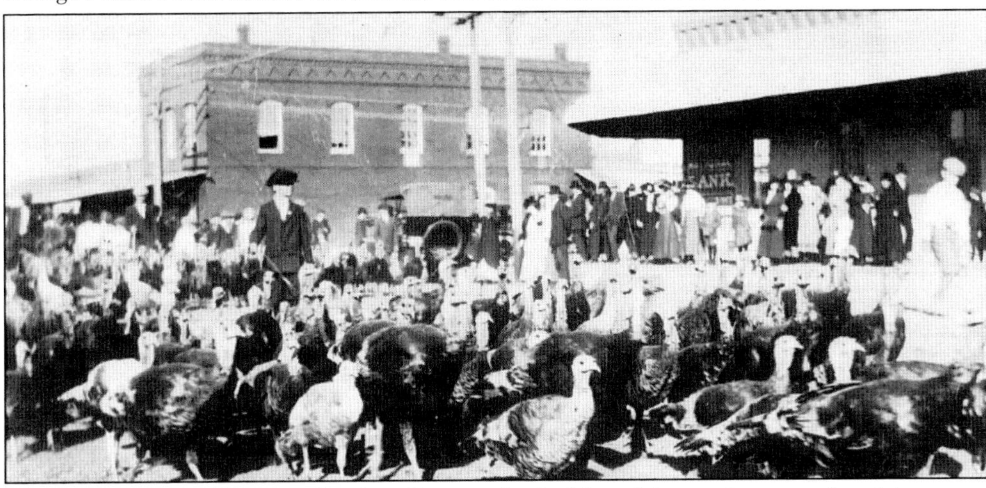
Cattle drives are well known, but Lee County also had hog drives and even turkey drives.

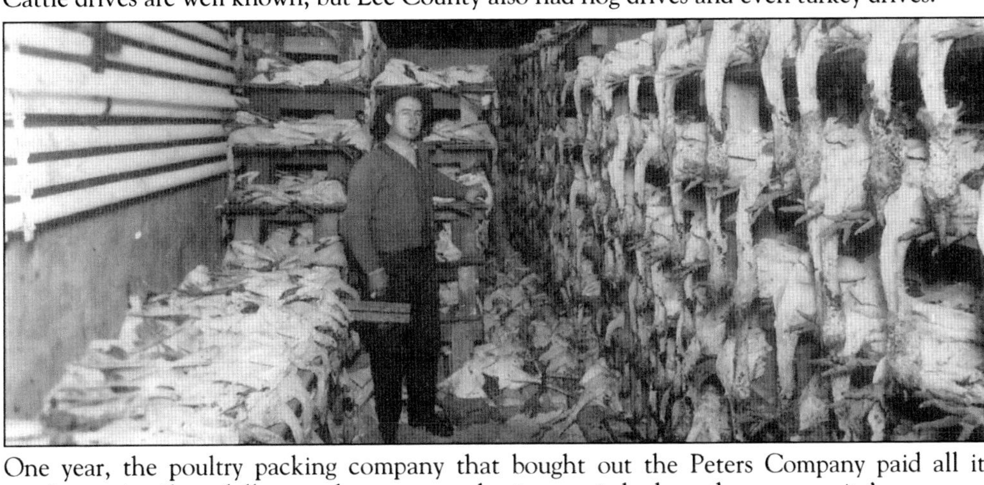
One year, the poultry packing company that bought out the Peters Company paid all its employees in silver dollars to demonstrate the impact it had on the community's economy. (Courtesy Texas Wendish Heritage Museum Archive.)

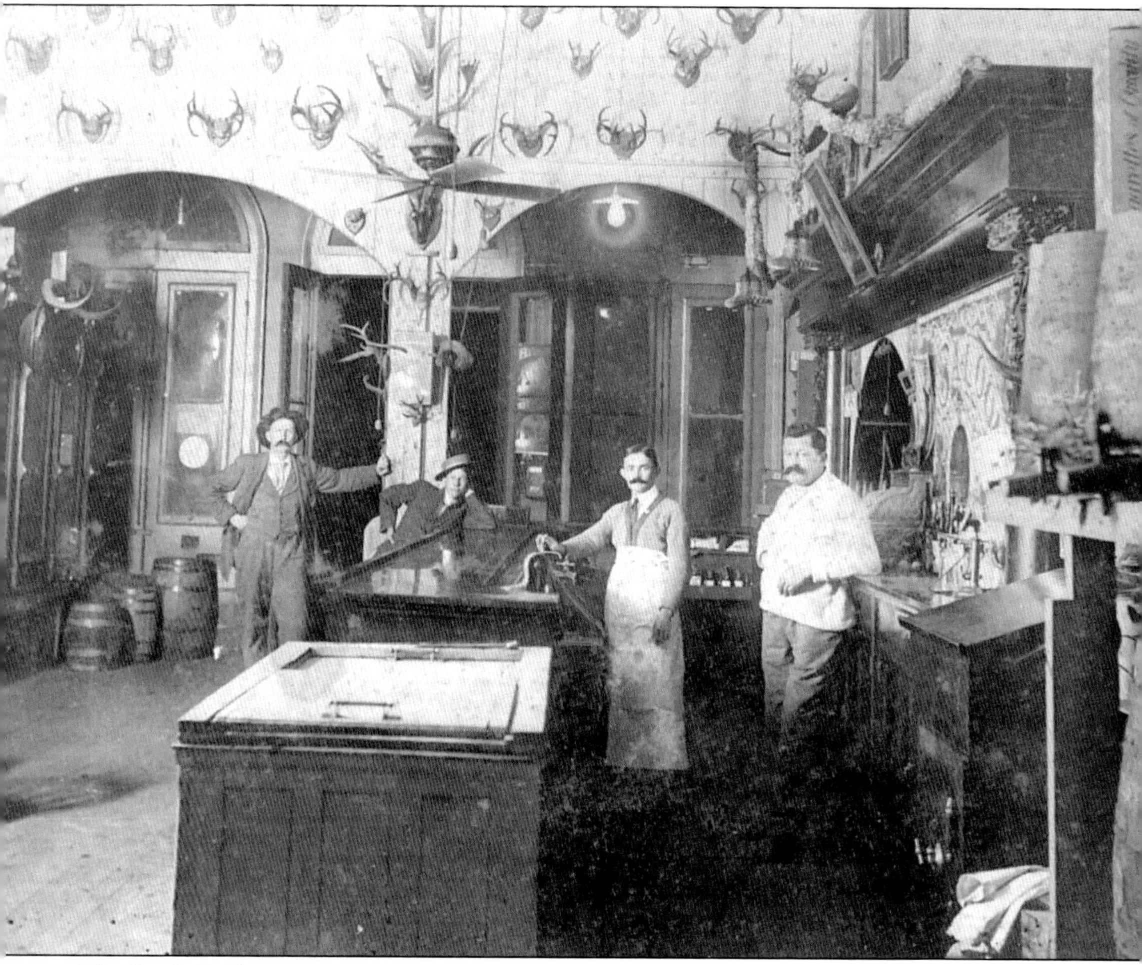

The lively Bull Frog Saloon, clearly a man's retreat, was on Burleson just north of Austin Street. Gus and Karl Kriegel are behind the bar. The ceiling fan was essential in the Texas summer heat.

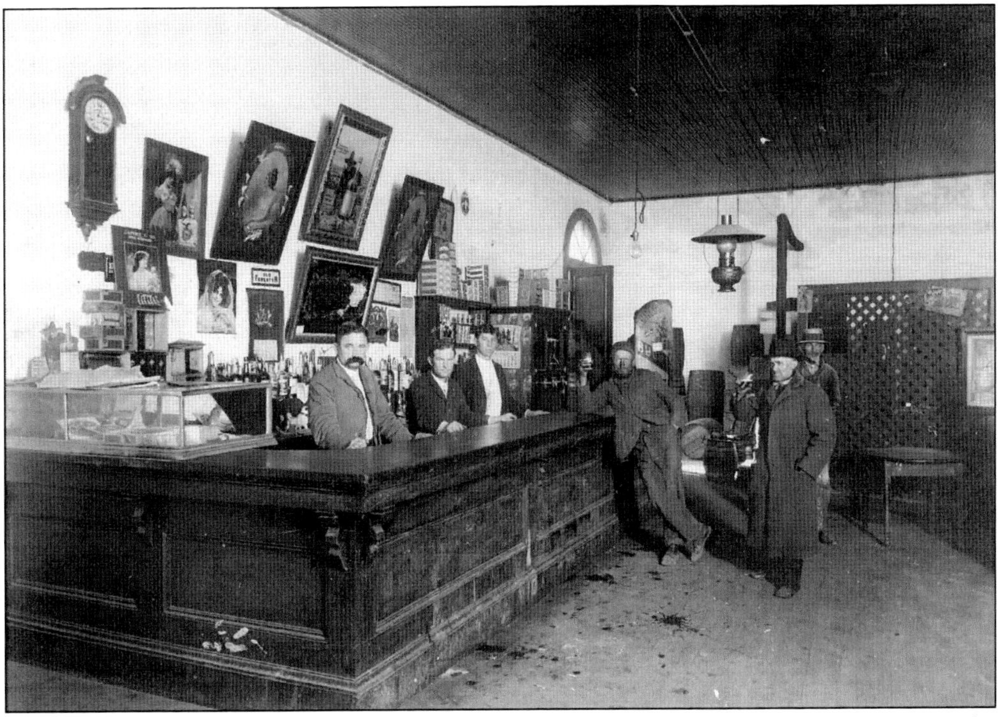

Another Kriegel saloon was located behind the grocery across Highway 290 on the corner. The saloon had a front entrance and also a rear entrance for those less inclined to be seen entering. Karl and Ernst Kriegel are pictured behind the bar, along with pictures of various lovely ladies.

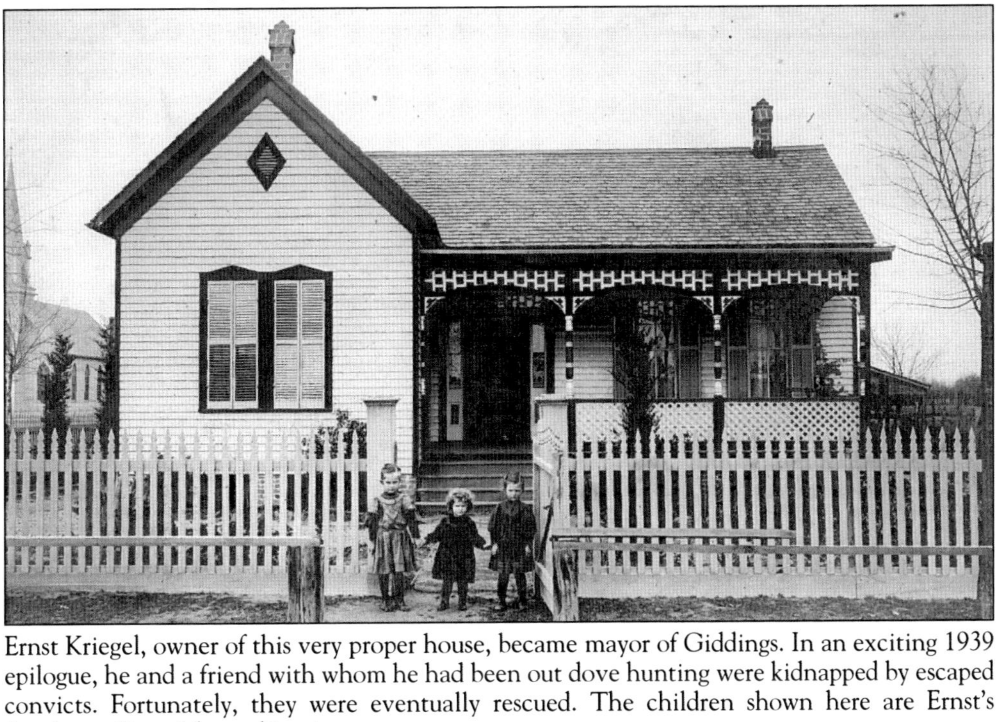

Ernst Kriegel, owner of this very proper house, became mayor of Giddings. In an exciting 1939 epilogue, he and a friend with whom he had been out dove hunting were kidnapped by escaped convicts. Fortunately, they were eventually rescued. The children shown here are Ernst's daughters: Erna, Ida, and Louise.

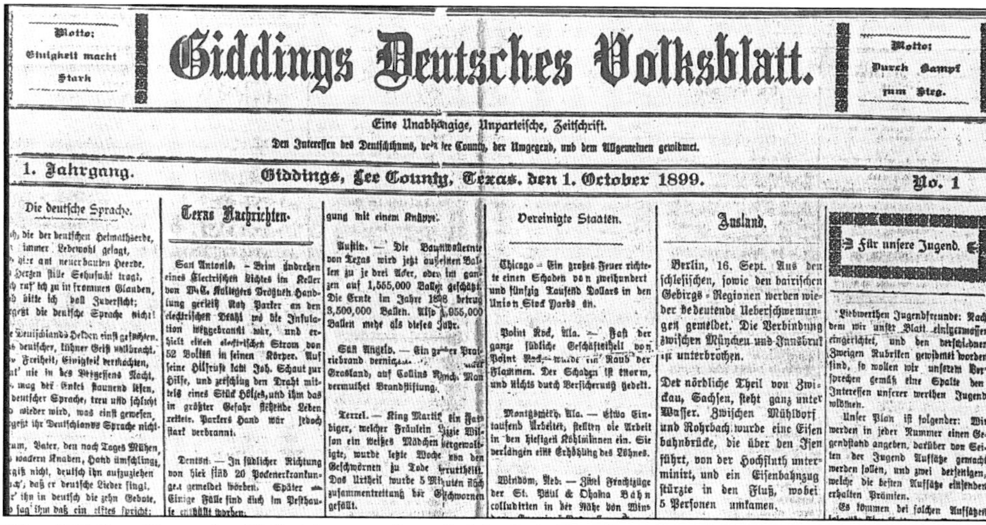

Motto: Einigkeit macht Stark

Giddings Deutsches Volksblatt.

Motto: Durch Kampf zum Sieg.

Eine Unabhängige, Unparteische, Zeitschrift.

Den Interessen des Deutschthums, von Lee County, der Umgegend, und dem Allgemeinen gewidmet.

1. Jahrgang. Giddings, Lee County, Texas, den 1. October 1899. No. 1

Die deutsche Sprache.

Texas Nachrichten.

Vereinigte Staaten.

Ausland.

Für unsere Jugend.

The *Giddings Deutsches Volksblatt* was founded by J.A. Proske in 1899. It was printed in German, but featured columns in Wendish for the Serbin community. Ads were printed in German, even for the Grange store and non-German lawyers.

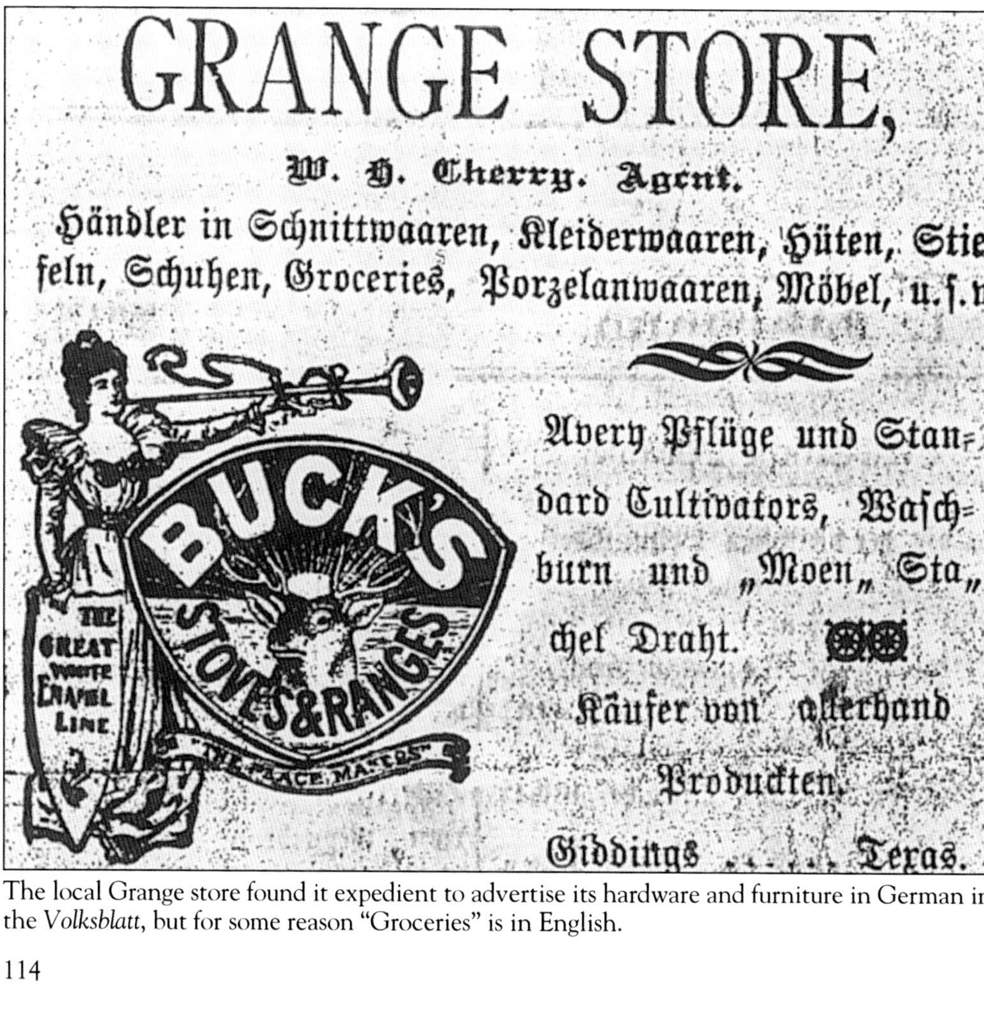

The local Grange store found it expedient to advertise its hardware and furniture in German in the *Volksblatt*, but for some reason "Groceries" is in English.

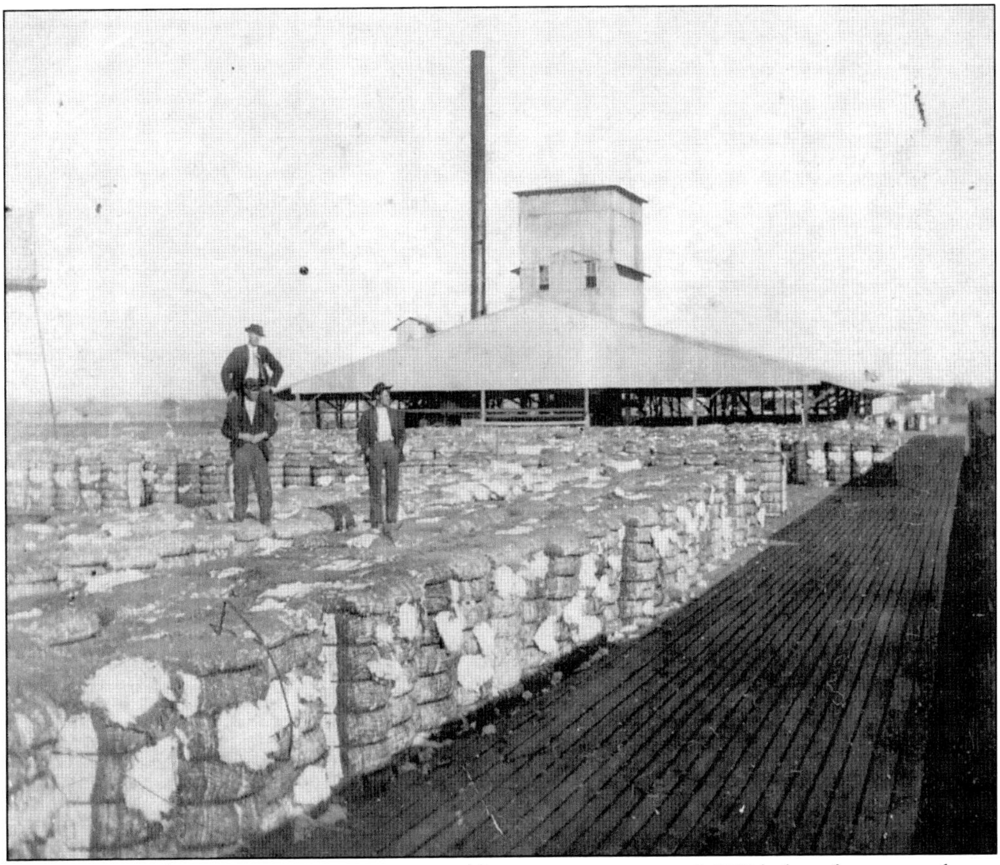

Built in 1901, the Lee County compress could process as many as 1,200 bales of cotton a day.

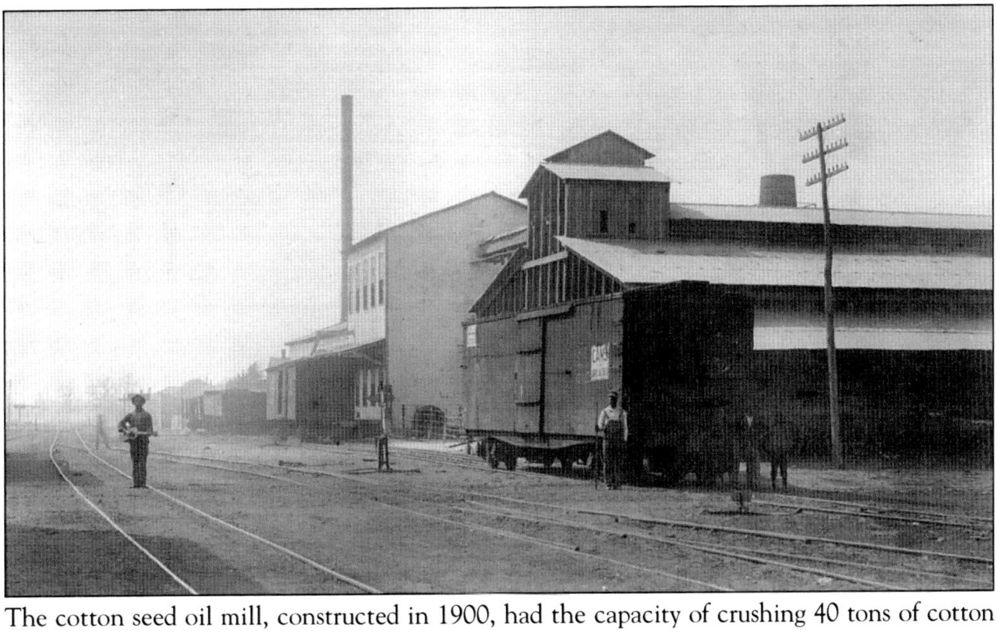

The cotton seed oil mill, constructed in 1900, had the capacity of crushing 40 tons of cotton seed a day.

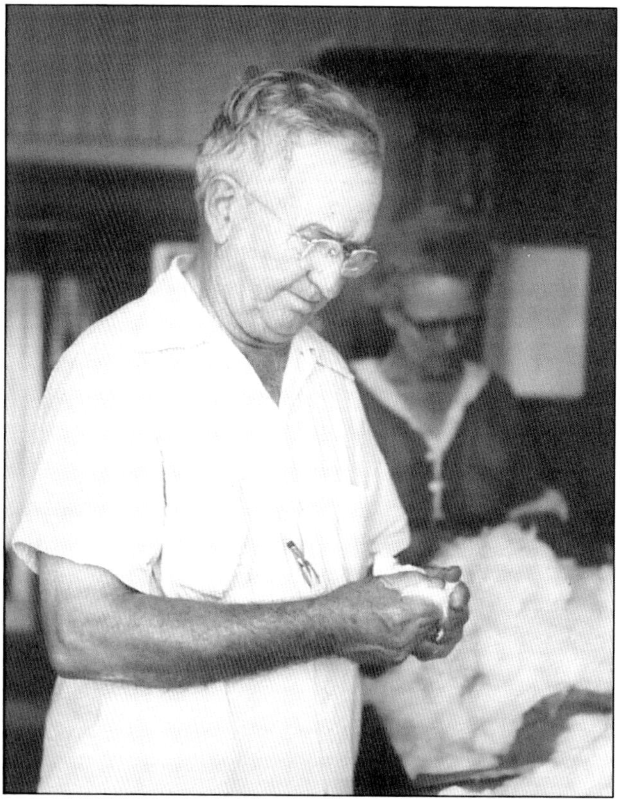

Cotton broker Ernest Collier, shown here classing cotton, had an office upstairs on the south side of 290, one block east of 77. Collier was also the Texaco dealer.

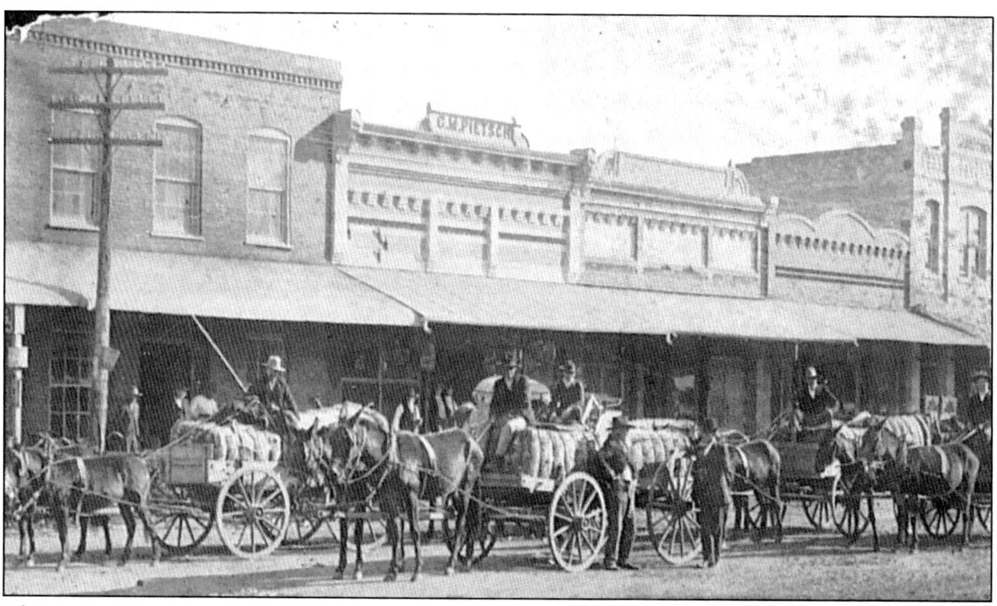

These ten bales of cotton sold for $619.10 in about 1910.

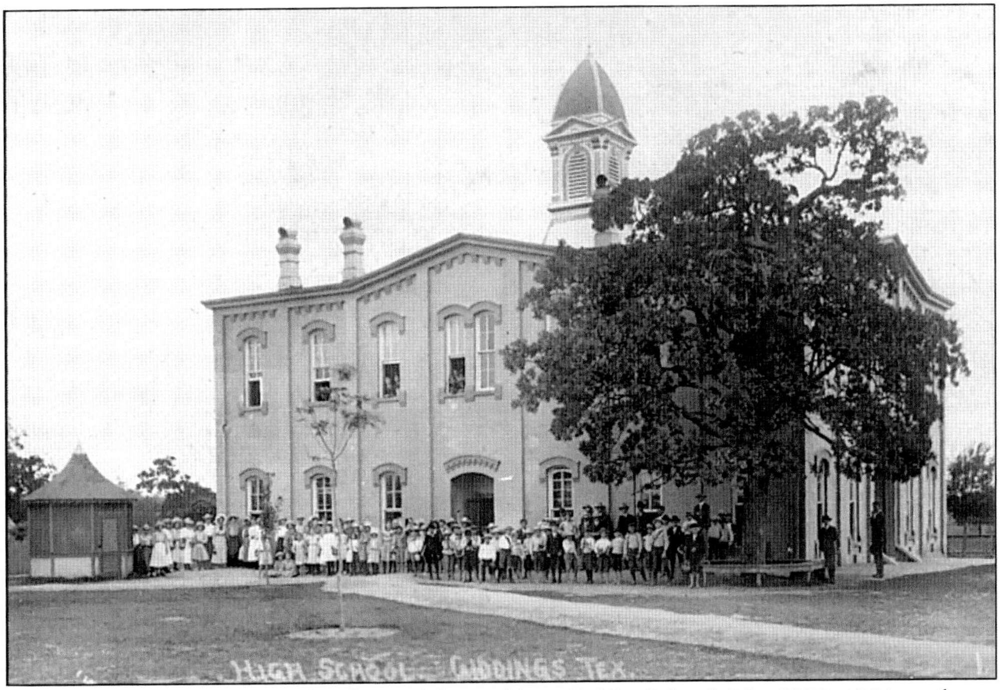

From 1892 to 1915, this building housed the Giddings Public School. The 1903–1904 catalogue of the school set the tuition at $3 per year, plus an optional $1 for Latin (Julius Caesar in the 9th grade and Virgil in the 10th). German was included as an optional subject, in the 10th grade featuring Lessing, Goethe, and Schuller. Mathematics went as far as spherical geometry and trigonometry. Zoology was taught in the 9th grade; chemistry, by lecture, in the 10th. That year seven of the eight students enrolled in 10th grade graduated.

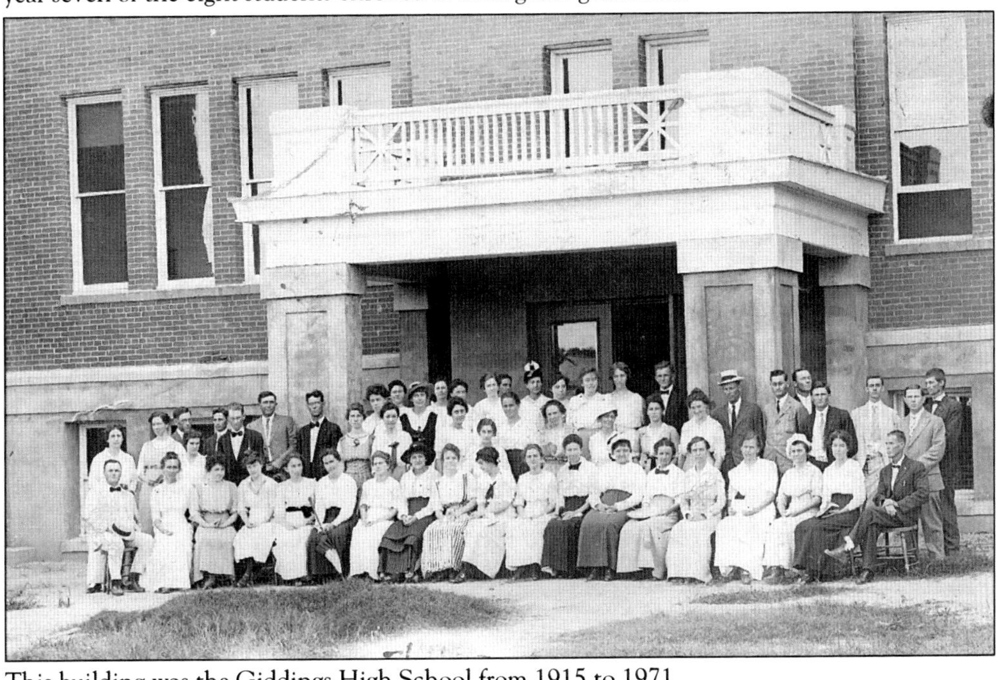

This building was the Giddings High School from 1915 to 1971.

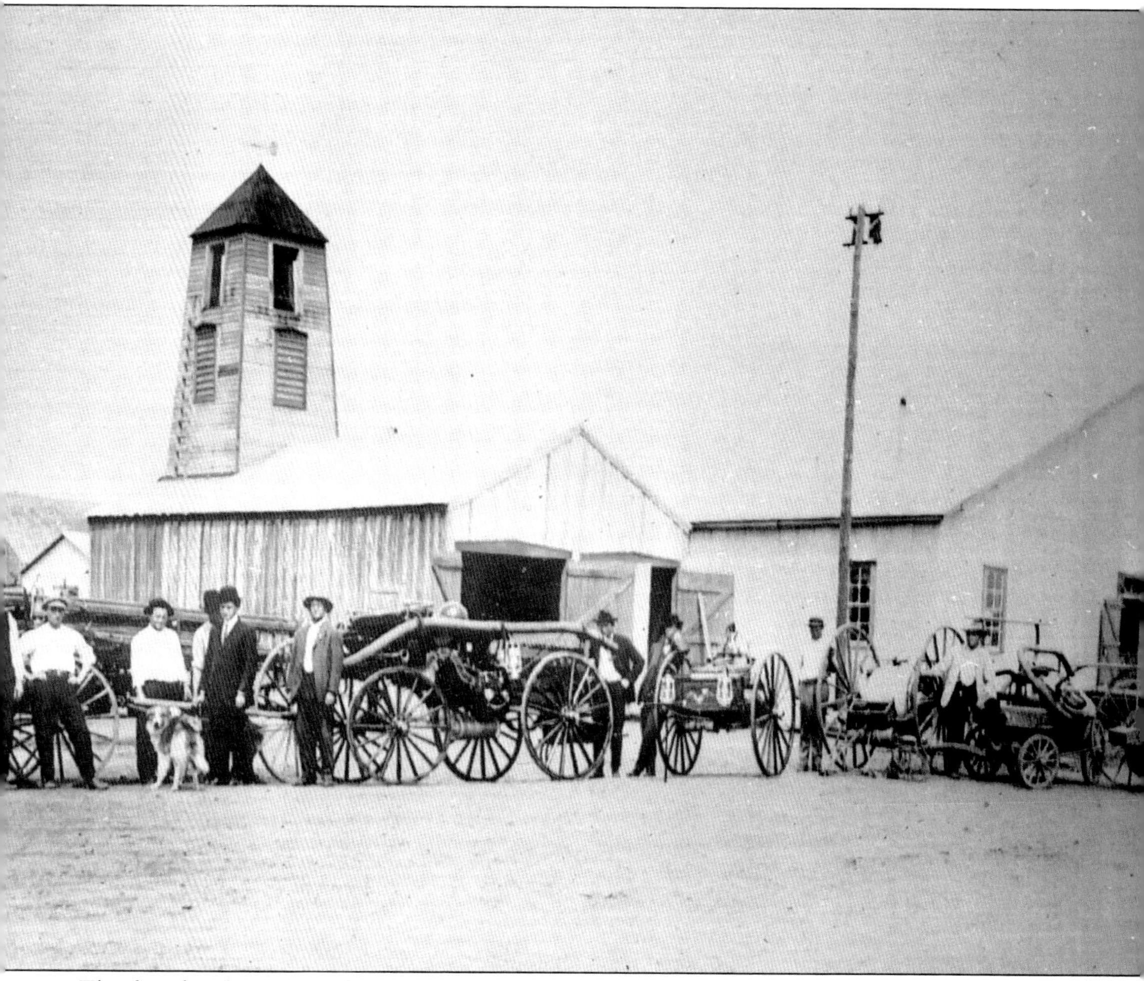

The first fire department had hand pumps that could not throw a jet of water high enough to save the courthouse. Water to fight fires was stored in 25-foot-deep brick-and-rock cisterns. John Newman, grocer and partner of Frederick Raube, died of pneumonia in 1893 after fighting a fire on January 25, 1893. "Mr. Newman died at 7 o'clock this AM. After breakfast I went over there. After dinner, went back to Mrs. Newman's, staid the evening. Mr. R went after supper to sit up with the corpse. Came home at one o'clock." On January 26, 1893, she wrote, "After dinner, went to Mr. John Newman's funeral services, walked out to the cemetery and back, stopped by Mrs. Newman's, then came home, feeling bad." —Rousseau diaries.

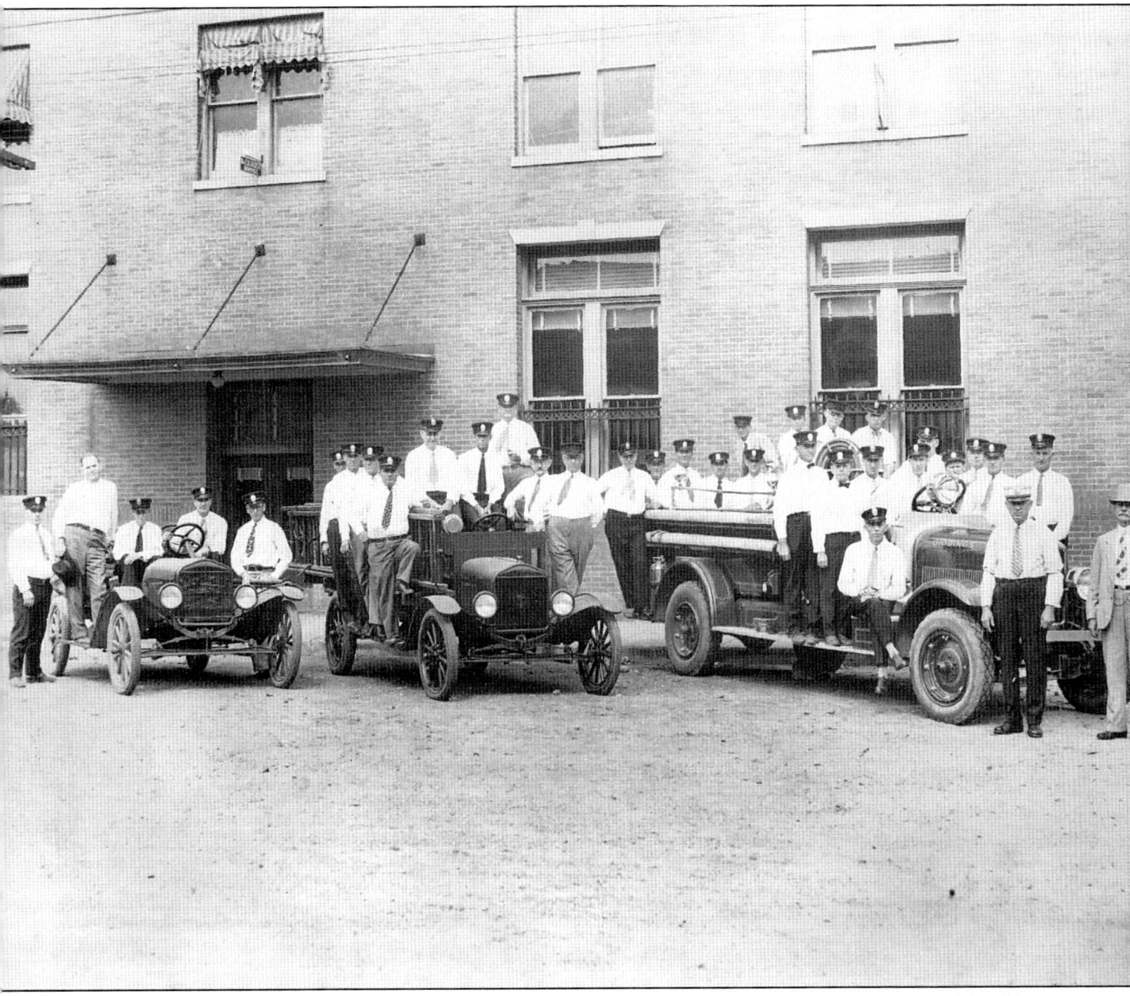

In 1928, the fire department was situated behind the First National Bank. The public library was located on the second floor.

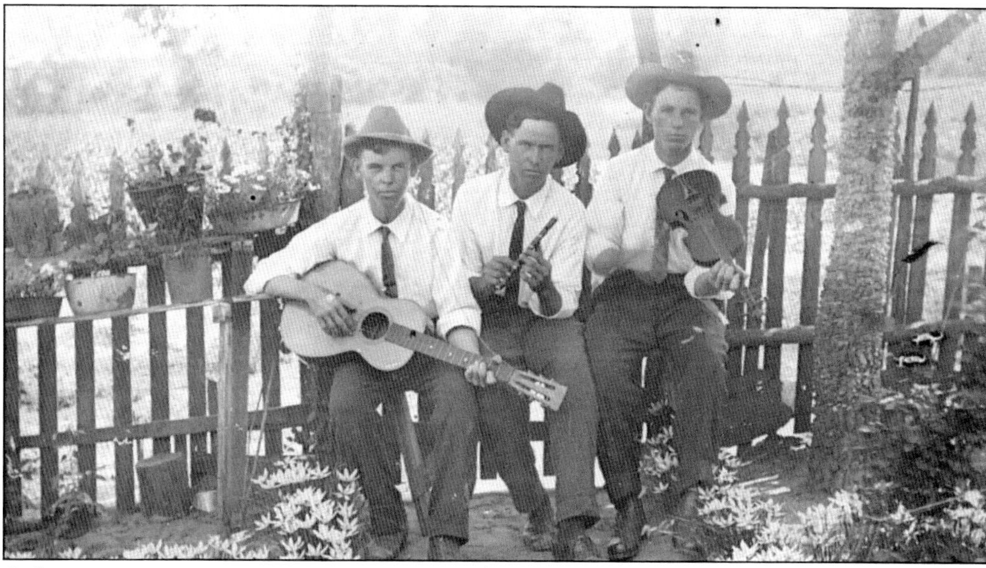

At home, music was a major entertainment. The Zwernemanns are on the flute and the guitar. The violinist is not identified.

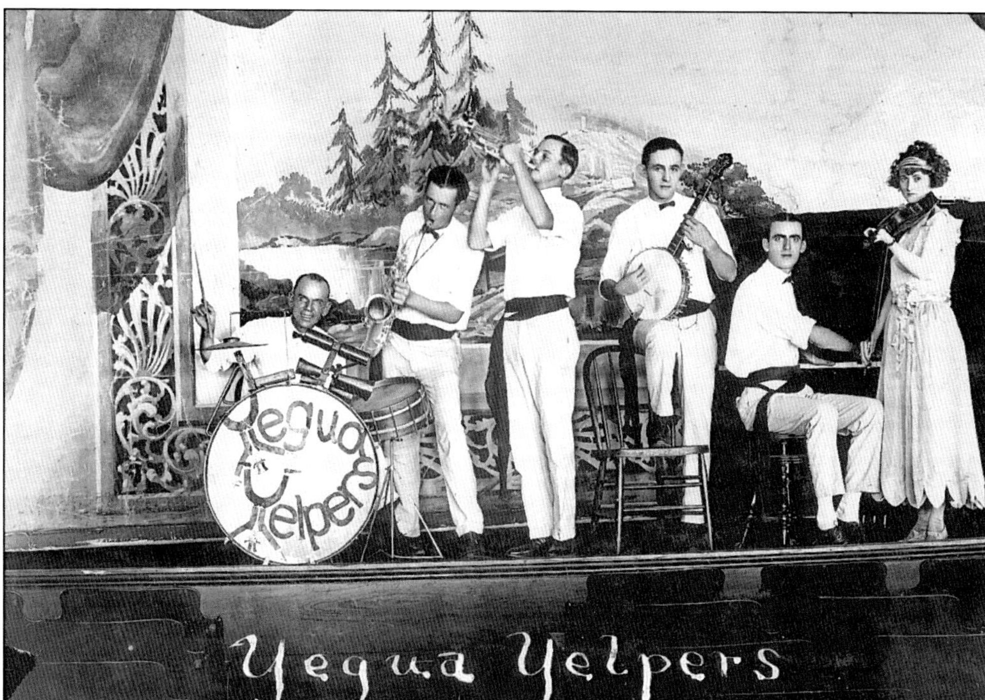

Ta-da! The Yegua Yelpers are on stage: Clifford Sparks on drums, Charles Hester on sax, Rudie Pietsch on trumpet, ? Laake on banjo, Roy Fletcher at the piano, and Eleanor Fletcher on the violin.

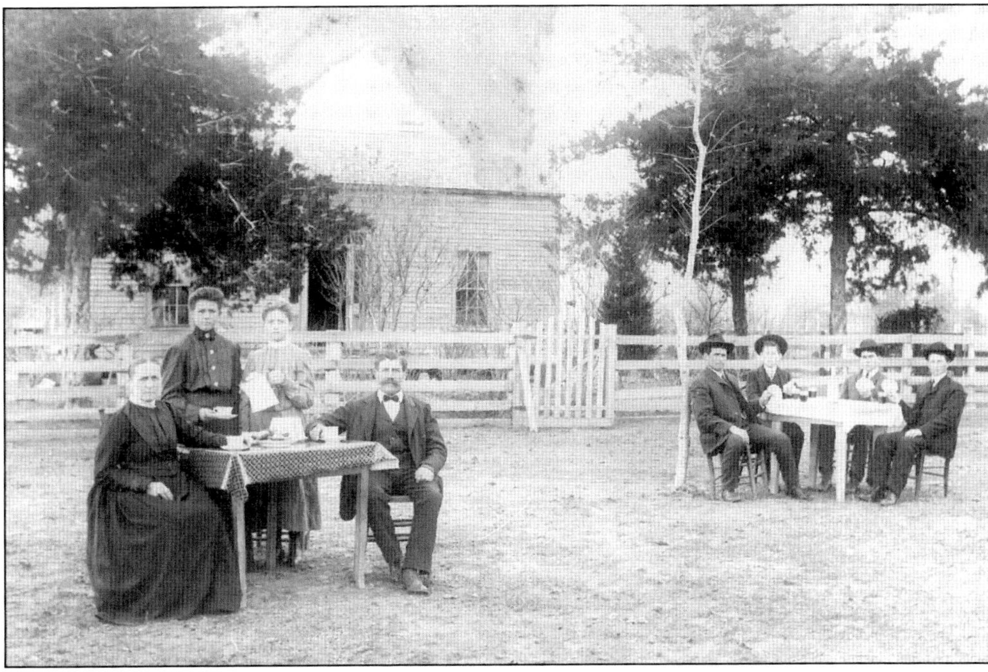

Families just outside of Giddings continued to find entertainment in the older ways such as playing the popular German game "Skat." Hoyle requires nine pages to summarize the complex rules and scoring of this basically three-handed game. It is named for the "widow," the cards dealt face down. Emily and Wilhelm Unger and their daughters, Mary and Ida, are the Skat players on the left; Clemens and Herman Unger and Fred and Richard Fischer are on the right.

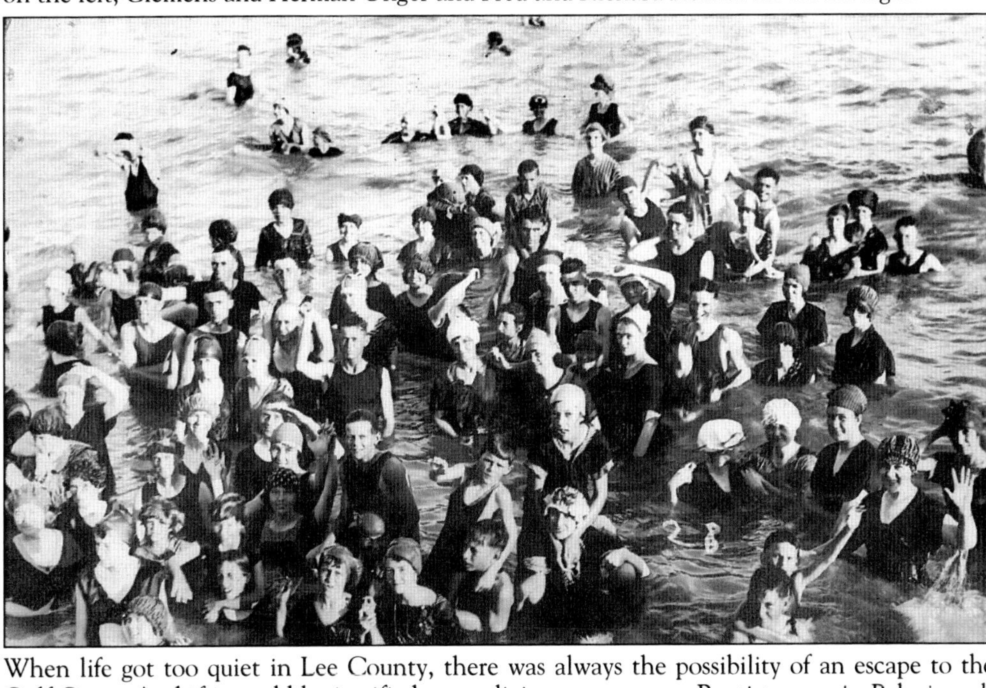

When life got too quiet in Lee County, there was always the possibility of an escape to the Gulf Coast. And if it could be justified as a religious retreat to a Baptist camp in Palacios, all the better.

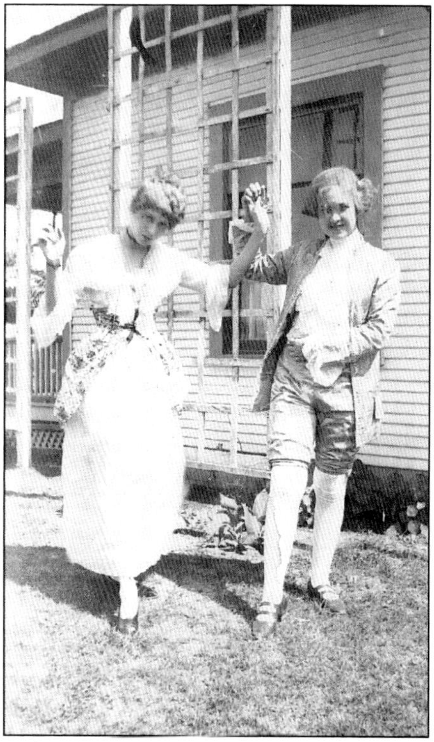

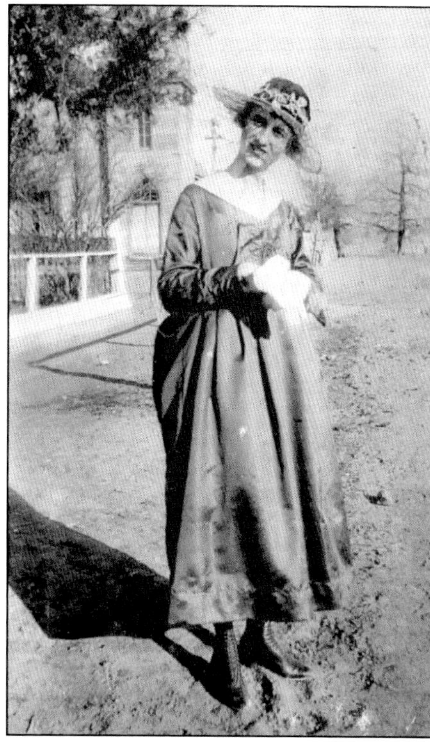

Left: This couple is likely costumed for amateur theatricals. *Right:* Roy Fletcher played maid of honor in an elaborate womanless wedding.

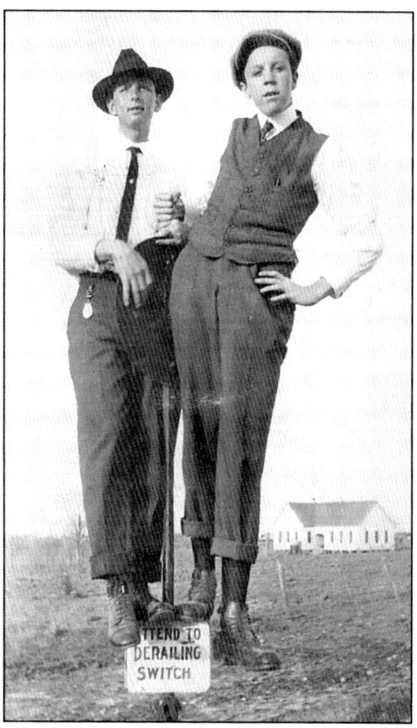

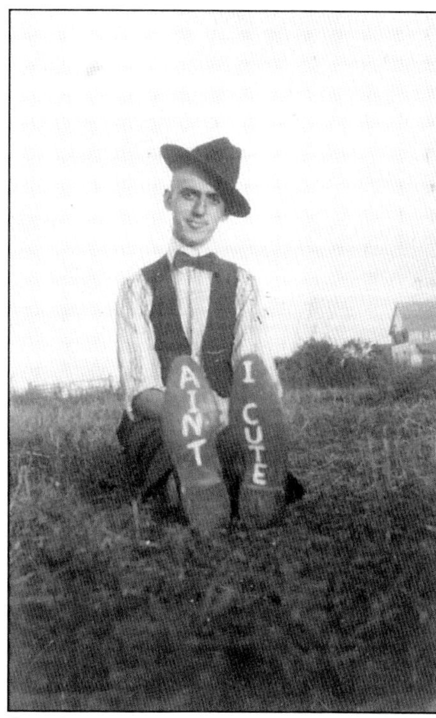

Left: The sign reads, "Attend to derailing switch." *Right:* This is more silliness, Fletcher-style.

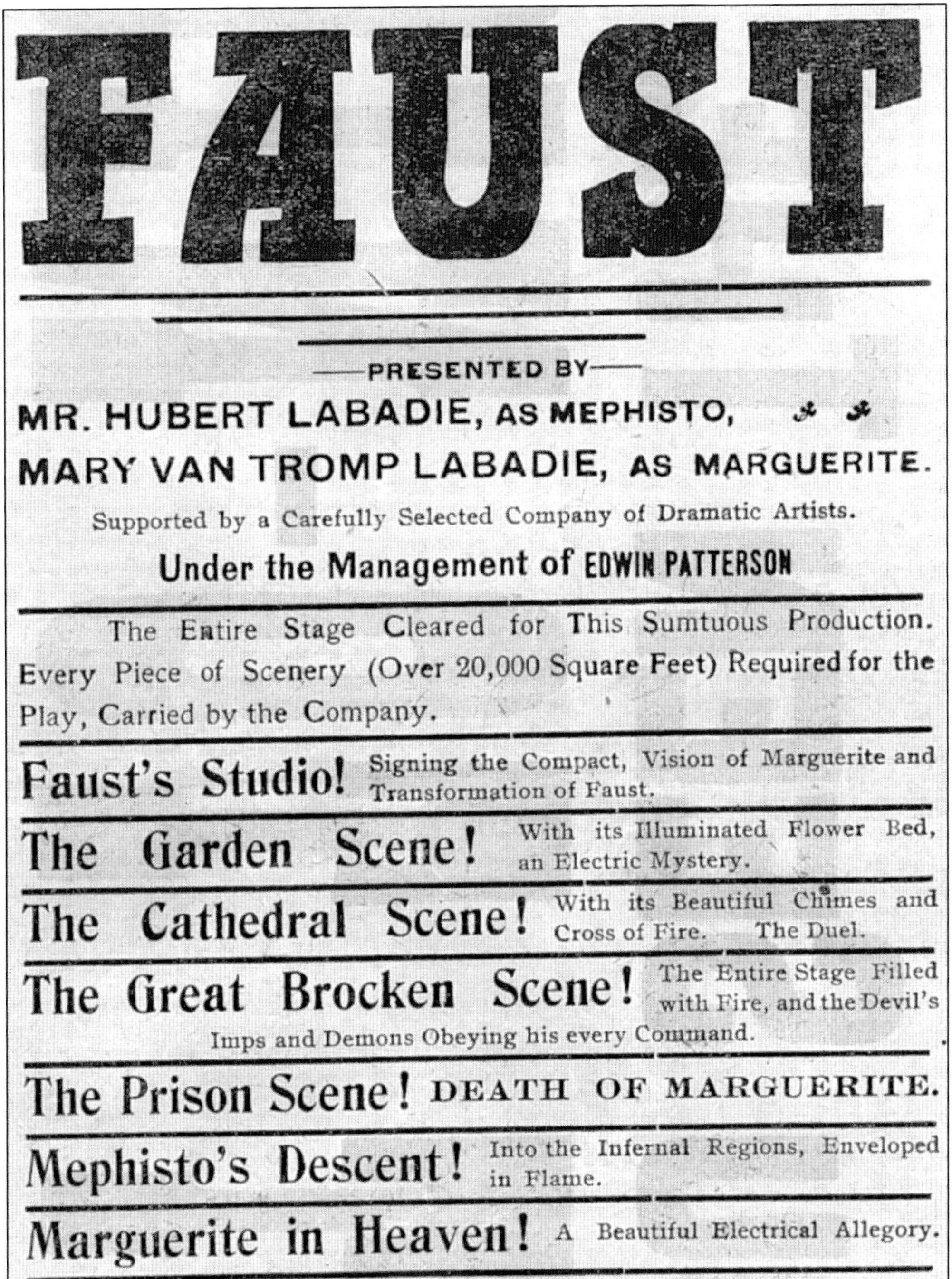

FAUST

—PRESENTED BY—

MR. HUBERT LABADIE, AS MEPHISTO,

MARY VAN TROMP LABADIE, AS MARGUERITE.

Supported by a Carefully Selected Company of Dramatic Artists.

Under the Management of EDWIN PATTERSON

The Entire Stage Cleared for This Sumtuous Production. Every Piece of Scenery (Over 20,000 Square Feet) Required for the Play, Carried by the Company.

Faust's Studio! Signing the Compact, Vision of Marguerite and Transformation of Faust.

The Garden Scene! With its Illuminated Flower Bed, an Electric Mystery.

The Cathedral Scene! With its Beautiful Chimes and Cross of Fire. The Duel.

The Great Brocken Scene! The Entire Stage Filled with Fire, and the Devil's Imps and Demons Obeying his every Command.

The Prison Scene! DEATH OF MARGUERITE.

Mephisto's Descent! Into the Infernal Regions, Enveloped in Flame.

Marguerite in Heaven! A Beautiful Electrical Allegory.

The play bill notes, "REMEMBER that all Tickets are Sold on a Positive Guarantee of a First Class Performance and that all Scenery will be Used." A diary excerpt from February 13, 1902, reads, "Mr. R and I went to the Hall to see Faust played. Mr. R paid $1.50 for our seats. Came home at 11 o'clock." —Rousseau diaries.

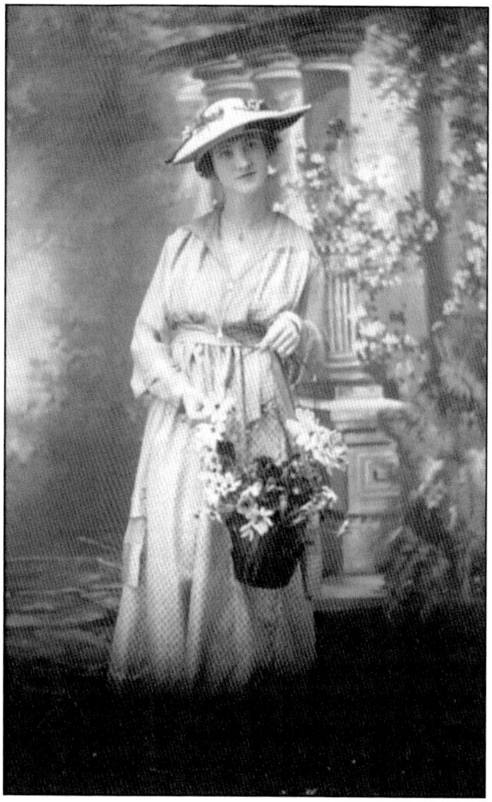

These lovely but unidentified ladies graced the Fletcher scrapbook.

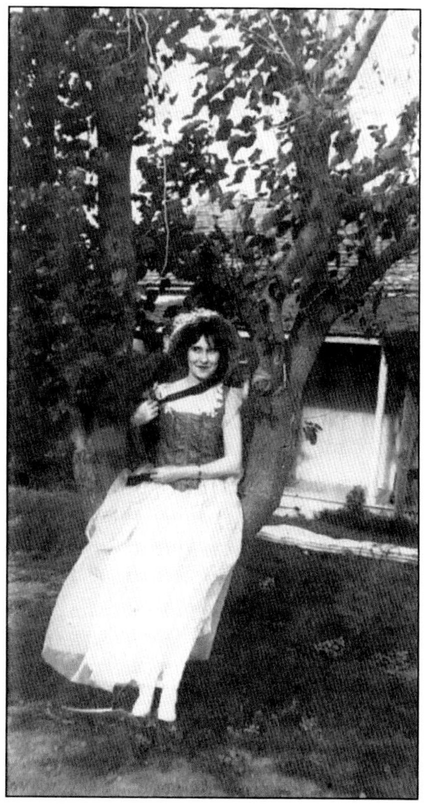

On the reverse side of this photo is the inscription: "A maid there was and she made her prayer, Even as you and I—To a rag and a bone and a hank of hair—"

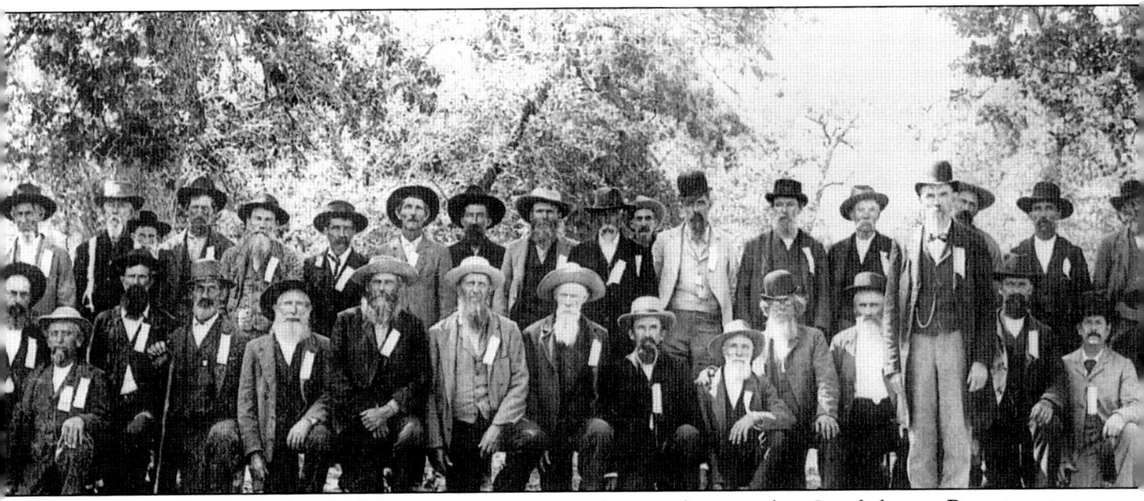

This is a section of a double panorama group photo taken at the Confederate Reunion in April 1895. Lee County was named in 1874 for General Robert E. Lee. Many veterans of the Confederate Army lived here; there were also veterans of the Union Army in Lee County, and occasional demonstrations of high emotion resulted. On February 6, 1900, Rousseau wrote, "Mr. Eren Bryan struck Mr. R in the eye. They were about the old war. Unexpected to Mr. R, his eye is swollen real bad. Mr. R attended lodge." —Rousseau diaries.

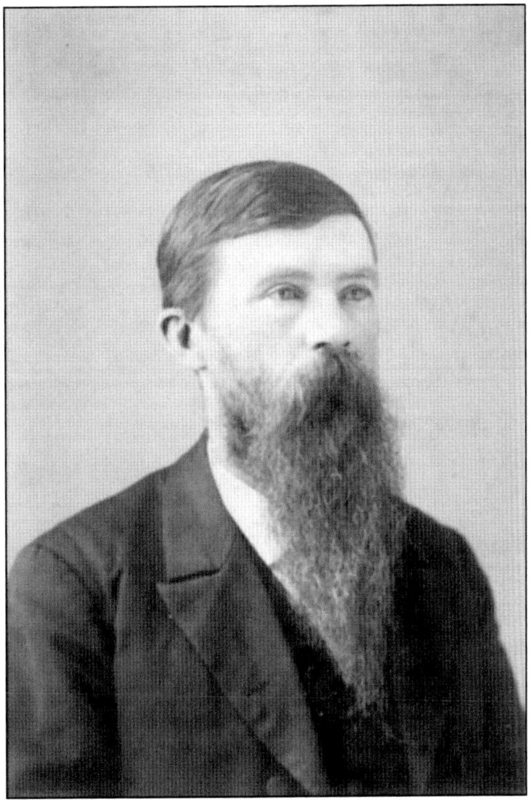

John Lovell Rousseau's wife, Annie, kept the Rousseau diaries. He volunteered to serve in the Confederate Army, was elected lieutenant, and then was court martialed for insubordination. Finally, he unofficially rejoined another unit. Judge Tate wrote in support of John's application for a pension, "No one here knows anything of his war record, but he has told me I expect as many as 50 times his war story before he ever thought of a pension."

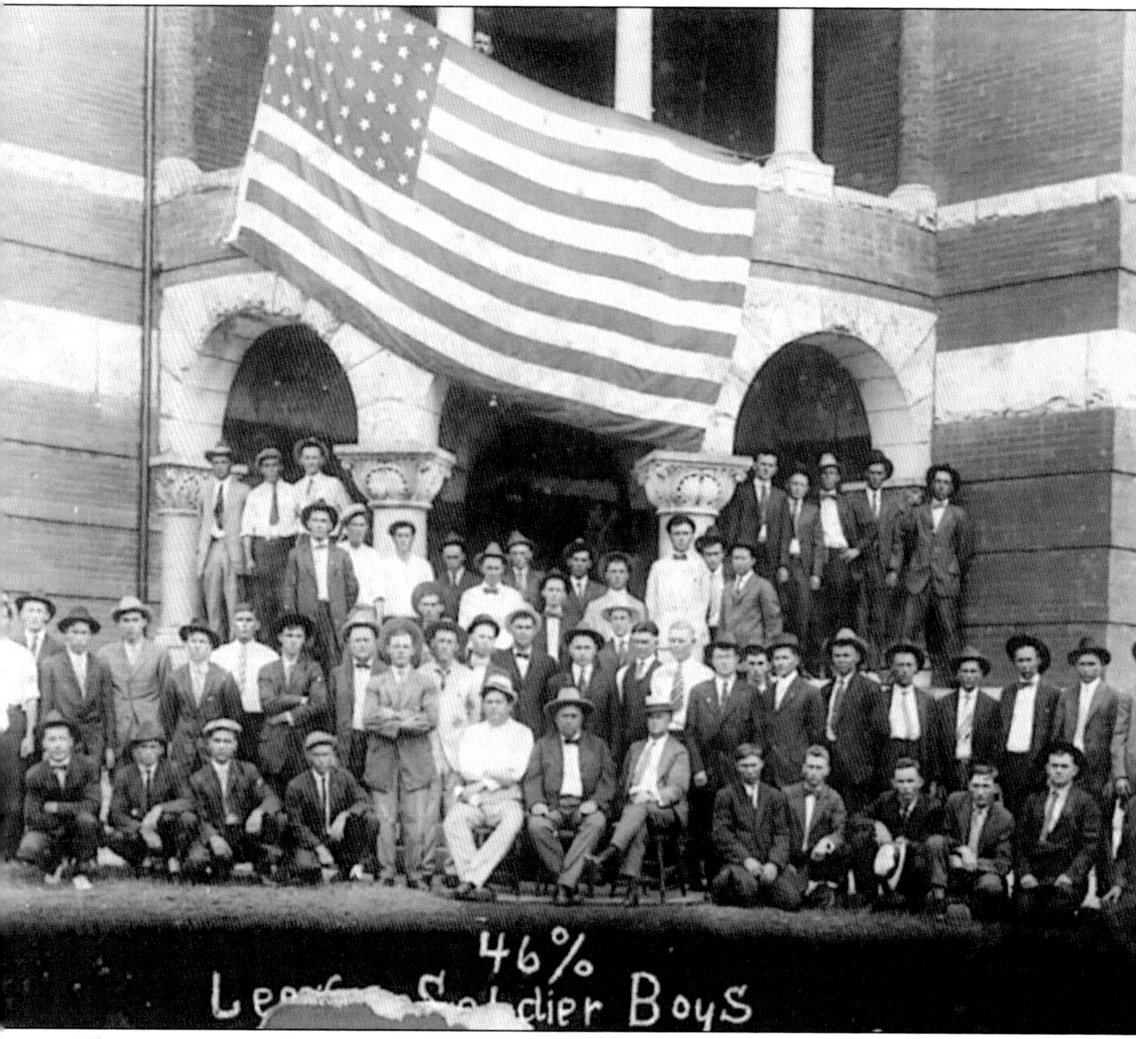

This picture was taken at induction in 1916–17. It is not known what the "46%" means. (Courtesy Texas Wendish Heritage Museum Archive.)

Henry Holt, who married Clara Hester in 1920, appears in uniform during World War I.

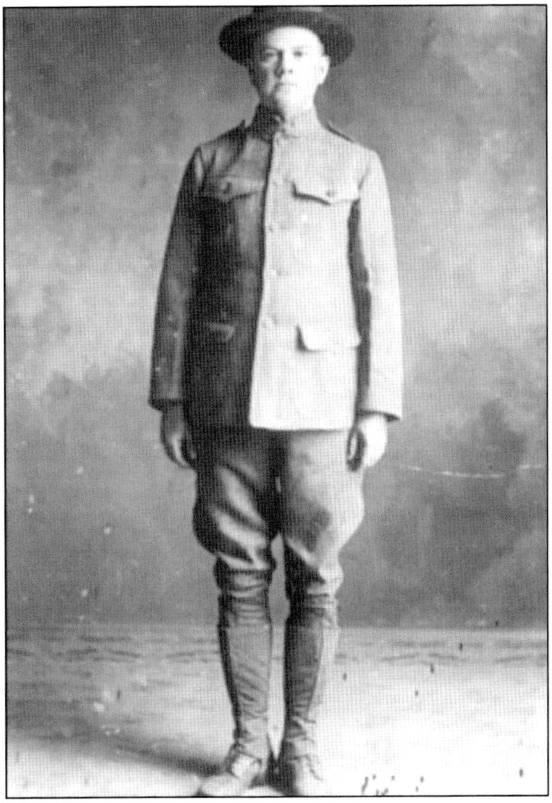

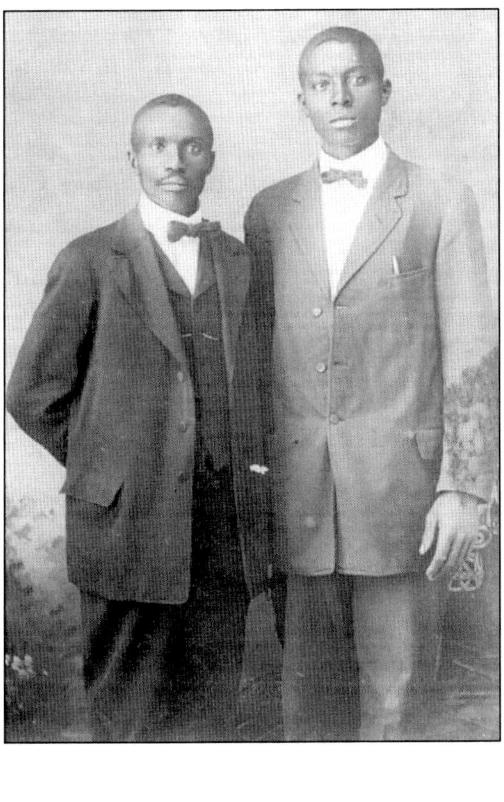

The Francis brothers were George (left) and Clinton. In 1917, Clinton went off to war, never to return. He died in service. George taught school for many years.

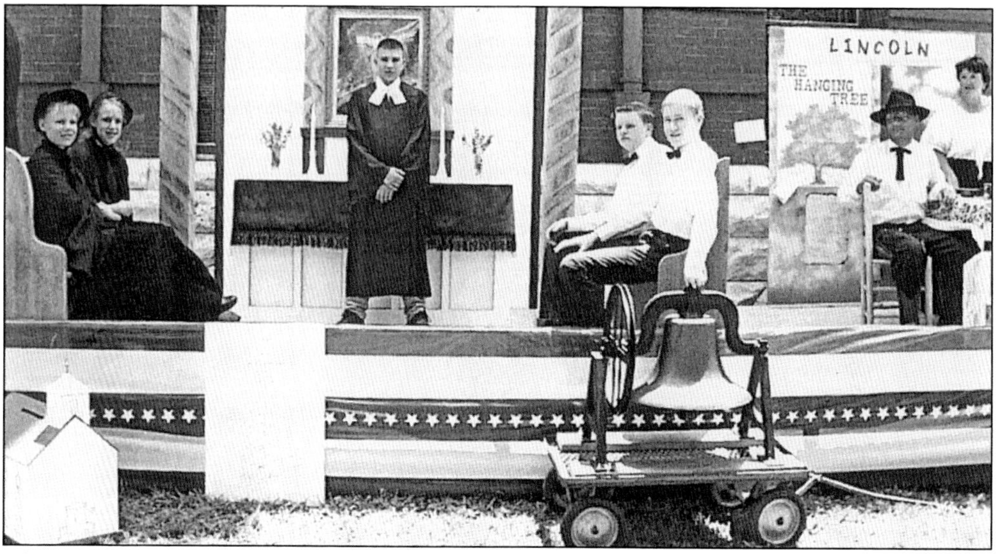

The 1999 centennial of the new courthouse displayed the continuing interest of the citizens of Lee County in celebrating their history. Well-known episodes of the past were recreated in a costumed pageant.

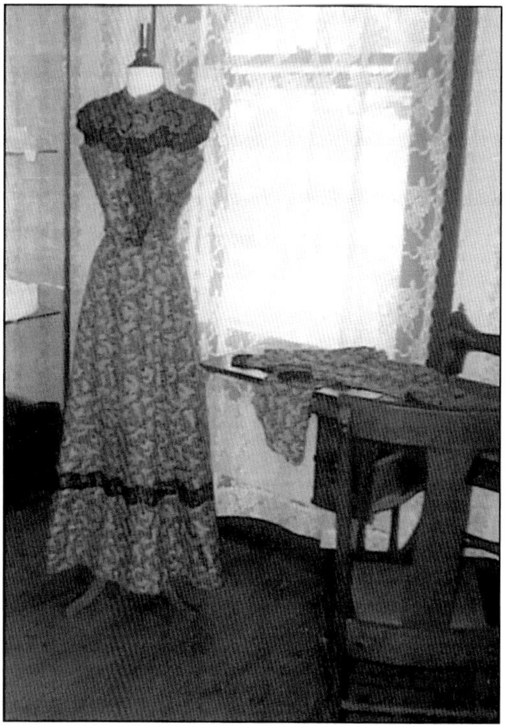

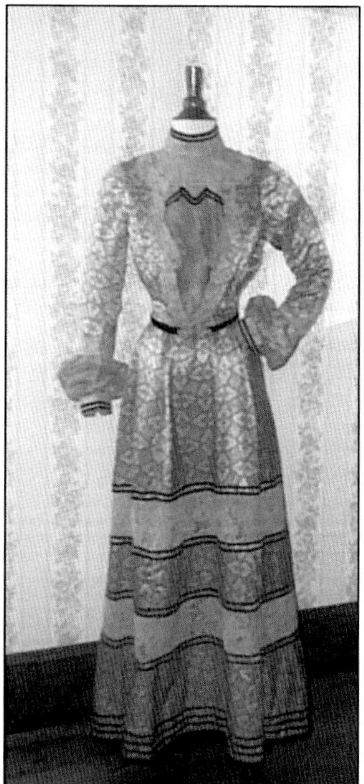

Dresses designed by Lena Zchuppe Mueller were on display in the Lee County Museum (the old York house), bringing sighs of admiration and nostalgia. Lena lived in Chicago and designed dresses for Marshall Field's before she came to Giddings to visit an uncle in 1901 and met the Reverend Wilhelm Mueller. She married him in 1903. Unfortunately, he apparently disapproved of her elegant dresses, so she stopped wearing them. Sad, but true. The past is to be treasured for what it was.